CIPR

# PR and Communication in Local Government and Public Services

LONDON  PHILADELPHIA  NEW DELHI

PR in Practice

John Brown, Pat Gaudin and Wendy Moran

**Publisher's note**

Every possible effort has been made to ensure that the information contained in this book is accurate at the time of going to press, and the publishers and authors cannot accept responsibility for any errors or omissions, however caused. No responsibility for loss or damage occasioned to any person acting, or refraining from action, as a result of the material in this publication can be accepted by the editor, the publisher or any of the authors.

First published in Great Britain in 2013 by Kogan Page Limited

120 Pentonville Road
London N1 9JN
United Kingdom
www.koganpage.com

ISBN      978 0 7494 6616 9
E-ISBN   978 0 7494 6617 6

**British Library Cataloguing-in-Publication Data**

A CIP record for this book is available from the British Library.

Typeset by Graphicraft Limited, Hong Kong
Print production managed by Jellyfish
Printed and bound in Great Britain by CPI Group (UK) Ltd, Croydon, CR0 4YY

# CONTENTS

## Appendices

# ABOUT THE AUTHORS

**John Brown FCIPR, CIPR Accredited Practitioner, MA (Hons)** is an independent PR consultant with over 35 years' experience in local government public relations and the media. He was Head of Public Relations for Strathclyde Regional Council (1993–1996) and subsequently Head of Public Relations and Marketing for Glasgow City Council (1996–2004). Served as chair of CIPR Scotland group, CIPR council member and in 2012 chaired the CIPR professional practices committee. Awarded the Sir Stephen Tallents medal in 2007.

**Pat Gaudin FCIPR, CIPR Chartered Practitioner, MSc PR, Dip CIPR, CIPR Teacher Training Certificate** has over 30 years' experience in public relations and communication in local government and the local public sector. Most recently Head of Public Relations and Corporate Strategy for Chelmsford Borough Council before becoming an independent consultant in 2006 and adding PR teaching to the mix in 2010. Served as chair of CIPR Local Government Group (2003–2006), CIPR council member and in 2013 chair of the CIPR professional development committee.

**Wendy Moran MCIPR, CIPR Accredited Practitioner, Dip CIPR,** is a Senior Lecturer in Communication at Manchester Metropolitan University, specialising in public relations across the local public services. Her background is in local government communication, which she has maintained through her Committee Membership of the Chartered Institute of Public Relations (CIPR) Local Public Services Group (LPSG). She is currently undertaking doctoral studies investigating the role of the PR practitioner in local government.

# FOREWORD

It has been 15 years since the last practice-focused textbook on public relations in local government, according to the authors of *PR and Communication in Local Government and Public Services*, and although that is too long, it has been worth the wait. This book is a gem and should be on the shelf of every practitioner in local government public relations and communication and of everyone who wants to know about it.

John Brown, Pat Gaudin and Wendy Moran have provided a thorough, thoughtful and accessible guide to one of the most challenging sectors of practice that there is. One where the accountabilities and transparencies required are unremitting and where the challenges are unrelenting, especially when resources are being ever squeezed. Yet, the local government sector also provides careers that are deeply satisfying for the professional communicator, in an environment where lives are touched and can be transformed and empowered.

*PR and Communication in Local Government and Public Services* begins by setting the recent historical context for local government and thereby mapping the changes over the last 20 years. From a service that pre-1995 concentrated on media relations, to one that between 1995 and 2009 focused on corporate communication with strategic plans for council reputation, changing culture, influencing policy and media relations, local government communication is now the guardian of council reputation and authenticity. Setting this platform then allows the authors to take an overview of how the modern public relations and communication team should be structured, pointing out the need for absolute professionalism, with an excellent discussion on the capabilities of practitioners, and indicating how performance can be measured. This leads to a chapter on communicating strategically, with a powerful section on reputation, before the book moves on to examine in detail the various areas of work and expertise demanded of the modern local government communicator.

The chapters that are practice-focused feature many expected topics, such as communicating with citizens and 'customers', employee relations, media and social media relations, crisis communications and of course putting together an effective campaign. In addition to this, a number of new, emerging and increasingly important subjects are given careful consideration. For example, partnership working and its challenges and opportunities; council branding – with a particularly helpful insight on the fact that behaviours are just as important as visual and communicative identity – and place promotion. All these topics are dealt with in detail, and with a careful balance between critical and excessive information being maintained throughout.

The authors write authoritatively and with deep knowledge, having all been involved in local government work themselves. There are liberal references to academic and wider texts and documents, many from the public sector, accountancy bodies and government, which inspire confidence in the material. There are numerous, varied and helpful case studies that provide guides to action and several of these are complemented with visual materials, bringing key points to life. Tables and illustrations are scattered throughout the text, helping to crystallise, summarise and re-enforce material, and the quotes introducing each chapter are pertinent and informative. These, combined with the checklists and keywords which round off chapters, draw the learning together in a succinct and memorable way. The book also features several detailed appendices containing essential information for operating in the public sector with its particular constraints: for example, Codes of Practice on local authority publicity in England, Performance Frameworks and the CIPR Code of Conduct.

The last chapter in this excellent book is called 'Communicating with confidence'. It exhorts practitioners to hold three principles dear: public interest, truth and transparency. This should be a mantra not just for the public sector, but for all those who would call themselves public relations professionals. This book is one which seeks to equip its readers with the capabilities required to be an excellent communicator. It is a book that teaches you and then enthuses you to go out and 'do'... with confidence.

*Professor Anne Gregory*
*Series Editor*

# ACKNOWLEDGEMENTS

Forty years ago, Geoffrey Lewis, a fellow and past president of the Institute of Public Relations, wrote the first practice textbook, *Public Relations for Local Government* (IPR/Business Books 1973). Since then there have been several books focusing specifically on local government public relations and marketing in the United Kingdom. We mention especially Tom Richardson's *Public Relations in Local Government* (Heinemann, 1988), Dick Fedorcio, Peter Heaton and Kevin Madden's guide *Public Relations for Local Government* (IPR/Longman, 1991), Keiron Walsh's *Marketing in Local Government* (Longman, 1993), David Walker's *Public Relations in Local Government* (Pearson Education, 1997) and Mark Fletcher's *Managing Communication in Local Government* (Kogan Page, 1999).

This is the first practice textbook on local government public relations in almost 15 years. The first this century. It reflects the current challenges in delivering professional public relations in a changing landscape for both communications and the delivery of local services. In bringing together the chapters for this textbook, the authors are indebted to the support and advice they have received from many colleagues in the CIPR Local Public Services Group, in councils and in other public relations and communication departments across the United Kingdom.

In particular, we thank Liz Azyan, Sue Appleby, Georgina Bentley, Caroline Binnie, Christine Birchall, Kate Bridge, Mike Browne, Jason Boyce, Geoff Coleman, Rod Cook, Emma Croll, Lucie Culkin, Louise Cumberland, Polly Cziok, Caroline Dixon, Kasia Figiel, Mark Fletcher-Brown, Sara Hamilton, Joanna Hannam, Beverley Hill, David Holdstock, Lee Jorgensen, Nigel Kay, Gill Kirk, Will Mapplebeck, Campbell Martin, Phil McCusker, Lynne McEwan, Alice McPhie, Nicky Mee, Joyce Nisbet, Alison North, Liz O'Rourke, Pauline Palmer, Mel Powell, Helen Reynolds, Eleri Roberts, Vicky Sargent, Marc Schmid, Fay Scadden, Ashley Scott-Wilcox, Ronnie Semley, Audrey Sharp, John Shewell, Laura Skelcey, Dan Slee, Cormac Smith, Dean Spurrell, Caroline Stamper, Tom Stannard, Ceri Sumner, Diane Talbot, Dan Thompson, Jenny Tozer, Robin Treacher, Sue Vanden, Simon Wakeman, Graeme Watson, Robert Webb, Carl Welham, Ruth Woodbridge and Rob Yeldham.

Additionally we acknowledge the particular help we have received from Alan Anstead, Rosie Boston, Elizabeth Gammell, Liza Greaves, Tom Holmes, Rhion Jones, Mikalis Kavaratzis, Jim Laikie, James Lland, Christine Richard, Andrew Stevens, Alan Stewart and John Wallace. And the staff at CIPR headquarters, especially Mark Birkin, Koray Camgoz, Maha Jamil, Kim

McCarthy, Phil Morgan, Alison Steel and the CIPR President for 2013, Sue Wolstenholme.

We would also like to express our special gratitude to the Kogan Page team who have worked with us, and encouraged us, throughout the 18 months, in particular our assistant editor Nicola de Jong, production editor Fiona Dempsey and the *PR in Practice* series editor Professor Anne Gregory.

*John Brown*
*Pat Gaudin*
*Wendy Moran*

PR in Practice Series

**Published in association with the Chartered Institute of Public Relations**
Series Editor: Anne Gregory

Kogan Page has joined forces with the Chartered Institute of Public Relations to publish this unique series, which is designed specifically to meet the needs of the increasing numbers of people seeking to enter the public relations profession and the large band of existing PR professionals. Taking a practical, action-oriented approach, the books in the series concentrate on the day-to-day issues of public relations practice and management rather than academic history. They provide ideal primers for all those on CIPR, CAM and CIM courses or those taking NVQs in PR. For PR practitioners, they provide useful refreshers and ensure that their knowledge and skills are kept up to date.

**Professor Anne Gregory PhD FCIR** is Director of the Centre for Public Relations Studies at Leeds Metropolitan University, UK. She has authored over 70 publications, as well as being editor of the Kogan Page/CIPR series of books which she initiated, she is Editor-in-Chief of the *Journal of Communication Management*. Anne also leads specialist commercial research and consultancy projects from the Centre working with prestigious public and private sector clients. She is a non-executive director of Airedale NHS Foundation Trust. Originally a broadcast journalist, Anne spent 12 years as a senior practitioner before moving on to academia. She was President of the Chartered Institute of Public Relations (CIPR) in 2004, leading it to Chartered status and was awarded the CIPR's Sir Stephen Tallents Medal for her outstanding contribution to public relations in 2010. In May 2011 she was voted Chair-Elect of the Global Alliance of Public Relations and Communications Management, the umbrella organisation of over 60 public relations institutes from around the world.

Other titles in the series:

*Creativity in Public Relations* by Andy Green
*Effective Internal Communication* by Lyn Smith and Pamela Mounter
*Effective Media Relations* by Michael Bland, Alison Theaker and David Wragg
*Evaluating Public Relations* by Tom Watson and Paul Noble
*Online Public Relations* by David Phillips and Philip Young
*Planning and Managing Public Relations Campaigns* by Anne Gregory
*Public Affairs in Practice* by Stuart Thompson and Steve John
*Public Relations in Practice* edited by Anne Gregory
*Public Relations Strategy* by Sandra Oliver
*Risk Issues and Crisis Management in Public Relations* by Michael Regester and
    Judy Larkin
*Running a Public Relations Department* by Mike Beard
*Writing Skills for Public Relations* by John Foster

The above titles are available from all good bookshops. To obtain further information, please go to the CIPR website (**www.cipr.co.uk/books**) or contact the publishers at the address below:

Kogan Page Ltd
120 Pentonville Road
London N1 9JN
Tel: 020 7278 0433
Fax: 020 7837 6348
**www.koganpage.com**

# 01
# The communicating council

*Most people just think that the council collects the bins and they haven't the faintest clue of the vast range of services that town halls provide. From cradle to grave, councils provide over 800 services to improve people's lives and help them get safe and sound through the day.*

SIR SIMON MILTON, CHAIR OF THE LGA 2007–08

*The challenge facing public sector communicators has never been greater. Teams and delivery budgets are being cut across the sector but the expectations of public service leaders, and the communities they serve, have not been diminished. Rising to this challenge requires professionalism, creativity, ingenuity and resilience.*

PAUL MYLREA, CIPR PRESIDENT 2011,
SPEAKING AT THE LOCAL PUBLIC SERVICES CONFERENCE

**P**ublic relations and public services go together. They are intrinsically linked to a belief in both the public service ethos and public interest. This makes the task of council and public services communicators particularly demanding. It may not have the cachet or glamour of work in other sectors, such as consumer, fashion, arts, sport or entertainment. But communicating and engaging with the public – as citizens, clients, patients, service users and consumers – on the wide range of issues or priorities that the public services throw up is both exciting and challenging.

Communicators have a special public responsibility. Providing information about services is one way to help people and communities function better and support their wellbeing. Engaging with the public is equally crucial to ensure the public's trust in the councils and organisations that deliver these services. The pressure on public spending – with real term cuts to council budgets of around 30 per cent over the next few years – is forcing councils to think of new ways of running services. Engagement is becoming increasingly important.

No other public relations sector offers the variety, range and challenge of the local public services, from family finding campaigns for children in care to boosting council recycling efforts to avoid landfill costs and protect the environment.

A snapshot of the work can be seen in the 2012/13 CIPR awards of excellence in local public services communications (see online resources at **http://www.koganpage.com/PRGov**). These range from campaigns to reduce hospital accident and emergency admissions on bank holiday weekends (NHS Milton Keynes and Northamptonshire) and tackling local youth unemployment by promoting apprenticeships (Medway Council) to addressing issues around primary school placement requests by 'promoting local schools for local kids' (City of Edinburgh).

Derbyshire County Council received 'consultation excellence' for their web-interactive 'your community, your choice' campaign prioritising spending of services. Liverpool City Council and 2012 Olympics-host London Borough of Hackney had award-winning place promotions.

The public sector is defined by the Office of National Statistics (ONS) as comprising central government, local government and public corporations. The local public sector encompasses local councils and the many services that fall under the council umbrella, from schools to social services, parks, libraries, museums to street cleaning, bin collections and recycling, and regulatory services such as consumer protection and licensing, planning and building control, the police, fire and rescue services, and the local health services under the NHS. Here, we focus primarily on public relations for local councils and their services.

Increasingly local services are overlapping, through partnership working and shared services across council boundaries. For public relations, this means getting together to ensure consistency of information and messages. It makes sense, saves money and benefits the public, baffled by the organisational divisions that often hinder the joined-up delivery of services, for example between health and social care. But it is not free from conflicts. For example, the police publicising efforts to tackle knife crime or anti-social behaviour could be at odds with the council promoting the same area to new business. Also, working together does not avoid a blame-game between services.

But, as Gregory (2003) has pointed out, public relations has been a force for good in society and has a 'major emancipating and empowering effect':

It has brought onto the public agenda many worthwhile issues that would not otherwise have been aired. Campaigning groups, whether they be for human rights, environmental issues or minority concerns have used public relations effectively to bring informed debate into society. There is ongoing work in the public sector, for example in local authorities, the health service and education where the 'engagement' agenda has provided service users and supporters with an opportunity to shape and promote the services provided for them.

# The development of local government public relations

Several researchers highlight the significance of local government in the development, growth and professionalisation of public relations in the United Kingdom (L'Etang, 2004, 2008; Bates, 2006; The Global Alliance for PR and Communication Management, 2010; Anthony, 2012). L'Etang (2008) explains that the growth of citizens' rights in the early 20th century was a turning point for local government communications: 'The burden of communicating change and new citizen rights and responsibilities fell on local government officers who imbued their work with strong notions of public service and communication that was both accurate and educational.'

According to L'Etang (2004), British public relations developed its 'own unique characteristics'. She identifies three distinct strands: the commitment of local government officers to provide information about their services; the production of film documentaries to explain public services, exemplified by John Grierson's most acclaimed 'Night Mail' about the post services in 1936; and the development of propaganda around the second world war, through the Ministry of Information, which subsequently became the government's COI (Central Office of Information), abolished by the coalition government in 2012.

The first two strands were the most meaningful in shaping the embryonic profession last century. The documentary movement contributed 'an idealism about democracy and a sense of responsibility and mission to educate an organisation's publics' and 'local government in Britain developed key public relations concepts and contributed in an important way to public relations ideology, particularly in relation to concepts of professionalism and public service ethos' (L'Etang, 2004).

Two organisations were especially influential, according to L'Etang (2004) in her definitive early history of public relations in Britain. These were the Institute of Public Administration and the National Association of Local Government Officers (NALGO), founded in 1905. The Institute's journal *Public Administration* included some of the early articles on public relations and by the 1930s there was an 'understanding of the importance of good public relations to facilitate smooth administration'.

NALGO members saw the need to shrug off the 'poor law' image and embarked on 'educating the wider public about local government and its role in society'. For the next 40 years, NALGO led the way in promoting professionalism among their members, countering negative publicity about council work, defending librarians and others under attack, supporting the local rates much criticised by business, mounting letter-writing campaigns, issuing pamphlets and organising exhibitions, public lectures and a 'civic Sunday'.

During the Second World War local authorities, especially in London, developed their press and public relations using mass communication to inform the public of evacuations, ration books and the effects of bombing. But it was after the war, post-Beveridge, that public services PR took off. NALGO's reconstruction committees recognised that effective local government had to be 'a partnership between the citizen, the elected representative and the local government officer... for the good of the community as a whole'. The new welfare, health, housing and social provisions needed explaining and a 'whole lot of legislation had to be put in plain language and interpreted' (L'Etang, 2008). More councils started appointing public relations officers.

Local government officers were the 'driving force' and the 'nucleus' behind the setting up of the Institute of Public Relations (IPR) in February 1948. Stephen Tallents, who became the IPR's first president, had attended an earlier NALGO conference of 500 local government officers and commented on both their 'keenness' and their 'isolation and loneliness' (L'Etang, 2004). The 'municipal group' formed IPR's first special interest group and had a key influence in promoting their views of professionalism and public ethos within IPR. Their sense of 'public interest' soon came into conflict with other IPR members who saw their paymaster, their client or employer, as foremost.

Seymour (1948), in the first edition of IPR's journal *Public Relations*, underlined the importance of 'truth' in public relations: 'It is the responsibility of the serious practitioner in public relations to convince those in authority that whatever the object, truth is the best weapon.' The IPR's first code of professional conduct talked about observing 'high professional standards', 'with respect for the public interest' and a 'positive duty to maintain trust, accuracy and good taste'.

By the late 1960s local government reorganisation was on the agenda with Royal Commission reports for England (Redcliffe-Maud) and Scotland (Wheatley), but the new map of councils was statutorily different from the commission's recommendations, especially in England. These reorganisations, during the 1970s, were the next opportunity for public relations to assert itself, as many councils had no public relations officer. The Bains Report (1972) highlighted the problem:

> The forthcoming reorganisation of local government will bring into sharp focus the deficiencies of public relations within many local authorities. In our view the

public have a right to information about the affairs of their local council and access to the committee and council meetings may well stimulate the public's desire to be better informed. A number of local authorities have, of course, given specific recognition to the importance of public relations... but our impression is that a great many authorities have paid insufficient regard to this function. This may be due to the doubt which exists in some areas about the propriety of some PR methods used in other spheres. We are in no doubt however that local authorities have a firm duty to inform the community of their activities and to put the council's view on matters of concern to that community.

The Bains Committee (and the Patterson Committee in Scotland) recommended new councils include a 'full-time public relations and information unit' with suitably qualified staff in their administrative structure. Public relations should also provide information support to councillors. And for the many thousands of staff working for councils, Bains stressed the value of internal communications:

to keep their own staff informed, particularly on matters which have, or are believed to have a direct bearing on them. This is important at a time of simultaneous organisational change within every authority... This is not just a question of the interests of the staff, important though these are. The success or failure of any organisational change depends largely on the willingness of the staff to make it work.

A year later, the first practice textbook on *Public Relations for Local Government* was published by IPR. Its author, Geoffrey Lewis (1973), was then deputy director of the public information branch at the Greater London Council and president of IPR: 'In its simplest terms the duties and objectives of a local authority public relations department is to tell the public what is happening in the town hall and then to supply the council with information about public reaction and attitudes.' For Lewis, council PR officers, should have 'diplomacy and tact... and a feeling for political issues', as well as the following ideal 'qualities':

1  An ability to communicate, clearly and concisely, both orally and in writing.
2  An ability to understand quickly complicated situations and to explain them in simple terms.
3  An ability to appreciate the council's objectives and a desire to explain them.
4  An ability to handle several subjects without exasperation.
5  An alertness to political situations.
6  An even temper and an acceptance, without bitterness, of rejected advice, yet a determination to press home a sincerely held opinion.
7  A knowledge of what the media want and how they 'tick' and how to make use, where appropriate, of the tools of the trade.

**8** A knowledge of local government and what makes it 'tick', or the ability to learn this quickly.

**9** An understanding of people and sympathy with their problems – including members and fellow officers.

**10** Experience in the tools of communication of one sort or another and preferably several sorts.

**11** An inborn ability to act as a full-time organiser and a part-time manager.

**12** An appropriate qualification, preferably membership of the Institute of Public Relations.

**13** A sincere belief that democratic government, for all its faults, is worthwhile government.

In 1975 Strathclyde Regional Council, serving almost 2.5 million people in the west of Scotland, was one of the first councils to have a corporate PR department, with around 30 staff, and divided into three sections: 1) 'Press', with six press officers covering specific services, such as education or social work; 2) 'Information', dealing with public enquiries, talks and present-ations, preparing publicity on services; and 3) 'Publications', co-ordinating corporately all publications, exhibitions, graphics and design. Head of public relations Henry Dutch (1993) summarised the year's work:

- 16,000 media enquiries dealt with;
- 808 press releases issued;
- 10 editions produced of *Strathclyde*, the council's newspaper;
- over 30,000 enquires from the public dealt with;
- re-launch of the council's employee publication 'Insider' (to 100,000 staff);
- launched the 'Strathclyde Works' campaign about the council's services;
- met increased demand from departments for print and exhibition materials;
- advertising savings of almost £500,000 in commissions and discounts.

Strathclyde, along with some 30 or so other councils across the United Kingdom, had a 'central advertising unit', modelled on an advertising agency. The unit managed all the council's advertising including public notices, re-cruitment and promotional and negotiated rates direct with the media, with considerable savings on rate card.

This was aided by the setting up of the National Association of Public Service Advertisers (NAPSA) in 1984, with some 130 councils as members. During its first 10 years, NAPSA offered training to staff on advertising and was a resource to councils on media buying (Wonnacott, 1994). Since 2000, most council ad units have ceased, with new procurement procedures and less advertising, particularly recruitment. But the costly legal requirement, dating back to the 1930s, of placing public notices in a paid-for newspaper, rather than in a council publication or website, remains an issue.

Roger Haywood (1991), the IPR's president that year, commented that some of the most effective PR in the country was being practised in local government. It is 'one of the toughest and most exposed arenas in which to operate':

> PR is part of our information democracy presenting options, expanding choice, opening discussion, disseminating information and listening to the perceptions and views of the public... If the public are to trust the authority, council or other community body then the communications must be prompt, open, honest, truthful and fair. Hardly the recipe for closed government.
>
> The reality is that the more open the government is, the better the service that is being offered, the more responsive the authority, the tougher the challenges... then the more important will be the quality of the public relations support.

# From public relations to reputation guardians

The Audit Commission put a high priority on promoting better communication in local government; it had identified communication as one of the eight success factors for 'the competitive council'.

In 1994, the commission issued guidance on how to present and publicise the new citizen charter performance indicators. And a year later *Talk Back* (1995) was published, with 20 recommendations and actions for councils, including giving priority to 'good communication with the public in everything the council does', 'becoming a listening council with the public relations unit acting as a catalyst' and developing a strategy and monitoring corporate standards for the authority's public relations approach.

This was followed by a project called 'Connecting with Communities', aimed at improving communications in a modernised local government. It was led by the Deputy Prime Minister's Office, involving the Local Government Association (LGA), Improvement and Development Agency (IDeA) and the Audit Commission, and drawing on research by MORI. Their report 'Five years of Communications' (2002) found that the majority of residents knew little about their local council and there was confusion over who ran specific local services:

> Those who feel they are well informed about the council tend to be more positive about the authority on a wide range of issues. They are much less likely to feel that the council is remote and impersonal or out of touch with local

people... more likely to feel that the authority offers local people good value for money and provides good quality service overall. Improving communications can have a positive effect on these image ratings and also on overall satisfaction levels.

The 2002 report marked a change in emphasis for local government public relations and communications – with engaging, dialogue, consultation, listening and feedback becoming increasingly important. By now 85 per cent of councils in Britain had full-time public relations or communications staff. But these staff were still over-concentrated on media relations (Wakeman, 2012) or delivering the 'public information... end of public relations' (Harrison, 2000). There was a recognition that local government public relations had to move from 'passive information giving' (Yeomans, 2009). 'The shift demands a new mix of skills and experience from the public relations practitioner working within this sector' (Wakeman, 2012).

Reputation became the focus for action. In 2005, the LGA launched its reputation campaign. Using MORI research and council performance indicators, the LGA set out 12 core actions that councils should undertake to improve public satisfaction. Seven focused on cleaning and environmental issues, such as dealing with 'grot spots'. Five were communication-specific: consistent branding, more effective media relations, producing an A–Z of services and a regular council magazine or newspaper, and stepping up internal communications 'so staff become advocates for the council'.

Based on further research, and drawing on the government's Place Survey 2008/09 to develop a reputation index for councils, the LGA together with LGcommunications published the *New Reputation Guide* (2010). It is a must-read for those in public services communication (included in online resources and available at **www.lga.gov.uk/reputation**).

The *Guide* charts three phases in council communications. Pre-1995 the public relations phase when it was mainly about building and maintaining relationships with the local media. From 1995–2009, the corporate communications phase with a strategic plan for council reputation, driving media coverage, changing culture and influencing policy. The latest phase is being the guardian of council reputation and authenticity. This requires creating and influencing networks of advocates, stewarding the council's brand, values and reputation, shaping culture and behaviours, and advising on policy and delivery of services, as well as involving employees as communicators.

Improving reputation is a collective challenge, the *Guide* says, if people are to have trust in the 'council' and 'public service' brand. The three big ticket issues are leadership – 'having clarity about what the council stands for and making sure it is understood by the whole organization'; brand – 'having a clear sense of purpose and believing and living your values'; and strategic communications – 'having the right skills to improve your reputation' (see Chapter 2, page 45).

Once we have a clear way of explaining what we stand for, which is in tune with what residents want and the way our staff deliver services backs this up, we need strategic communications to become the guardians of our reputation. Too many of our communications leaders are not yet providing this stewardship role.

(New Reputation Guide, 2010)

Julia Corkey (2013), Westminster's new director of communications and strategy, has underlined that the job of asking residents to pay council tax is harder in times of financial austerity. This means reinforcing the 'council brand' of quality and trusted management. It is now even more important to stress the range of services provided, avoid council-speak and show that the council tax offers value for money. To turn a cut into a reputational benefit, says Corkey, referring to Westminster shutting its three one-stop shops, is to make sure that alternative provision is first class and any changes are publicised widely and clearly.

The latest research by the LGA (Polling on Resident Satisfaction with the Council), tracking public opinion nationally, indicates that satisfaction levels with councils has remained fairly constant, with 16 per cent saying 'very satisfied' and 57 per cent 'fairly satisfied'. Seven out of ten feel the council keeps them very well or fairly well informed about its services. But only 51 per cent agree or tend to agree that councils provide value for money and 33 per cent think councils do not act very much or not at all on the concerns of local residents. Clearly, as cuts impact on services, councils will need to engage their residents more in decisions about priorities.

# Information, publicity and the law

The raison d'être for today's public relations is enshrined in statute, the Local Government Act 1972, particularly Section 142 for England and Wales and Section 88 of the Local Government (Scotland) Act 1973 with the bureaucratic title 'Provision of information etc, relating to matters affecting local government'. This legislation specifically allows local councils to fund, provide and publish information to the public about local services and the functions of the authority.

Such information could be conveyed through publications, exhibitions, films, pictures, lectures or holding discussions – the examples in the Act. This was extended in 1986 to include the promotion of economic development in the authority's area and in 2003 to include broadcasting, through an 'electronic communications network or service', but under the oversight of the UK's broadcasting legislation.

In the 1980s, the legislation was put to the test. A number of councils, particularly Labour councils, were in battle with Mrs Thatcher's Conservative government over rate capping, funding and resultant service cuts. Labour-controlled Greater London (GLC) and Lothian Regional councils were first challenged in court. GLC was forced to abandon one 'political' campaign that exceeded the information remit. In the Lothian case, the council's

Conservative group leader, Brian Meek, argued that the articles in the council's newspaper were not simply informative about services and function, but persuasive and political. The Court of Session in Edinburgh recognised that councils were political in make-up and held that information to the public could include justifications, explaining the council's position.

But in 1983, the English courts deemed unlawful a £650,000 advertising campaign by the Labour-run Inner London Education Authority (ILEA) opposing rate-capping. The campaign – with the theme 'what do you get if you subtract £75 million from London's education budget?' – was aimed at informing the public about the effects of the cuts. Conservative-run Westminster City Council raised the successful court action against ILEA and the court, in this instance, ruled that where the primary purpose is persuasion, the information did not meet the requirements of Section 142.

It was publicity campaigns by the GLC, under Ken Livingstone's leadership from 1981 to 1985, which annoyed Mrs Thatcher's government most; none more so than their two-year award-winning campaign 'Say No to No Say' against the GLC's abolition. The government, angry that some councils were deliberately abusing the 1972 Act powers to publish information, asked David Widdicombe QC who was chairing an inquiry into the conduct of local authority business to investigate.

The Widdicombe Report (1985) recommended that there should be a clear statutory prohibition on publicity of a party political nature. This was followed by legislation, first in 1986 and then in 1988. The term 'publicity' was introduced; publicity covered 'any communication, in whatever form, addressed to the public at large or to a section of the public'. Today this embraces all council websites and social media. Part 2 of the Local Government Act 1986 (amended in 1988) set out the restrictions that currently apply:

Prohibition of political publicity

**(1)** A local authority shall not publish any material which, in whole or in part, appears to be designed to affect public support for a political party.

**(2)** In determining whether material falls within the prohibition regard shall be had to the content and style of the material, the time and other circumstances of publication and the likely effect on those to whom it is directed and, in particular, to the following matters

**(a)** whether the material refers to a political party or to persons identified with a political party or promotes or opposes a point of view on a question of political controversy which is identifiable as the view of one political party and not of another

**(b)** where the material is part of a campaign, the effect which the campaign appears to be designed to achieve

**(3)** A local authority shall not give financial or other assistance to a person for the publication of material which the authority are prohibited by this section from publishing themselves.

The 1986 Act brought two other substantial changes: first, the introduction of a Code of Recommended Practice on Local Authority Publicity as regards 'the content, style, distribution and cost of local authority publicity or such related matters' and second, the requirement for councils to keep a separate record of their publicity expenditure, which can be inspected 'at any reasonable time'. The government-initiated Code has to be approved by Parliament, after statutory consultation. Councils are required to 'have regard to the provisions of any such Code in coming to any decision on publicity', but there are no stated sanctions for breaching it. A breach complaint would have to be considered by a council's chief executive or monitoring officer and if illegal spending is alleged, the council auditor.

To date, the UK Parliament has approved three codes: the first in 1988, which was amended in 2001 and the third in 2011, a full revision for England only (see Appendix 1, page 261). The 1988 Code still applies to Scotland and Wales respectively; local government is a devolved responsibility and the Scottish Parliament and Welsh Assembly are responsible for future revisions. In March 2013 a new revised Code for Wales was published for consultation. The 2011 Code is framed under seven principles – lawfulness, cost-effectiveness, objective, even-handedness, appropriate use, equality and diversity and care during periods of sensitivity (election times).

For over 25 years, the 1986 Act and the Code have placed restrictions on local authority publicity (see checklist). Additionally, any council staff member whose remit is dealing with journalists or broadcasters – or communicating on behalf of the council through the web and social media – is politically restricted, which means they cannot take any active part in politics or electioneering, except voting (see Chapter 2, page 37).

## Checklist on the 2011 publicity code

(Refer to full code in Appendix 1)

### Be lawful

- No 'party political' publicity
- No 'political' advertising on TV and radio
- Follow rules on publicity for any local referendum
- Restrict publicity just before and during an election period
- No publicity to persuade people to sign a petition

### Be cost-effective

- All publicity and campaigns must show 'value for money'
- Reproducing publicity by others must demonstrate local benefit
- Council funded advertising must not 'subsidise' any organisation

## Be objective

- Reference to any government policies/proposals must be balanced
- Explaining council plans/policies must be factual and objective
- No campaigning to persuade public on questions of policy
- Avoid anything likely to be seen as political comment
- But council can 'correct erroneous material' published by others

## Be even-handed

- Present fairly the different views in matters of political controversy
- The local work of councillors can be publicised, with riders
- Councils can host blogs and postings by third parties, if moderated

## Be appropriate

- Council publications should not 'emulate commercial newspapers'
- Council newspapers/magazines should not appear more than quarterly
- All council publicity to be clearly identified as such on the front page
- No spending on services of lobbyists
- Councils should not fund displays at party political conferences

## Be equality and diversity aware

- Publicity can address people's attitudes to health, crime, safety etc
- And promote the eliminating of discrimination
- And the advancement of equality
- And the fostering of good relations

## Be election aware

- Avoid publicity just before and during elections or referendums
- This will include council blogs, postings and web forums
- No council publicity of any candidate(s) standing in elections

The Code sets out the parameters for publicity. It is 'not designed to curtail communications or to undermine them', according to LGcomms (2011). The government's explanatory memorandum to the 2011 Code underlines the positive role for today's communicators, still very much in accord with the public relations objectives of council predecessors almost a century ago:

> For a community to be a healthy local democracy, local understanding of the operation of the democratic process is important and effective communication is key to developing that understanding. Local authority publicity is important to transparency and to localism, as the public need to know what their local authority is doing if they are to hold it into account... in order to hold it into account the public need to have information about what their council is doing and why it is doing it.

(See also Chapter 4, page 79.)

There are two other pieces of legislation that have forced councils to be more open and accountable. The Public Bodies (Admission to Meetings) Act 1960 ensured press and public were allowed by law to attend council meetings, although the press had rights going back to 1908. The Freedom of Information Act 2000 gave any member of the public rights of access to information held by councils and public bodies.

## Publicity Code breaches

The restrictions in the Publicity Code have been assimilated and overall well managed by councils and public relations professionals. But any detailed look through council newspapers or magazines, press releases, websites and social media traffic, will throw up numerous instances of breaches, mostly unintended, but some clearly party political. A Commons Select Committee (2010) reported that most council newspapers were 'informative', but considered a few veered towards 'political propaganda', a clear breach. Several English councils, following a council decision, still publish their residents' newspaper more frequently than quarterly, another breach of the 2011 Code.

However, few actual breaches have been formally reported. But these raise critical issues for all council public relations teams. In 1988, after complaints about 'illegal expenditure', the Commission for Local Authority Accounts in Scotland questioned the Labour-run Edinburgh District Council's 'Improving Services-Creating Jobs' campaign, which mirrored the GLC's campaigning. Council vehicles, banners, posters, badges, balloons and T-shirts all featured the slogan. In a significant ruling, the Court of Session recognised the use of slogans or headline messages in publicity, but ruled the campaign was unlawful. The slogan did not convey information. If the council had added a phone number (or today a website address), the slogan and the campaign could have been deemed legal.

The Scottish Public Standards Commissioner (2011) identified breaches when he was asked to rule on two complaints: quotes in the April/May 2011 issue of *Glasgow*, the council magazine by the Labour leader of Glasgow City Council, Councillor Matheson, when he criticised by name Scotland's SNP Finance Minister over funding decisions during the Scottish Parliament elections. And secondly, a complaint about a council letter from Councillor Matheson, with his picture, promoting the city's Christmas events to homes in his city centre ward. The Commissioner judged that Councillor Matheson had not contravened the Councillor's Code of Conduct (separate from the Publicity Code) because he had not 'requested or authorised' the offending quotes or 'approved' the actual content of the letter.

But he stated there were breaches of the 1986 Act caused by an 'unacceptable standard of governance' at a senior level, a failure to exercise proper editorial control. The letter breached paragraph 39 of the 1988 Code (inappropriate use of council resources to publicise an individual councillor). The magazine quotes breached paragraphs 13 (comments should not be prejudicial or political) and 43 (publicity at election-time). The offending *Glasgow* magazine was withdrawn and its door-to-door distribution to 180,000 households halted when the complaint was raised. The Commissioner stated:

> The comments attributed to the respondent (Councillor Matheson) in the magazine article should have been restricted to a factual explanation of the impact of the central government funding allocation on the Council's 2011/12 budget and spending plans. To ensure this, the article should have been edited by senior officers of the council to remove any party political comment.

For the Commissioner's full judgment, see online resources at **http://www. koganpage.com/PRGov**).

The London Borough of Tower Hamlets – and its elected Mayor – was the subject of the most recent publicity code breach. Mayor Rahman was featured in a 30-second TV advert paid for by the council to promote its plans to build 4,000 new and upgrade 9,000 council houses. The advert, both in English and Bangladeshi, was shown extensively on five local TV channels in January 2012.

Ofcom (2013) – the UK broadcasting regulator – adjudicated the adverts were a breach of Section 321 of the Communications Act 2003, which bans any 'political', not just party political, advertising. In defence, the council argued unsuccessfully that the adverts were informing residents about housing services; referred only to the borough's independent mayor and were not broadcast during an election or referendum period. Providing a contact phone number and web address, in this case, did not exempt the TV ad from being political. Ofcom ruled that paragraph 6 of the 2011 Publicity Code had been clearly broken: 'political' advertising on TV and radio is a breach (Ofcom judgment, see online resources at **http://www.koganpage.com/PRGov**).

The Tower Hamlets case was raised in the House of Commons on 14 February 2013 and the local government minister, Brandon Lewis MP, stated that the government is considering making the Publicity Code statutory in England to stop the 'corrosive abuse' of council taxpayers' money.

The use of taxpayers' money for political campaigning is simply not acceptable, and this is in addition to Tower Hamlets' disregard of the Code of recommended Practice on Local Authority Publicity through its continuing publication of its weekly propaganda newspaper *East End Life*. Such actions are not just a misuse of public funds, they are ultimately harmful to local democracy and an independent, free press. It is also further evidence of a worrying pattern of divisive community politics and management of council staff and resources by the mayoral administration.

(Hansard, Col 840W. 14 February 2013)

In April 2013, the coalition government issued a consultation on introducing new legislation to make the 2011 Code mandatory in England and to give the Secretary of State new power to direct a local council to comply (DCLG, 2013).

# Getting the basics right

Too often it is a breakdown in communications – and trust – that generates local dissatisfaction, community concern, online activity and media attention about service failings or simply an organisation's inability to listen or respond. Media coverage on child protection failures and neglect in care homes and hospitals can seriously dent public confidence; headlines about chief officers' salaries or pension payoffs jar with the public when the same council or fire authority is looking at ways of saving money; and rows about the reduced frequency of bin collections or accusations of one-sided public consultations show councils have lost touch with the people they were set up to serve.

Communication breakdown is a backdrop to many of the individual complaints reported by the Local Government and Health Services Ombudsmen (2011/12). For example, complaints by visiting blue badge holders about Cherwell Council's failure to provide signs at its car park entrances informing disabled drivers about a new charging policy resulted in a rebuke from the Ombudsman and a cancellation of £11,600 in parking charges; the Ombudsman stated, 'the work the council had done to raise awareness was not adequate'.

More recently, Birmingham City Council (2012) agreed to pay out over £53,000 after being found guilty of maladministration causing injustice because of delays and failings to meet the assessed needs of a severely disabled adult, Mr N. The Ombudsman concluded that without Advocacy Matters, a voluntary organisation, 'making many telephone calls and sending many e-mails to the council', and the resolve of Mr N's family, the complaint would not have reached the Ombudsman and the injustice would not have been remedied.

The boundaries between our public services and their publics are 'porous' and the interactions both ways, between staff and public, impact on how services and organisations are perceived. 'Front line people are the most important and least acknowledged corporate communicators', highlighted the Audit Commission (1995) some 20 years ago: 'The response of the refuse collector to an angry resident about rubbish spilt on the garden path has more immediate impact on a council's reputation with that resident than the most carefully worded press release or keenly-debated committee decision.'

David Walker (1997) underlines that often-ignored factor in PR strategies that all employees – not just the PR team – have a role in both listening better to and communicating better with the public:

> Every action by an agent of the council performed in public sends a message about the organisation. What it implies is, first, that since communicating with the public occurs virtually everywhere on the external boundary, all councillors and staff need to be aware that they leave a trace, an impression, a message wherever they are in contact with the public. That means, second, that public relations can only be a subset of a wider programme of contact between the local authority and its environment.

Poor communication with citizens and complainants is listed as one of the main barriers to good complaints-handling in the report 'Aiming for the Best' (2011). 'Complaints', the report underlined 'can be a rich source of citizen insight... and should be valued as illustrating what the "customer journey" may be like for the citizen in practice. Complaints can help councils identify risks and weaknesses across services that should inform future planning and commissioning decisions.'

Forty years of the Plain English Campaign has made some differences to how public bodies communicate, but unfortunately has not ended the gobbledygook and lack of clarity in all official communications, offline and online. Sandwell Council's leader, Councillor Darren Cooper was quoted in *Plain English* magazine in 2012 as saying training council staff in clearer communications will 'in the longer term save the council money'. But still many public services websites, now a first port of call for information, remain impenetrable, with vast arrays of official reports and poor search engines.

Also job titles are open to derision as 'non jobs', an easy target for criticism at any time, but more so when cuts are being made to local services. In April 2010, the *Daily Telegraph* listed the 'ten most ridiculous job titles', mostly in councils, including 'waste management and disposal technician' (rubbish collector) and 'wet leisure assistant' (pool attendant). The Taxpayers Alliance's (**www.taxpayersalliance.com/waste**) 'non-job of the week' campaign to root out wasteful spending highlighted the £42k a year 'policy and performance enhancing manager' post for Tower Hamlets Council's parking enforcement services; this 'ridiculous job title' had an accompanying 2,000-word job description.

The Plain English Campaign founder Chrissie Maher said her favourite was Peterborough Council advertising for a 'Head of City Vibrancy': 'What's wrong with head of business investment, if that is what they are after?' (**www.plainenglish.co.uk/examples/job-titles-to-get-the-city-vibrating**). For its jargon and 'difficult language', Maher nominated the first consultation report from the new Humberside police and crime commissioner for the 2013 Golden Bull Awards: 'this is definitely an example of how not to communicate clearly' (*Yorkshire Post*, 2013).

Recent medical research (South Bank University, 2012) found that patient letters from doctors or hospitals, drugs labels and patient information were 'too complex' and open to misinterpretation by 42 per cent of the adult population. Official letters or e-mails from councils also fail the comprehension test. More sensitive listening and clearer communications face to face, on the phone, in letters and e-mails, in texts and tweets, in leaflets and signage could prevent much misunderstanding. All public services should regularly review their written communications.

Public support is further undermined when local public services managers get it wrong in naming or describing new services. The words may mean something to managers – but little to the public. In 2003, Greater Glasgow Health Board launched a major consultation to replace two local Victorian hospitals in the city with 'ACAD's', ambulatory care and diagnostic units. The £130-million state-of-the-art 'units' offered day surgery, investigations, therapies, treatments and a host of outpatient clinics and services. Using the acronym 'ACAD' caused confusion and added to the controversy about perceived loss of hospital services.

It took five years and was well into construction before the health board changed its mind, dropping 'ACAD' for 'hospital' and launching a new information campaign 'to explain clearly what these new hospitals will do'. The board's now chief executive, Robert Calderwood (2008) admitted: 'The initial names given to the hospitals, "ACADs" and "Ambulatory Care Hospitals" have not proven to be successful. Ambulatory is not an everyday word; it has served to cloud – not help – people's understanding of the major role to be played by these new hospitals.'

Poor communication and poor consultation with the public can cause confusion, cost money and even put lives at risk. It undermines trust in public services and the reputation of the council, the hospital or authority responsible for delivering the service. Public relations is integral to service delivery. 'Public relations are there to be made, not endured,' according to Walker (1997): 'Local authorities can reshape the way they are perceived.'

All public services rely on professionals – accountants, solicitors, doctors and nurses, teachers, social workers, engineers, architects, planners, surveyors, food analysts – to deliver specific services. So it should also be for public relations. Central to public relations are the people – citizens, customers, clients, patients or service users – the organisation is set up to serve.

> Identifying and understanding people's opinions and desires and developing them alongside the organization's objectives requires enormous creativity, knowledge and ability to move with the times. This has been, and always will be, the key to public relations excellence.
>
> (Gordon, 2011)

That is the task of the public relations team.

# 02
# The communication team

*Respect and resourcing for local government communication teams falls in and out of favour. There is nothing like a crisis or reorganization to help put better resources into communications. But when will leaders and chief executives understand that this is often too little, too late. The councils with most support from their communities are the ones who make a genuine effort every year, often as a result of their excellent communications.*

**ROBIN TREACHER, CHAIR, CIPR LOCAL GOVERNMENT GROUP 2006–08**

The public relations or communication team should be at the heart of every council and local public service organisation. Its purpose is not just to handle and oversee day-to-day communications with the media, local community and stakeholders, but to provide a strategic communications direction for the organisation. That direction must always be linked to the objectives and priorities of the council or local public service body and to the safeguarding of its overall reputation internally and externally.

Good public relations and communication are not just the province of the team; it should be the hallmark of everyone working in public services; everyone from department heads to service managers, school head teachers and lead planners right down to the front-line staff, receptionists and call centre colleagues, social workers, nurses, home carers, refuse collectors and enforcement officers. The way they interact with citizens and customers impacts on service satisfaction and council reputation.

Ipsos MORI, the polling organisation, in their research work with councils over the last decade have shown that there is a correlation between councils that communicate well and deliver services well: 'If residents feel informed about what their council does, they are more likely to be satisfied with its services. If they believe they receive high quality local services, they are more likely to think they get good value for money. It is a virtuous cycle' (Ipsos Mori/LGA, 2008).

Today's council or local public services communication team will bring together a wide range of communication skills and from different disciplines, including public relations, marketing, journalism, design and graphics. Many teams now include specialists in social media and web content management, consultation, health promotion campaigns, arts promotions, events management and, occasionally, research.

A few teams have additional responsibilities, customer services running information desks or one-stop shops and managing the call centre and web enquiries, dealing with Freedom of Information matters or facilitating TV and film production in their area. Several councils and local public bodies are working together on communications, some contracting comms services from each other, some sharing; this trend is likely to increase. Given that the role of a communications officer in public services communications is wide ranging, Phil McCusker has put together a very useful outline performance framework for reference (see Appendix 2).

# The team's responsibilities

So what are the responsibilities – strategic and operational – for public relations or communication teams serving local public services in the United Kingdom? Here is an extensive list of all responsibilities identified from the authors' study of communication teams across the country – it highlights what could or should be under the 'public relations or communication' umbrella. But in practice most teams do not cover all.

## Strategic

- Strategic priority – putting in place an agreed public relations and communications strategy and plan (for one, two or three years ahead) based on the objectives, strategy and priorities of the organisation and local services.
- Leading on communication – setting the style and tone throughout the organisation, internally and externally.
- Reputation – safeguarding the reputation of the organisation and the services it provides, having a strategy to improve reputation, initiating action when there are reputational risks.
- Brand – reviewing and protecting the council's or organisation's brand, its USP (unique selling point) and DNA.

- Consultation/public engagement – there are duties, some statutory, on public services to consult on priorities, services and service changes, council tax and budgets.
- Lobbying – being an advocate for the area and its residents/service users to government and other public bodies, on key issues, including legislation changes.
- Emergencies planning – being an active partner in civil emergencies planning, with other local and national services and communications teams.
- Evaluation – quantitative and qualitative research to inform decision making; surveys, citizens' panels, focus groups to check satisfaction and reputation; monitoring voice and reach across all media.
- Procurement – not all PR and marketing services can be delivered in-house and deciding what should and should not be is a strategic decision.
- Supporting the policy makers, elected councillors, appointed board members, the chief executive and directors, giving strategic communications advice to help shape decision-making.
- Partnering – taking an overview of public sector communications locally and actively pursue partnerships to provide more effective communications to the public.

## Operational

- The media – dealing proactively and reactively with journalists and programme makers in the local, national and international press, TV, radio and online media on local public services stories and issues.
- Digital and web – overseeing the organisation's digital sites, micro sites, ensuring accessibility for all audiences; maintain, update and develop content, search engine optimisation and analytics.
- Social media – developing the organisation's use and voice on social media, Twitter, YouTube, Facebook, LinkedIn, Flickr, etc, including protocols for staff.
- Campaigns – initiating well-researched local campaigns on a wide range of issues, from recruiting foster parents to promoting recycling, from public safety issues to paying council tax.
- Internal communications – keeping staff at all levels informed and engaged on priorities and changes (this is often seen as a personnel/HR function).
- Crisis communications – ready to take immediate stock and respond 24/7 to a crisis impacting on a service and corporately.

- Emergencies – able to roll out communications during civil and other emergencies (for example severe flooding).
- Social marketing – to promote or 'nudge' behavioural change to improve individual and community health and wellbeing. (In England, public health promotion transfers from NHS to councils during 2013.)
- Place marketing – marketing the local area, city or town for business, investment, tourism, or visiting for shopping, heritage, culture, leisure. (Several cities have separate marketing organisations, for example Glasgow, Manchester, Liverpool.)
- Local services marketing – from schools admissions to free school meals, personalisation of care to promoting local parks.
- Publications – overseeing and managing all publications, including leaflets, reports, and ensuring they are consistent in style and cost-effective in both print and digital formats, and accessible to all audiences.
- Graphics and design – providing an in-house service for graphics and design for print and digital.
- Brand identity – ensuring the logo and name is consistently applied, with rules for any third party usage.
- Photographing/video – commissioning photography and managing the stills, video library, on or offline.
- Copywriting – preparing clear, concise but creative copy for print and digital.
- Information services – providing easy-access information on services, for example one-stop shops, information kiosks and digital terminals.
- Events – event management of local festivals, community consultation days, formal openings of facilities/services, award presentations.
- Speech writing – drafting speeches and presentations for council leader, mayor or provost, cabinet members, chief executive, service directors or board members.
- Supporting councillors in their ward work – publicising their role, their surgeries both on and offline.
- Advertising – placing all paid-for advertising cost-effectively, and managing messages, content and style.
- Complaints – handling and responding to complaints corporately.
- Freedom of Information – corporate point of contact for dealing with FOI requests from the public, and meeting the requirements of the FOI Act.
- Film office – bringing to the area and facilitating TV and film productions, a practical economic generation function.

# Shaping the team

The organisation and positioning of public relations, marketing and the wider communication function varies markedly across the local public services. The UK Audit Agencies defined the communications function in a public services organisation in 2010 when they set out for the first time performance indicators for communications (see Table 2.1).

**TABLE 2.1** Communication function for public service organisations

**Internal communications**
*Staff whose roles primarily involve:*
Employee engagement
Change management
Internal channel management

**Digital/social media**
*Staff whose roles primarily involve:*
Using electronic media to target audiences, both internal and external to the organisation. Key channels include internet, intranet and social media

**Strategic communications**
*Staff whose roles primarily involve:*
Strategic communications advice
Stakeholder engagement
Customer insight

**Corporate communications**
*Staff whose roles primarily involve:*
Brand management
Corporate reputation management
Corporate publications (eg annual reports)
It may also involve digital communications, stakeholder engagement and internal communications

**Marketing**
*Staff whose roles primarily involve:*
Campaign management (eg agency management, campaign evaluation, events)
Sponsorship and partnership marketing
Customer insight
Research and evaluation
Stakeholder engagement
Publications, including print procurement, design and editorial/copywriting of printed, customer-facing communication materials

**TABLE 2.1** *continued*

**Media/press**
*Staff whose roles primarily involve:*
Media handling
Media-focused events/ministerial visits etc
Media planning (eg managing a grid)
Public relations
Speechwriting
Public affairs

**Senior management**
Senior managers whose role is not tied to a discipline, ie directors or heads of communication. (Senior staff tied to a discipline, for example a head of marketing should be reported under the category above)

**Support staff**
Support staff are included when they spend over 50 per cent of their time supporting the work of communicators (either within the central communication function or supporting embedded communicators in other departments/sections). For example, administration staff, business manager, personal assistant, team support officer, diary secretary.

**NOTE:** Communication posts are defined as those where staff spend more than 50 per cent of their time on the above activities.

UK Audit Agencies *Communications Performance Indicators*, UK Audit Agencies, June 2010, licensed under the Open Government Licence.

Police and fire services tend to opt for a very centralised and corporate communication team, now often managed by a civilian head but usually reporting to a senior uniformed officer at assistant or deputy chief constable level. In the local health services – health trusts or health boards – public relations and media relations are also mainly a corporate function. Although in England with the abolition of the primary care trusts, this will change with health promotion responsibilities moving to local councils and clinical commissioning groups deciding whether to commission a localised PR/communication service (privately or through a local council) or through a nationally planned service.

In local government the picture is more complex; each council, whether by design or default, has its own structure, with the communication function differentially split, but separately managed, corporately and departmentally. Corporate communications, mainly dealing with the media, is based within the council's chief executive's or corporate services department, while service departments often run their own communications, particularly promotions, campaigns and publications. With the current pressures on council budgets, communications and its delivery is under the spotlight; a move to a more integrated and corporate approach to council communication is gaining pace. It is not just about saving money, although that is a factor, it is about councils taking a more strategic approach, aligning communications to the council's objectives and priorities. In this section we will look at some recent examples.

Council communications have developed in an ad hoc way over the last 50 years. Three distinct strands have emerged: dealing with the press; providing public information; and the promotion or marketing of facilities and services. The 'press' function was usually delivered centrally, frequently headed up and staffed by former journalists. The 'information' and 'marketing' functions were mainly delivered departmentally or responsibilities uneasily split with the central team. Staff were recruited who had experience in marketing, journalism, public relations or promotions.

Service departments, rather than the council corporately, were better at grasping the need for marketing and public relations, and convincing their service committees at the time for budget and staffing. So social services, education, roads, leisure and cultural departments, for example, appointed their own dedicated staff, embedded within the department, with a variety of job titles – information officer, publicity officer, promotions manager, sponsorship officer, campaigns officer, welfare rights officer and sometimes press officer. Their job was mainly to publicise services, run campaigns and support events. Their responsibility was to the department, not the council overall. Their communications priorities were departmental, often with little or no reference to the council.

For example, Leicestershire County Council – the 2009 winner of the *Local Government Chronicle* 'Council of the Year' Award – had in the same year 46 staff undertaking communications work across the council, spending in total around £3 million a year. Approximately 60 per cent of the spend and the staff were in four service departments, namely children and young people, adult social care, highways, transport and waste, and community services. The 'central' functions were divided between two departments: PR, press and design in the chief executive's; and internal communications and the website in corporate services. Westminster City Council's communications consultancy, Westco Trading, was brought in to review the structure; its review was thorough and its conclusion blunt. This approach is 'ineffective'. A step change is required starting with 'a clear message, carried through a coherent one council communications strategy' (Corkey, Wholey and Compton, 2009a).

Councils have been slower than private sector companies to embrace integration and a strategic approach to corporate communications. Westco's research found managers in Leicestershire supported a more proactive and planned communications approach, but could not agree on the best way for this to be structured. There was a three-way split – 37 per cent supporting centralised communications, 35 per cent retaining function with departments, and 28 per cent wanting some more centralised, but not all (Corkey, Wholey and Compton, 2009a). This is not surprising. Department directors and managers across councils are often the most resistant to corporate change; most cannot see beyond the department's priorities and some would prefer to promote the department, rather than the council, as a brand. It is also their comfort zone. Understandably, there is a fear about loss of control, as resource and budget moves away. But there is a genuine worry that moving marketing, PR and promotions from the department to the centre could impact adversely on their services, or the department's trading income.

Leicestershire, albeit a large council, is typical of many councils with split communication functions, only the scale will be different. A study in 2009 of English councils highlighted that just over half of all councils' communications staff were located in a centralised or corporate team. But there were significant variations. District councils had the highest number of staff (72 per cent) and county councils the lowest (22 per cent) in a central team. The proportion for London boroughs was 52 per cent, and for metropolitan and unitary councils 31 per cent and 33 per cent respectively (LGcomms, 2009a). Liza Greaves' (2012) survey of 69 councils confirms the trend towards centralisation in districts and boroughs but other councils still have comms staff 'not under the aegis of the central team'.

Westco's conclusions for Leicestershire could be applied to all councils with a split communications function; the council's voice is diluted by departmental messages and a myriad of departmental publications, and no overall communications strategy. Westco made a series of recommendations for change: a move to 'unified communications' and a corporate communications planning model to identify priority campaigns in service areas for executing corporately (Corkey, Wholey and Compton, 2009b). Leicestershire has restructured its communications with a new corporate communications team of 25, focusing primarily on media relations and proactive campaigns, but with an emphasis on the latter (see Figure 2.1).

Bolton Council was one of the first councils to radically restructure and integrate its communications, around the imaginative and award-winning 'Bolton Brand' (Bolton Council, 2006).

A communications and marketing agency was established in 2006 within the council 'to drive greater efficiencies, both qualitatively and quantitatively, across the council's consultation and research, marketing, design and communications activities' and to build and manage a positive reputation for both the town and the council. The three integration drivers to create a 'holistic' way of managing communications were present – market and environment, communication and organisation (Cornelissen, 2008). For Bolton, there was a clear business case: efficiency savings in consolidation, reputation management benefits and delivery benefits.

An assistant director responsible for communications and marketing headed up the new integrated set-up, with four teams each having a lead manager – marketing (supporting services), communications and media (including council publications), strategic development (marketing Bolton) and, significantly, consultation and research, which would 'evaluate council policies, monitor customers and stakeholders satisfaction and gather supporting evidence to shape council services'. The agency promoted itself across the borough and sought service level agreements with, among others,

**FIGURE 2.1**   Leicestershire County Council Communications Team 2012

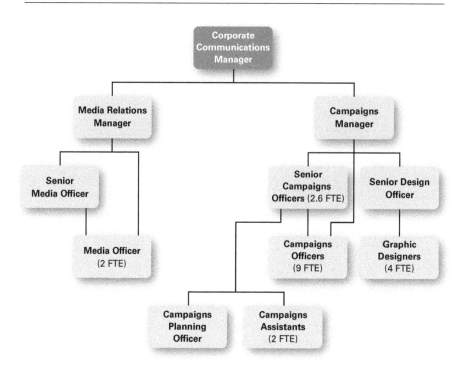

a major leisure provider and the local primary care trust. Since 2010, with council cuts and reduced income from trading, the Bolton communications and marketing team has been significantly downsized, but within the basic 2006 framework.

Other councils have reshaped their teams differently. In 2012, Scotland's biggest council, Glasgow City Council, restructured and renamed its section 'communication and service development' with the head of service reporting to the chief executive. The city council is, like many councils, in the midst of a transformation programme for 'tomorrow's council' and the new section is seen as an enabler. There are six teams under the same umbrella: corporate customer care; corporate service reform; marketing and internal communications; organisational development; public relations and press office; and web development. The 10-person press office 'promotes the council's activities and protects its reputation in the media'. Marketing and internal communications is responsible for brand management, campaigns, promoting policies and services, council advertising and the publication of the quarterly staff magazine *Insider* and the now twice-yearly council magazine *Glasgow* (Glasgow City Council, 2012).

Over recent years, several of Glasgow's council services have been spun out into arm's length external organisations (ALEOs) wholly owned by the council. These include Glasgow Life (formerly the city's cultural and leisure services), Cordia (home care, school meals, catering and cleaning services, lollipop wardens), City Building (construction and building repairs and maintenance) and City Parking. Each is responsible for their own separate branding and communications. Glasgow Life has its own in-house team and City Building and Cordia contract external contractors for public relations, media relations and marketing. Although the council corporate team work closely with the ALEOs, the separate structures and branding distance these services from the council, yet it is the council that ultimately picks up the bill. For the council taxpayer, there must be confusion when visiting a leisure centre or one of the city's museums or receiving a home care service. This makes it impossible to achieve integrated communications. It highlights one of the issues now facing councils – and their communications – when more and more services are contracted out to arm's length or private companies, partnerships or voluntary organisations.

The best examples of communications being reorganised and aligned to council objectives are in Derbyshire and Essex.

Derbyshire County Council radically reshaped its communications function in 2011/12. For the last 20 or so years, public relations was organised traditionally around four teams: press office; promotions; graphics/technical; and the Call Derbyshire call centre. The council's policy is that communications should always be delivered by a corporate team at the heart of the organisation; some communication posts and projects continue to be directly funded by services, for example to promote fostering and recycling, but the work is managed corporately.

The new structure (see Figure 2.2) creates three multidisciplinary teams, a digital web and development team, along with the existing contact centre. The multidisciplinary teams are responsible for 'corporate issues' (finance, culture, regeneration and the council leadership), 'children and young people' (education, youth, children and families) and 'adults and environment' (adult care, highways and transport, technology and recycling). These responsibilities ensure a much closer link with council objectives and service plan priorities. The teams cover all communications channels, including campaigns, internal and external publications, advertising, proactive media relations, internal communications, marketing, events and roadshows. Four communications officers work on a rota basis to staff a 'news desk' to deal with day-to-day media activity, ensuring the planned work of the teams is uninterrupted.

The digital team manages the council's digital infrastructure, including the Tridion content management system, the corporate GIS (geographic information system) of maps and data for council services and the public, web services such as SiteImprove and GovDelivery, and a portfolio of 22 council websites. A publications panel of the council leader and communications director and deputy oversee the council's branding and scrutinise the case for all the council's print; already they have saved £250,000 in the first year.

**FIGURE 2.2** Derbyshire County Council Communications Team 2012

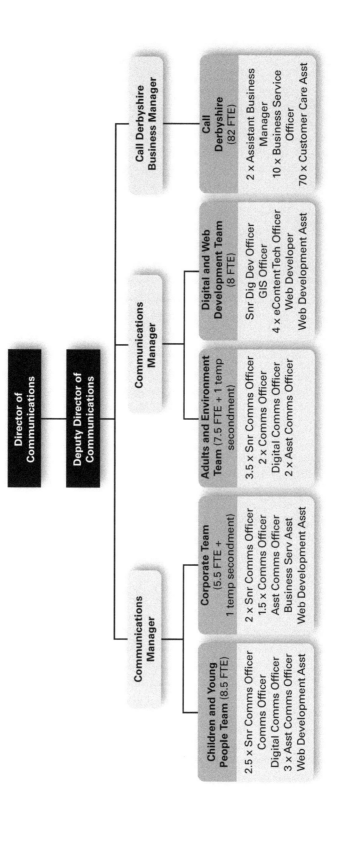

Director of Communications

Deputy Director of Communications

Communications Manager

Communications Manager

Call Derbyshire Business Manager

**Children and Young People Team (8.5 FTE)**
2.5 x Snr Comms Officer
Comms Officer
Digital Comms Officer
3 x Asst Comms Officer
Web Development Asst

**Corporate Team (5.5 FTE + 1 temp secondment)**
2 x Snr Comms Officer
1.5 x Comms Officer
Asst Comms Officer
Business Serv Asst
Web Development Asst

**Adults and Environment Team (7.5 FTE + 1 temp secondment)**
3.5 x Snr Comms Officer
2 x Comms Officer
Digital Comms Officer
2 x Asst Comms Officer

**Digital and Web Development Team (8 FTE)**
Snr Dig Dev Officer
GIS Officer
4 x eContentTech Officer
Web Developer
Web Development Asst

**Call Derbyshire (82 FTE)**
2 x Assistant Business Manager
10 x Business Service Officer
70 x Customer Care Asst

Derbyshire has won more than 100 awards and accolades for its public relations work over the last five years because of a 'professional, creative and focused' approach, emphasising, they state, 'substance, not spin'. They work to tight budgets and invest in staff training (Tozer, 2012). Their communications focus is on:

- creating a better understanding between council and customers;
- delivering key messages about the council and its services;
- ensuring high take-up of services and benefits by local people;
- securing wide coverage of council decisions and activities;
- monitoring public perception and views about council services.

Following a major review undertaken by Westco, Essex Council's external communications were rationalised and centralised, with a one-off saving of more than £1 million. Essex Communications was set up in 2009 as a 'full account managed service' for both clients, the service departments in Essex County Council, and external clients, including the local enterprise partnership and other councils. The team brings together skills in public relations, marketing, e-comms, design, campaign management, events, lobbying, brand management, publications and research (CIPR PRide Awards, 2012).

Essex Communications states its mission is:

> to promote the work of Essex County Council, to enhance and protect its reputation, to win resources for the organisation, to attract and retain quality members of staff, to increase access to and awareness of services, to increase residents' satisfaction and to promote the wider county of Essex as an unrivalled place to live, invest, learn and visit.

However, what makes Essex Communications different is how it is structured, under its head of external communications and marketing (see Figure 2.3).

There are three core teams, each with an account manager and each responsible for focusing on one of the three key areas of the council's corporate strategy and delivery programme, EssexWorks – our people, our economy and our world. People deals with policies and services affecting residents and their quality of life, increasing educational achievement and skills, promoting health and leisure, and supporting the vulnerable. Economy covers transport, promoting sustainable economic growth and delivering value for money. World includes recycling and reducing waste, promoting a cleaner, greener Essex and making communities safer. Through organising communications under these remits, the council's strategic priorities are operationally married to communications objectives, and a proactive communications activity.

Each team – people, economy and world – is a multidisciplinary corporate campaign team, with at least six communications staff: manager, two/three account executives, senior designer, press officer and events co-ordinator. Additionally, Essex Communications has a fourth team handling day-to-day corporate communications. This includes the editor of *EssexWorks*, the

**FIGURE 2.3** Essex Communications 2011

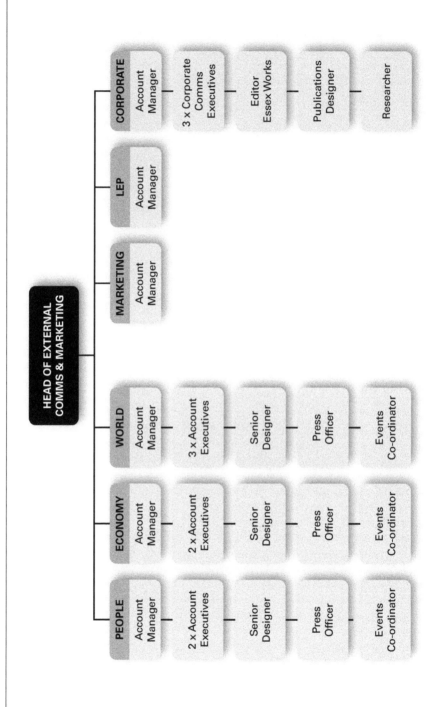

council's magazine, a publications designer and three corporate communications executives. Part of their work is overseeing the council's publications, now corporately, rather than departmentally, controlled and branded. A separate account executive provides communications support (media, website and social media, and events) to the local enterprise partnership under contract. Staff also undertake work for other councils and partners. There is political and senior managerial buy-in. Essex Communications is governed by a strategic communications and public affairs board, which includes the leader of the council, cabinet members and directors. The board interrogates the business case for proposed campaigns, further ensuring that communications and campaigns are in tune with the council's agreed priorities.

Building on the success of EssexWorks, a new EssexWorks corporate plan for 2012–17 was approved by the council in 2012, along with a five years communications strategy linked to it. This sets out the three communication priorities. First, developing a small number of intelligence-led consumer marketing and cross-cutting campaigns to support the council's key priorities. Second, marketing and resident research to take forward the council's commitment to externalise some council services and, if so, how they should be council branded. Third, developing the council's capacity to engage with and influence key audiences. This, states the strategy, will require capacity building in the team, more expertise in market research, evaluation, customer engagement and social media (Essex County Council, 2012).

The clarity and focus of the Essex Communications team approach has brought dividends. The team and their campaigns have notched up over 20 industry awards in two years; for example 'Drive Essex' targeting 17–30-year-olds to change their driving behaviour and 'Good for Essex' promoting volunteering – and the big society – in partnership with many of the county's district and parish councils. The team was the regional CIPR PRide outstanding in-house team of the year in 2011 and 2012. Their work and focus has been listed as a factor in protecting the council's reputation following the much-publicised arrest in 2011, and subsequent court case and jailing, of Essex's council leader Lord Hanningford (Paul White) over fraudulently claiming parliamentary expenses (CIPR awards entry, 2012).

# Leadership

How communications are effectively delivered – strategically and operationally – depends much on the leadership of the communication team. Does the leader have the confidence of the chief executive, the strategic directors, the board or the council's leadership? What are the attributes and competencies required of a director of public relations or head of communications? The titles 'head' or 'director' are used differently and can imply status in terms of pay grades, but for our purposes they mean the most senior person charged with the management of communications, public relations and marketing within a council or local public service.

Professor Anne Gregory (2008) in her study into the competencies and behaviours of senior communication practitioners in both the public and private sectors found that 'investigating and analysing' and 'preparing thoroughly' featured in the top 10 for the private sector, but not on the public sector list. 'The more obvious business-orientated behaviours of analysis and investigation, thinking strategically and preparation are demonstrated more overtly in the private sector where a focus on business performance is critical,' stated Gregory. Public sector competencies, such as building strong relationships and consulting, were weighted heavily towards people and collaborative and consensual working (see Table 2.2). Business environmental scanning – a key contribution public relations can make at the top level – was 'not required as much' in the public sector.

**TABLE 2.2**   The 10 competency titles, descriptions and summary behavioural indicators for public sector communicators

- *Understanding the bigger picture:* Demonstrates a comprehensive understanding of the impact of organisational strategy on own responsibilities.
- *Taking action:* Makes prompt and clear decisions, empowers others to do the same.
- *Consulting and involving:* Works with staff, 'customers' and the wider community to ensure successful consultation and support.
- *Presenting and communicating:* Ensures audience understanding through the use of an appropriate and interactive communication style.
- *Creating and innovating:* Seeks out new ways of doing things and implements change purposefully but sensitively.
- *Persuading and influencing:* Gains clear agreement and commitment to an agreed course of action through effective persuasion and negotiation.
- *Upholding the reputation of the service:* Behaves consistently with clear personal values which complement those of the organisation and wider community.
- *Building strong relationships:* Relates well to a broad range of people, building and maintaining an extensive network of contacts.
- *Managing under pressure:* Finds ways to enable self and others to cope with difficult challenges, demonstrates clear thinking and keeps problems in perspective.
- *Formulating strategies and concepts:* Thinks broadly, conceptualises clearly, creates a vision and develops solutions.

From Gregory, A (2008) Competencies of senior communications practitioners in the UK: An initial study, *Public Relations Review*, Vol 34, p 220 © 2008 Elsevier.

Senior public sector communications were, according to the study, under more pressure than their private sector equivalents; this was because they were much more involved in day-to-day implementation matters, including reacting to the media agenda. Even two of the listed top public sector competencies 'formulating strategies and concepts' and 'creativity and innovation' were, on further analysis, more to do with operational work, such as planning for campaigns on tight budgets, than strategy.

This picture of senior public sector communicators was mirrored in a report 'The Chief Executive's Challenge', a study by LGcommunications into the perceptions of council chief executives and political leaders into their communications function and its leadership. They concluded that there was a lack of strategic focus (LGcommunications, 2008).

Heads or directors of communications were seen as 'effective channel managers' rather than 'business strategists'. Main weaknesses identified were little proactivity in handling the media, insufficient political nous, not enough understanding of local government and its financing, and a lack of ability to persuade or influence other senior directors or politicians. To meet the challenge and to gain their confidence at the top level, the chief executives bluntly stated that communications and public relations heads had to up their game. In effect, they had to make a shift from communications to corporate business management and show how communications can strategically add value to the top table.

That challenge was picked up a year later with the publication of 'The commission on competencies for senior communication roles', a significant report by experienced strategic communicators from councils, consultancies and academia (LGcommunications, 2009b). It set out and details six competencies and qualities necessary for leadership in communications:

1  Strategic communications
2  Leadership influence and experience
3  Excellent communications effectiveness
4  Truthfulness, integrity, honesty
5  Resilience
6  Political nous

What separates a good communications director from a leading communications director is fulfilling that strategic role, 'connecting communications to the vision of the organisation'. This involves 'horizon scanning and creativity' and embracing those business-orientated behaviours and competencies Gregory found in her study to be missing in the top 10 for public sector communicators.

To be strategic, the report emphasised, communication directors must not just have an understanding of the business of local government, but be experts in local government and what matters in policy terms. They have to understand business strategy, local government finance and funding, so they can fully contribute to the corporate discussion. They must 'not only be in touch with their own organisation but attuned to other stakeholders and the public'; that also requires understanding the whys and wherefores of stakeholder engagement.

Credibility depends on that strategic understanding of the business – whether the setting be local government, police, the fire services, health trusts or boards or local enterprise partnerships. Chief executives and leaders expect their communications head or director (and the team) to deliver excellent communications, but are also looking for stronger proactive media management including social media; better evaluation and research on communications effectiveness; political savvy to work effectively across the management/political divide; and resilience to cope with conflicts. Integrity and honesty is paramount to earn the trust of senior colleagues internally and externally in dealing with a crisis or sensitive matters.

Greaves' (2012) latest survey shows that communications 'influence' in authorities appears disturbingly low. Only 11 out of 69 comms heads interviewed sit on the management team and a further 30 report directly to someone on the team. That means one in three comms heads have no direct or indirect voice at the top table. More worrying is that only one in four comms heads can attend key senior officer/political meetings 'by right'. Most can only attend 'if invited'.

This snapshot adds to the ongoing debate about whether or not the head or director of communications should be included in the strategic management team. An experienced communications consultant to councils, Mark Fletcher-Brown (2012) has stated the 'obsession' with the top table is often misplaced. It is better to have 'walk in rights with your chief exec'. And through that you can contribute more, but only if you are 'thought useful, get to the point quickly and bring solutions to today's, and anticipate tomorrow's, problems'.

The debate should be less about who should sit at the top table. It is more about who *must* sit at the top table. And that 'must' is earned and recognised by all others around the table. The 'must' requires the communications head to take a leadership role, bringing something significant to the table's decision-making: not just advice in managing communications, but taking a strategic 360-degree view of the organisation and the current and future issues it faces.

Leadership may be the 'best vehicle to showcase the true power of public relations' according to Moss and DeSanto (2012). Their detailed study underlines that there is 'more than a semantic difference' between leadership and management. Leadership is being innovative, creative, proactive and looks beyond the status quo to reinvent: 'Public relations is a natural component of leadership because it is concerned with short term and long term actions and changes, in that it constructs the language of actions and changes for organizations.'

# Professionalism

Leadership, too, is about developing professionalism in the team and making sure staff are both skilled for the tasks they do and know the rules, including the political rules, under which they operate. This is particularly important for council and public services communications staff. It is also vital to be up to speed on the latest thinking and technology. Daljit Bhurji (2012), managing director of integrated PR agency Diffusion, puts it succinctly:

> Keeping on top of trends and expanding knowledge across as many areas of PR and social media as possible should be our goal. But the skills we choose to develop need to be more specific to our strengths. The jack of all trades but master of none will have limited value in the future.

Members of the PR team come from different backgrounds and via different routes – some through marketing, some through journalism, some directly from a course in communication or public relations, others from PR in other sectors or with experience in, for example, digital communications and content management.

Colleges and universities offer diploma and degree courses in public relations, many available part time or online. In an increasingly competitive work environment most will want to develop their professional skills.

All public sector organisations will have at least annual staff assessments, although for many it can be seen as a box-ticking exercise. For members of the PR team, there is an opportunity to link such assessments to a continuous professional development (CPD) scheme run by the Chartered Institute of Public Relations (CIPR) or the Chartered Institute of Marketing (CIM) through training courses, webinars, in-house training, conferences, study days, networking, personal learning and gaining professional qualifications. Such a link can give a focus to both the individual's career development and the employer's team development. This is operating successfully for public relations and marketing staffs in several public services organisations, as well as in-house teams in the private sector and consultancies.

Membership of a chartered body promotes professionalism. CIPR and CIM members have to abide by a code of practice and to commit themselves to professional development. Through personal learning and skills training, members can widen and update their knowledge, understanding and skills base. The most experienced practitioners might support and encourage the development of others and gain CPD points for doing so. Whatever career stage, CPD gives a framework to plan and manage personal and professional development. CIPR members on CPD can earn points and progress to become an accredited practitioner and CPD is an essential part of becoming a chartered practitioner.

A host of relevant courses, conferences and online training or study guides – which can add CPD points – are also available from a range of bodies, including CIPR and its Local Public Services Group, Public Relations

Consultants Association (PRCA), LGcommunications, Consultation Institute, Local Government Information Unit, Local Government Association and the National Union of Journalists. LGcommunications runs an annual leadership academy for communicators.

Gregory (2009a) suggests that there is an obligation on PR practitioners to be as professional as possible – taking education and training as seriously as other professions, such as colleagues in finance and accountancy, law, medicine, building surveying, pharmacy or architecture: 'It is right and proper that organizations expect the highest standards from their communicators, just as they would from corporate lawyers or accountants.'

Improving public relations ethics has been a key component in achieving greater professionalism (Day, Dong and Robins, 2001). Professional public relations institutes across the world, including CIPR, align themselves with the Global Alliance Code of Ethics (see **www.globalalliancepr.org/website/ page/code-ethics**). All CIPR members agree to abide by a code of professional conduct, which is based around the three principles of integrity, competence and confidentiality (see Appendix 3). Through ascribing to the code, CIPR members fulfil the purpose set out in the Institute's Royal Charter 'to promote for the public benefit high levels of skill, knowledge, competence and standards of practice and professional conduct on the part of public relations practitioners'.

Practitioners have to think about conflicting loyalties and duties – to yourself, to your employer, to your council, to your organisation, to your profession, to your publics, to society. Key considerations are:

- doing what you believe to be right, just and fair;
- making sure you have the skills to do the work assigned to you;
- keeping your knowledge, skills and expertise up to date.

Operating with integrity and respect will deliver the highest professional and ethical standards and will not bring the profession into disrepute (Parsons, 2004). When Dr Jon White undertook a series of scenario planning meetings with PR practitioners across the country in 2011, he found their expectations for the profession in 2020 were to be 'confident, committed to professional development and working to well-developed codes of conduct' (see Appendix 4).

# Political nous

Political nous is essential for every member of the communications team. All local public services organisations are 'political' – they are either run by elected councillors, elected mayors or elected police and crime commissioners (PCCs), or exist because of local and national political decisions and are funded mainly by the taxpayer. So the communication team is working in a 'political' environment. Their campaigns, activities, statements, tweets and blogs can be interpreted – or misinterpreted – as 'political', or even 'Political', party political.

Everyone in the communications team should be clear on the law and the rules. In summary, the Local Government Act 1986 states: 'a local authority shall not publish any material which in whole or in part appears to be designed to affect the public support for a political party.' The 'Recommended Code of Practice for Local Government Publicity' is an essential reference. It was first published in 1988 and amended in 2001, and completely revised in 2011 for England only. Because of devolution, the 1988 Code still applies in Scotland and the Welsh Assembly published and revised the Code in 2013.

The latest 2011 'Recommended Code of Practice for Local Government Publicity' for England (see Appendix 1a) continues to ban the publication of any material that could be deemed party political but sets out other restrictions, on lobbying, and the frequency of council newspapers or magazines. There is a 'purdah' on most publicity during election periods. All councils and public bodies and their communication teams have to consider carefully any departure from recommended practice.

LGcommunications and Solicitors Bevan Brittan LLP have prepared a helpful guide, called 'Cracking the Code', based on the 2011 Code of Practice (LGcommunications, 2011). The guide sets out what the Code means for local government communicators, dispels some myths, and highlights the comms role in the 'promotion of local democracy'. It says the Code is 'not designed to stop us doing our jobs' but understanding the Code fully will enable council communicators to do their job with confidence.

Any member of the council communications team – or in fact anyone in the council – who speaks 'on a regular basis to journalists or broadcasters' is deemed 'politically restricted' under the Local Government and Housing Act 1989. This means they cannot take any active part in politics, canvass, hold office in a political party or stand as a candidate in an election. The 1989 Act has not been amended to take account of the development of social media. But the Local Government Political Restrictions Exemptions Adjudicator for Scotland is advising Scottish councils that the terms of the Act now includes dissemination of information to the general public through social media.

> The intention of the LG&H Act 1989 was to ensure that political restrictions applied to every post holder whose job was to brief the media in matters which the local authority wished to disseminate to the general public. In the parlance of 1989 that meant speaking to the press. In 2012 it includes direct broadcasting through social media. I therefore take the view that political restrictions should apply to the holder of a post under a local authority all or part of whose job involves the dissemination to the general public of information on behalf of the local authority, whether that information is disseminated through journalists or broadcasters or directly through social media.
>
> (Marjoribanks, 2012)

This inclusion of staff 'speaking' on behalf of the council through the social media could be applicable across the United Kingdom. In Wales it would be a matter for the Welsh adjudicator. In England, it is now up to chief executives to decide who is politically restricted. Communications and other council staff providing content for the web and communicating through social media should check their position before engaging in any political activities.

# Measuring performance

Measuring communications activity – a fostering, road safety or public health campaign – is easier than measuring the performance of the communications team. Overall, evaluation has proved to be the 'Achilles heel' of the communications function, according to Moss and DeSanto (2012). They suggest moving towards an 'impact measurement'. The problem is separating out the overall impact of the communication function and the success or otherwise of the organisation. What indicators should be measured? Does the function and team add value to the overall delivery of public service? What is that 'added value' and can it be measured? Is the team and its communications activity cost-effective? How does the team compare with other communications teams in the same sector (council, police, fire services, health) or across the public services?

Two very different approaches have been developed to measure and evaluate communications in local public services. The first, by the UK's five audit agencies (Audit Commission, Audit Scotland, National Audit Office, Northern Ireland Audit Office and Wales Audit Office), was part of a series of corporate performance indicators assessing value for money. And the second, a performance test based on reputation advocated jointly by the Local Government Association and the network for senior local government communicators, LGcommunications; their view is that assessing reputation should underpin any communications measurement.

The audit agencies' communication indicators are not mandatory, but were published as a guide and catalyst for public services organisations to benchmark PR, marketing and communications. They defined for the first time 'the scope of the communications function' (see Table 2.1, page 22) and set out to identify 'the requirement of a modern, value for money communications function'. There are five communication indicators (see Table 2.3. These are detailed in the online resources at **http://www.koganpage.com/ PRGov**).

The first three are numbers driven, dealing with total costs and staffing. Much of the data required aggregates totals for staffing costs (including temporary staff and consultants), other operational and programme costs and staffing numbers under the communications umbrella. The Audit Agencies guide sets out in detail what actually should be included within the complete communications function of a council or public services organisation (UK

**TABLE 2.3** Communication performance indicators

(as set by the UK Audit Agencies 2010)

*Indicator 1:*
Communication costs as a percentage of organisational running costs

*Indicator 2:*
Communication staff as a percentage of total staff

*Indicator 3:*
Professional communication staff as a percentage of communication staff

*Indicator 4:*
Internal client and stakeholder satisfaction index

*Indicator 5:*
Management practices

Audit Agencies, 2010). This is both the central communications team/function and all 'embedded communicators' who spend half their time or more on communications, and are based in other departments or sections and often costed under separate budgets.

These totals provide an annual 'level of investment in communication activity' and 'should be a reflection of the communication challenge facing the organisation, not the size of the organisation'. That gets to the heart of what the auditors want councils to focus on – are the costs of running the communications function in proportion to the resources that are being managed? Are they spending more or staffed more than other councils with similar challenges and why? An analysis of embedded and central staffing and programme spend could highlight whether 'efficiencies can be driven by centralising expenditure'.

Professionalism is underlined in Indicator 3. Councils who have a significant proportion of communicators who are not termed professional should be looking at ways of improving the ratio, through training and professional development.

Indicator 4 assesses the views or perceptions of the users of the communications services. It builds a picture of satisfaction based on five statements where clients and stakeholders are asked to score on a scale of 1 (strongly disagree) to 5 (strongly agree). For example, the first is: 'The communication function delivers good quality, professional advice to develop communications activity in support of my business.' The integrity of this indicator does depend heavily on how extensively and honestly views are gathered from clients. These clients are usually other departments or sections within the organisation or external public bodies.

Indicator 5 focuses solely on specific management practices; according to the auditors these are key and help to indicate whether or not communications is a 'well run, capable and mature function'. Its 10 sound management practices (see Table 2.4) should be adopted by all councils, public services organisations and their communication managers. Greaves (2012) in her annual survey found that at least three out of four comms teams achieved indicators 1, 2, 4, 5 and 10. Teams fell short on indicators 6 (evaluation) and 9 (professional development). The Audit Agencies, in drawing up this indicator, recognised it may need to be upgraded once most bodies achieve all 10 practices.

**TABLE 2.4** Management practices for communication: Performance Indicator 5

(as set by the UK Audit Agencies 2010)

*Score out of 10 number of practices adopted by the central communication function*

1 Communication strategy and activity is explicitly linked to organisational business objectives.

2 Communication activity, for the most part, is underpinned by a recorded communications strategy.

3 Communication strategy and annual plan are signed off by the relevant board or equivalent governance group.

4 Communication strategy, plan and activity are based on customer/audience understanding and insight where appropriate.

5 External communication activity is integrated across channels and includes an appropriate mix of marketing, media, digital and stakeholder activity.

6 Communication outputs and outcomes are evaluated through appropriate methods and the findings used to inform future activity.

7 The most senior officer in the organisation with a dedicated communication role is a member of or has a direct report to the board or equivalent management group.

8 Communicators regularly advise policy and business delivery colleagues in the development of strategy.

9 The organisation offers continuing professional development for all our communication staff and all members of staff undertook this activity over the last year.

10 The organisation has driven down the cost of acquiring procured communication products and services this year (ie procured services included in Indicator 1: Costs), based on a like-for-like comparison with the previous year.

Communications was the last of the corporate indicators published by the UK audit offices, an acknowledgement in part that it was one of the most challenging to develop. What it does provide is a common baseline for evaluating public services communications and its costs; but there are significant gaps.

There are no indicators to evaluate wider public perceptions or the impact the communications function has on the services, people and area, and on the work the public services body is there to support. Nonetheless, the UK Audit approach has been welcomed and adopted nationally and internationally; the Scottish Government and the UK Government Cabinet Office have, among others, used the indicators as a key benchmarking tool for communications. The New Zealand Government Treasury has introduced a communications management practice metric based on Indicator 5. The Chartered Institute of Public Finance and Accountancy (CIPFA) offer a benchmarking service to public bodies using the UK Audit Office's five recommended communication performance indicators for its member councils and public services. CIPFA's individually tailored reports assess each organisation's communications performance, benchmarked against others on areas such as spend and staffing, helping public bodies to pinpoint their strengths and weaknesses (CIPFA, 2010).

Using data from councils in 2009/10 and 2010/11 for indicators 1 and 2, CIPFA's analysis shows that the average cost of running the communications function is 0.4 per cent of the total organisation's running costs, but total communications staff (both central and embedded) averages 0.5 per cent of the organisation's total staffing. CIPFA's recent work confirms the continuing importance of media relations in particular, along with corporate communications in the total activity of council communications (see Figure 2.4). The two areas account for almost half (48 per cent) of the communications staff workload carried out. Internal communications is the third most important activity, accounting for one-sixth of the average communications workload. Digital/social media emerges as the fourth main activity, followed by marketing and strategic communications.

Performance measurement is as important for the communications function as for any other service area. The audit agencies' approach through CIPFA offers a route in default of any statutory communications indicators. Having a detailed breakdown of annual costs, staffing etc for an organisation's communications, together with information on how it compares with others, is a starting point to understanding best value. For public sector communication managers and their organisations, these reports should assist in more informed decisions on budget and improvements to the communications function.

Benchmarking and performance comparisons should not be 'an end in itself', warns Audit Scotland (2012), rather an opportunity to ask questions. Why are others performing better or cheaper than us? 'Benchmarking can be a powerful tool for managers to improve services, but used inappropriately it can also be expensive and can fail to deliver benefits.'

**FIGURE 2.4** Average communications staff time spent on communications activities in 2010/11 (excluding support staff)

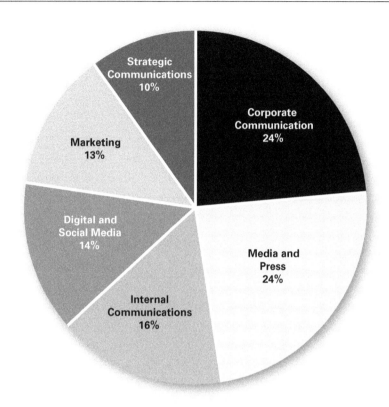

SOURCE: CIPFA 2012, **www.vfmindicators.co.uk**

The second – a 'reputation' approach to communications performance – was first developed as part of the Local Government Association's Reputation Campaign in England in 2005 to set performance targets and actions.

Using the annual council best practice performance indicators (BVPIs) and Ipsos MORI research into individual councils and their services, its focus was on the difference councils and their communications activity can make to individuals and communities. Performance was all about improving public 'satisfaction' and reputation. Satisfaction was measured through council-commissioned surveys into residents' views, residents' panels and focus groups. Initially, 12 core actions or minimum targets were set and a council's performance was self-assessed and graded 'gold', 'silver' or 'bronze'.

Seven of the 12 actions were around environmental issues, which scored poorly in resident satisfaction surveys at the time, for example adopting a visible council branding for the council's cleaning operations, dealing with 'grot spots', setting up a report line, and removing abandoned vehicles. The five specific to communications were consistent council branding of services, media management to promote and defend the council, produce an A–Z council services guide, publish a regular council newspaper or magazine to inform residents and a focus on internal communications so staff became advocates for the council.

Over 200 councils signed up to the 2005 Reputation Campaign. Its focus on core actions helped to turn around Norfolk County Council and the London Borough of Hammersmith & Fulham's performance; both were in the bottom quartile for council satisfaction in 2003/04, five years later they achieved the top quartile. For Norfolk, much of the improvement was attributed to a step change in staff communications and engagement. Broadland District Council, already in the top 30 per cent of best performing councils in 2003/04, moved to the top 10 per cent in 2008/09. Broadland, rated 'gold', was seen as a 'star performer', highest district scores on litter removal, second highest on value for money, third highest on place satisfaction and informed (residents felt informed) ratings and in the top 10 for acting on residents' concerns. In contrast, Lancashire County Council, rated 'bronze', didn't see any improvements to reputation, but it learnt a significant lesson. There was 'no coherent one council approach to communicating the council's message' to internal or external audiences (LGA/LGcommunications, 2010).

In 2010 a *New Reputation Guide* was published by the LGA and LGcomms following a review and research into the 2005 exercise. It once again underlined the importance of reputation: organisations that work to improve reputation, it stated, perform better, are more efficient, provide better services and improve resident satisfaction. The new guide was also able to draw on the government's 2008/09 Place Survey in England, which measured council performance in 352 councils (Place Survey Online, 2008).

For the first time, the 2010 Guide developed a 'reputation index' for councils. This is a weighted council satisfaction score. It recognises that deprivation and other population factors impact on satisfaction levels and uses the Place Survey data for the weighted reputation index – the expected satisfaction score given a level playing field. The difference between the two scores – the overall satisfaction score and the reputation index – is the 'reputation gap'; positive is performing better than expected and negative is underperforming in terms of resident satisfaction. Councils were then scored on a scale of '4' (best) – '1' (worst) on 'reputation index quartile performance' using the 2008/09 data. For the councils mentioned above, their reputation scoring is shown in Table 2.5.

Reputation can never be a one-off measurement. And the Guide develops a three-steps evaluation for reputation progress. These are taking a reputation test, using a self-assessment form for senior managers exploring both perceptions and evidence; second, conducting a regular reputation tracker through regular surveys; and third being subject to a peer review, under the independent auspices of colleagues in the LGA and LGcommunications.

**TABLE 2.5** Examples of Reputation Index Performance Scoring

| Council | Overall Satisfaction | Reputation Index | Reputation Gap | Reputation Index Quartile Performance |
|---|---|---|---|---|
| Broadland DC | 63 | 79 | +16 | 4 |
| Hammersmith & Fulham LB | 59 | 60 | +1 | 4 |
| Lancashire CC | 40 | 38 | –2 | 2 |
| Norfolk CC | 44 | 44 | 0 | 2 |

**SOURCE:** *The New Reputation Guide 2010*, based on 2008/09 Place Survey data

This approach relies heavily on tracking reputation, particularly through regular surveys of council residents. Much depends on the questions asked and incorporated in tracking analysis; to date these questions have been elementary and at times not always standardised to allow comparisons. On satisfaction surveys and benchmarking, the Local Government Association and London Councils have issued specific guidance with a set of recommended questions; the hope is that councils commissioning such surveys will use their voluntary framework and then data is easily comparable and more robust for benchmarking (LGA/London Councils, 2012).

With a focus on improving reputation, there is an assumption that this will be reflected in higher satisfaction ratings. But that will not always be the case. An event or a crisis, or bad publicity, will test any public services organisation's reputation. During the wintry weather of January 2011, a national omnibus survey by Populus found that 70 per cent of people were dissatisfied with the way their council had cleared ice and snow from the pavements. National satisfaction with councils fell seven points to 62 per cent (a two-year low) at the end of that month. Negative press stories about bin collections and council salaries may also have had an effect. But satisfaction bounced back by summer 2011 to 67 per cent and hit 70 per cent in October 2011. Local satisfaction levels will vary. Regular tracking of reputation at a local level can help review what has happened and assist planning for similar disruptions in the future. To minimise reputation falls, councils have to be ready to be more responsive to real-time information from residents, complaints, tweets, blogs, e-mails and phone calls. Being responsive is part of reputation management.

The *New Reputation Guide* substantially takes forward the measurement of reputation. The guide is what it says: 'a resource' to measure and improve reputation, drawing its recommendations from the evidence in the extensive place survey work across English councils. It is focused but less prescriptive, setting out 'key themes' to address reputation – three big issues and the five rules of reputation, the most important drivers of resident satisfaction with their councils.

Councils, and their communications teams, are left to determine how these are best developed locally. The Stages of Reputation (see Table 2.6) could be easily adapted and applied to all local public services organisations, such as police authorities, fire and rescue services, and health bodies. This performance approach through reputation complements the work of the

**TABLE 2.6** The stages of reputation

1 **The Big Issues**

  **i** **Leadership** – promoting clarity of purpose and commitment from political, corporate and management leadership to embedding the vision and behaviours across the council/organisation.

  **ii** **Brand** – hallmarking 'what you want to be famous for' making sure managers and staff 'live and breathe' the council/organisation's values, and residents, staff and partners trust the brand.

  **iii** **Communications** – based on competence, articulated strategy linked to priorities and evaluation of agreed reputational goals.

2 **Building Local Reputation: the five rules**

  **i** **Proving value for money** – perceived value for money was seen as the 'most powerful driver for public's satisfaction'.

  **ii** **Always informing and engaging residents** – for example, informed residents are more likely to be satisfied with their council and councils that engage are more highly regarded.

  **iii** **Building trust and confidence** – developing mutuality, showing that there is a shared relationship and the council listens to what residents want or are concerned about.

  **iv** **Improving key council services** – the 'core reputation services' on the public's horizon. For councils, street cleaning, refuse collection, parks and leisure.

  **v** **Focusing on changing lives** – For example, supporting people to get on together, tackling anti-social behaviour and working on the jobs front.

3 **Assessing Reputation**

  **i** **Take the Reputation Test**

  **ii** **Conduct a regular reputation tracker**

  **iii** **Undertake a peer review**

**SOURCE:** The *New Reputation Guide* 2010, Local Government Association/LG Communications

UK Audit Agencies on communications indicators. The two sets of performance data can be benchmarked with other public services bodies in similar sectors. Taken together we have a more rounded picture of the impact and cost-effectiveness of the communications function.

Finally, one additional way to benchmark the team's work is to enter for one or more of the annual industry-recognised awards, including the excellence and other award schemes run by CIPR, CIM, PRWeek, and the PRCA. The CIPR Local Public Services Group (LPS) and LGcommunications have specific public services awards schemes. Such awards are sometimes criticised for being self-congratulatory events, costly to enter and even costlier to attend. But they do have a value: the work is independently judged by experienced professionals. Both those shortlisted and award winners frequently present their entries at conferences and seminars; PR courses and textbooks use the case studies as examples of good practice. So, entering awards is a positive way to showcase work, to sharpen all aspects of practice, including evaluation, and to learn and share practice with peers.

## Checklist

- PR/communication function is both strategic and operational.
- Match corporate objectives with communications objectives.
- Councils/organisations must know/oversee their total communication function.
- Clarify role of embedded (departmental) communicators and central team.
- Case for a unified or corporate communication team.
- All staff must have 'political nous', know the law and the Publicity Code.
- Leadership qualities and competencies are critical.
- Need for professionalism and continuous professional development.
- Measure and benchmark communications team performance.

## KEY WORDS

Responsibilities; strategic; operational; communications function; corporate; centralised; embedded communicators; unified communications; political buy-in; leadership; competencies; channel managers; business strategists; top table; professionalism; ethics; political nous; publicity code; place survey; reputation index; benchmarking; performance indicators; restrictions; reputation guide

# 03
# Communicating strategically

*The good news is that Public Relations/communication seem to be really coming of age as a recognised strategic function in local government. Comprehensive Performance Assessment (CPA) reports (thus far) have helped to highlight the need for good two-way internal communication as well as external communication. Increasingly our remit is widening to include public consultation and engagement, customer care and customer services, policy development, internet and intranet management.*

**PAT GAUDIN, CHAIR CIPR LOCAL GOVERNMENT GROUP 2003–06**

This chapter considers practical steps to developing a communication strategy underlining the importance of the strategy underpinning and contributing directly to the overall corporate and business strategy. It also makes the case for taking a strategic approach to all communications, be they large or small.

For strategies to be effective and to be 'owned', it is important to engage not only the PR/communications team but senior and chief officers and elected members; invariably seeking to demonstrate the importance of communications underpinning council/organisation strategies as a matter of routine rather than as a one-off or a 'bolt-on' at the end of the process. When working with 'non-communicators' it is also a critical way to illustrate to them the importance of planned communications as integral to their particular strategy, campaign or project, leaving them with something tangible with which to move forward over a given period.

How often is the PR practitioner asked by a service to produce a leaflet, to put information on the website, to issue a press release, without any context? The response invariably will be, 'Why? What are you trying to achieve?'

In recent years, increasing numbers of local councils have developed a communication strategy in support of their corporate plan. Different inspection regimes have influenced attitudes to communications – to the need to be customer focused, consulting and engaging local residents and to communicate with internal publics, partner organisations and other stakeholders.

A further change in emphasis has been from policy to strategy. Policies are geared to council objectives approved by councillors; strategies give direction as to the implementation of those policies. In the past a council's communications policy would have been geared to council and councillor communications, particularly via the media and various forms of one-way publicity about services provided. Increasingly there is evidence of communication strategies being taken seriously as part and parcel of the overall organisational goals:

> Building the communications strategy based around our corporate priorities ensures that communications issues are set firmly at the heart of the council's service planning and performance monitoring arrangements.
>
> (Wellingborough Borough Council, 2012)

# Research

Local government communications have also benefited and developed as a result of findings from national research. The Communities and Local Government report 'Perceptions of Local Government in England' (2006) provided strong evidence to suggest that clearly written, honest and transparent communications help to build trust among residents. Taylor and Williams (2006) also highlighted the importance of the need for councils to make a much greater effort to communicate 'effectively, openly and honestly', which they considered would lead to improved communication and also to help build greater trust between residents and councils.

The importance of two-way communication is stressed in research findings time and time again, suggesting the need to be seen to be listening to residents' views, and then, crucially, to be seen to act on the views obtained. The evidence suggests that when residents feel that consultation is only lip service, their trust in and satisfaction with their council will be negatively affected. Social media is making a considerable difference to the way that many residents (but not all) may communicate with their council and this is further explored in Chapter 10. What is refreshing is that local public sector organisations are recognising the value of social media as a key component of planned communication, not just as a one-way information tool but as a way to engage and develop a dialogue with residents and service users.

Research by the Ipsos MORI Social Research Institute also showed a strong link between resident satisfaction with their council and how well the council keeps them informed (Ipsos MORI, 2008). People who feel well informed about what their council does are much more likely to think it provides high quality services and that it offers residents good value for money. These two factors are believed to have most influence on satisfaction with council performance, helping to build and maintain public confidence not only in the local council but in local government overall (LGA, 2008).

Such findings are reflected at local level:

> Increasingly the message from different sources is that effective communications are important for local authorities. And that these communications need to be planned and managed and require a council-wide commitment... There is a direct link between effective communications and satisfaction with local government services. The more that people feel informed, the higher the overall satisfaction rating is likely to be.
>
> (Stevenage Borough Council, 2007)

There has, however, been a tendency to concentrate on promoting, publicising, informing external audiences with an emphasis on products. In the original Local Government Association (LGA) reputation campaign, councils were encouraged to keep residents informed by providing an A–Z guide to services or publishing a regular council magazine or newsletter (LGA, 2006).

These may be good ways to inform local residents but they are essentially one-way communications. What is important is that they are not 'stand-alone' but are elements of a coherent communications strategy, which has clear aims, objectives and ways to measure and evaluate their effectiveness. Do such communications reach the people intended? Are they read? Are they useful? Do they achieve their objective? Do they deliver an overarching council objective?

# Reputation campaign

The Local Government Association, together with LGcommunications, have reviewed and updated their reputation campaign to provide council leaders, chief executives and heads of communication with a route map to help improve the reputation of local public services: 'It does not publish a list of core actions for councils. Rather it examines themes of reputation; three big issues and five rules of reputation. It leaves councils to determine the best course of action for themselves to meet the new challenges outlined under these themes and those remaining from the original reputation campaign' (LGA, 2010). There is also an increasing recognition of the need to move away from information provision and one-way communication, to 'a two-way meaningful dialogue, where information is given in ways which attract and engage citizens, making it more likely that they will retain information and get involved with services, thus leading to good outcomes for the citizen' (LGA, 2008).

# Internal communication

It is important to make reference here to internal communication – any communication strategy must address its internal publics/stakeholders. Some authorities have a separate internal communication function locating it, for example, within Human Resources. Regardless of where in the structure the function sits it is vital that communication strategies address internal as well as external publics – internal and external communications are inextricably linked. Employees are often referred to as important PR ambassadors (Oliver, 2007) yet all too often staff complain that they first see something about their council in the media, or that, for example, a change in refuse collections is well communicated to the public but staff who receive public enquiries on reception desks and helplines are missed out of the loop.

It may seem obvious that councillors are key stakeholders who need to be informed about developments, initiatives, controversies, so they are able to respond authoritatively to their constituents. PR practitioners should therefore include councillors in their communication strategy at least on a 'need to know' basis. It should be remembered that elected members not only have regular contact with residents but also provide a valuable source of feedback. That is one of the benefits of identifying stakeholders/publics in a communication strategy – regardless of who has the lead to communicate with which public/audience, it is important not to miss any out (see Chapter 6).

# Strategy

There can be a great deal of confusion about the words strategic and strategy. Anne Gregory seeks to clarify by suggesting that strategic management involves making, implementing and evaluating decisions that will enable an organisation to meet its long-term objectives: 'It is a process that defines the organisational mission, vision and objectives and then develops policies and plans to achieve those objectives. Resources are then allocated to implement those policies and plans... In most large organisations there are several levels of strategy and public relations can contribute to them all' (Gregory, nd).

In the local government/local public services context it is important that public relations/communications is valued as a strategic management function, contributing to strategic management, rather than seen purely as a 'messaging, publicity, and media relations function' (Grunig, 2006). A communication strategy should underpin and support the council's corporate plan.

> Councils need to be confident that all of their communications are working for them and that they are using resources to best effect. There needs to be a coherent direction based on the council's corporate objectives that encompasses all communications with staff, residents and other key external stakeholders... It is only by developing, implementing and evaluating this approach that a council can make meaningful judgements about what its communications are achieving.
>
> (LGID, 2009)

> Councils who are among some of the best communicators demonstrate top level buy-in to the importance of communications. They understand the link between communications and reputation, and consider the communications implications at every point in the decision-making process.
>
> (LGA, 2012)

Local councils come in different shapes and sizes – unitary, district, borough, city, county – all with an extensive range of responsibilities with services organised through a number of departments or directorates each with its own strategic plan to support the corporate plan. Each department will also have different functions and projects they want communicated. Communications staff will either operate from a central corporate team or there will be dedicated communications staff within particular directorates (see Chapter 2).

Regardless of how they are organised they need to communicate with one another, ensuring consistency, co-ordination and coherence across the council, encompassing all communications with staff, residents and other key stakeholders/publics: 'seeing corporate communications as a strategic function requires the strategic involvement of communications practitioners in managerial decision making' yet 'in many organisations communications practitioners tend to be cast in the role of communications technicians rather than managers or strategists, and are not included in the dominant coalition responsible for the formulation of organisation wide strategies' (Cornelissen, 2005).

It is important that chief and senior officers and elected members are confident in what communications can deliver and in the advice they receive on the communications aspects of council policies. Councils that perform well also tend to be councils that communicate well.

## The Chief Executives' Challenge Report

In 2008, 50 chief executives plus some leaders and heads of communication were surveyed and the findings indicated that only a third saw communications as playing a full strategic role; another third either did not see this as the role of communications or did not feel that their communications staff were up to it; and a further third saw the strategic input in terms of functions run by communications, such as consultation and engagement (LGcommunications, 2008). What was encouraging, however, was that the majority of chief executives wanted their communications to be more strategic.

Increasingly the trend is for council communications strategies to support the council plan. Allerdale Borough Council, for example, has seven strategic priorities to help it achieve its vision of 'making Allerdale a great place to live, work and visit', and in its 2011 Communications Strategy it clearly expressed the role of council communications 'to articulate and communicate activities and services that support and deliver these priorities':

**1** Maintain a high quality, clean and green environment.

**2** Ensure the right mix and quality of housing to meet local needs.

**3** Ensure that communities stay safe and feel safe in their everyday lives.

**4** Support and encourage health and wellbeing for both residents and visitors.

**5** Attract and support new and existing businesses.

**6** Create an environment where business can flourish.

**7** Work with communities and partners to develop a flexible approach to delivering services to meet local needs.

Essex County Council's Communications and Marketing Strategy 2012–17 takes this approach a step further and provides an excellent illustration of supporting the council's strategic objectives, which are to:

**1** Protect and enhance the County Council's reputation.

**2** Elicit changes in audience behaviour that helps the County Council and its partners to:
   – save money and reduce future services demands/costs;
   – improve key outcomes for Essex communities; and
   – successfully market ECC's new commercial ventures and delivery vehicles.

In order to deliver on these objectives there will be no more than eight consumer campaigns that support the Council's key priorities.

> Once the eight key campaigns have been agreed, we work with service directors and their teams, on an ongoing basis, to determine where communication support is required. We will work with colleagues to develop detailed campaign plans. Each of these plans will set out the objectives of the campaign, tactical deliverables, clear timelines and milestones, and clear evaluation criteria.
>
> (Essex County Council, 2012)

North Ayrshire Council, in its 2012–15 strategy, takes an integrated approach to combining internal and external communications; introduces core communications standards across the Council and incorporates communications into the Council's business planning process.

The strategy also makes clear how it complements and supports other key strategies and plans including the Council Plan, the economic development and regeneration strategy, the organisational development strategy, the ICT strategy, the performance management strategy, the financial strategy and the emerging customer services and community engagement strategies.

**FIGURE 3.1**   Key interdependencies diagram

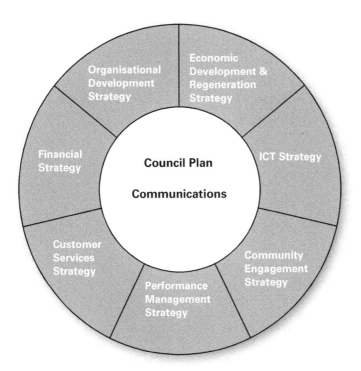

Figure 3.1, taken from the North Ayrshire Communications Strategy, shows the interdependencies and links between the communications strategy and other key Council strategies and plans.

This is translated in their strategy to be the golden thread – incorporating communications into the Council's business planning process:

> Communications must be at the heart of every Council project, programme and service if we are to achieve our key objective of ensuring that the Council's operations, priorities, core objectives, ambitions, values and challenges are better understood, both externally and internally.
>
> (North Ayrshire Council, 2012)

# Developing a communication strategy

There are many examples of how to develop a communication strategy in textbooks and on websites. Some councils include useful templates on their intranet sites, sometimes as part of a communication toolkit alongside examples of how, for example, to use the corporate brand on publications or PowerPoint presentations. Yet there can still be a gap between what is perceived as theoretical and/or strategic and day-to-day practice. What, therefore, is key is that the council communication strategy is owned internally from the top of the organisation to the front-line staff, if it is to be truly effective and receive the resources to make its implementation a reality.

## *Planning is crucial*

A communication strategy takes you from where you are now to where you want to be. It ensures that all communications are focused on priorities and are effectively targeted to the right people at the right time. To be effective, it has to be a live working document and should reflect the fact that communicating is a cross-cutting issue that affects the whole council. Individual departments should not be operating their own communications in isolation... separate directorate communication strategies should show how they contribute to the objectives set out in the corporate communication strategy, as well as setting more local objectives of their own.

(I&DeA, 2009)

There are various guides to help PR practitioners with the planning stages of developing a PR/communications strategy. Back in 1979 Marston came up with one of the best-known planning formulas for PR with the mnemonic RACE (Kelly, 2001):

- Research
- Action
- Communication
- Evaluation

Inevitably there have been developments through the years and a popular approach is to present a circular/continuous process emphasising four distinct phases:

1 Defining the PR problem – situation analysis.
2 Planning and programming – strategy.
3 Taking action and communicating – implementation.
4 Evaluating the programme – assessment.

**FIGURE 3.2**    Four-step PR planning process

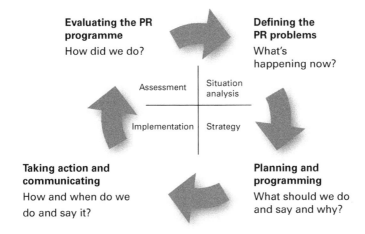

Evaluating the PR
programme
How did we do?

Defining the
PR problems
What's
happening now?

Assessment | Situation
analysis

Implementation | Strategy

Taking action and
communicating
How and when do we
do and say it?

Planning and
programming
What should we do
and say and why?

**SOURCE:** Cutlip *et al*, *Effective Public Relations*, 2000

**FIGURE 3.3**    Gregory's planning model

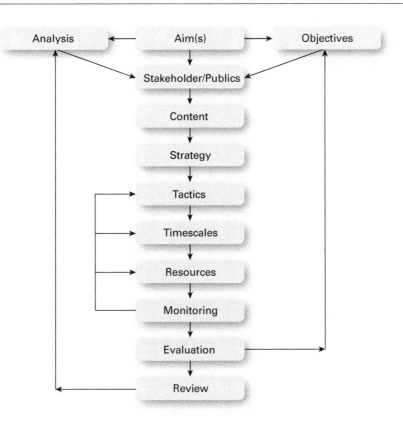

Analysis ← Aim(s) → Objectives

Stakeholder/Publics

Content

Strategy

Tactics

Timescales

Resources

Monitoring

Evaluation

Review

Gregory (2010) has expanded PR planning into a sequence of steps that add further detail to the process and provide a very useful framework for the overall communication strategy and for individual campaigns.

The research/analysis stage is important, including looking at what has worked elsewhere. Local authorities are very good at sharing best practice with one another, picking up tips and ideas and applying these to their own council's particular circumstances. Every strategy is of course unique and can benefit from a team approach, with the communications team and others working together, sparking ideas off each other. Drawing up a communication strategy is not a science and there are different ways to approach the task: 'Public relations practitioners carefully consider how programmes need to begin, and continue in a structured way to the benefit both of their organisation and to the "publics" their organisation interacts with' (Gregory, 2010).

## Conducting an audit/situational analysis

A communications audit can be an important starting point, especially if this is the first time a communication strategy is being developed. It will provide evidence of 'Where are we now? What are the issues?' and a baseline against which to develop and measure communication strategy objectives. The audit is likely to include both quantitative and qualitative research and should include:

- satisfaction ratings; employee survey results; resident survey results; national indicator information;
- internal perceptions of the council's external communications;
- external perceptions, for example from citizens'/residents' panels and inspection reports;
- media content analysis;
- analysis of external environmental factors using tools such as PEST (Political, Economic, Social, Technological), PESTLE and EPISTLE. For PESTLE add Legal and Environment (green); for EPISTLE also add Information (sources) (Gregory, 2009);
- a SWOT analysis of the council's strengths and weaknesses set against the opportunities and threats that confront it.

Approaches to situational analysis are further explored in Chapter 9.

North Ayrshire Council refers to in-depth research carried out over the course of a year, and Stevenage Borough Council's Corporate Communications Team started planning and research for their new strategy around 18 months before its publication. Both emphasise the importance of consultation at the outset, actively seeking views of, for example, managers, key partners and members of the public. North Ayrshire indicates some of the methods they used:

The communications strategy has been developed and revised as a result of input from elected members and our workforce and from discussions with external parties such as local and national journalists, other local authority communications managers and public sector communications professionals.
These included:

- Workforce survey conducted on the council's intranet (Navigate) with hard copy forms distributed to non-office-based staff
- Series of staff focus groups on internal communications involving office-based and non-office-based staff
- Series of manager focus groups on internal communications
- Series of staff workshops on developing internal communications channels involving office-based and non-office-based staff
- Customer satisfaction survey conducted with elected members, and
- Customer satisfaction survey conducted with senior managers
- Electronic survey of the Communications Services at other Scottish Councils

(North Ayrshire Council, 2012)

## *Starting with the basics*

There are fairly standard headings as to what should be included: Aims, Objectives; Publics; Key Message(s); Implementation; Resources; Timescale; Evaluation.

People frequently indicate that they have difficulty distinguishing between aims and objectives. Put simply:

- **Aims** are aspirational, direction setting, where you want to get to.
- **Objectives** are the measurable steps that help you to achieve those aims. How are we going to get there? Objectives should be **SMART**. There can be few who do not know what this acronym means but just in case it is well worth repeating:
  - Specific – eg relating to a particular public.
  - Measurable – you will be able to say whether the objective has been achieved – and make sure outcomes (not outputs) can be measured.
  - Achievable – within the PR planner's ability to deliver – only communication problems can be solved with communication solutions.
  - Resourced – people, money, physical resources (sometimes the **R** becomes Realistic or Relevant).
  - Time bound – has a stated end point (again there are developments such as **T** for Targeted and Timescale – the former might be picked up in **S** for specific but Timescale is useful in looking not just at the end point but considering the relevant milestones along the way).

## Expand each element

Using Gregory's framework above it can be useful to expand each element at the development stage as a reminder of exactly what is to be achieved at each stage:

- Aims – what do we aim to achieve? Goal?
- Objectives – set out **measurable outcomes** and guide the strategy (how are we going to do it? how will we measure success or otherwise?)
- Risks – identify any associated risks.
- Consider evaluation at the outset – how will we know if we have been successful?
- Publics – who do we want to reach (and what do we want them to do? become aware, understand, take action?). These are likely to include residents, including seldom heard/need-to-reach groups; the media; staff; partners; local businesses; opinion formers locally and nationally; elected members. In other words, not just those with a stake in the organisation (stakeholders) but those publics who have a particular interest or issue. Many of these are likely to be further subdivided to address, for example, different staff groups.
- Key messages – what we want our audiences to hear/receive.
- Implementation – the methods, the communication channels, the activities, the tactics, putting the plan into effect.
- Resources – people, skills, budget, costs, technology, etc.
- Timescale/timing – the period of time strategy covers and the milestones along the way.
- Review as we go; monitoring; having the flexibility to adapt if necessary.
- Evaluation – planned at outset and continuous throughout the time period. How will we know if we have been successful? How will we evaluate that each objective has been met and that each communication method has been effective? What performance indicators and evaluating measures will we use?
- Feedback – to inform the next cycle. How did we do? What was successful? What needs to be changed/amended next time around?

Stevenage Borough Council's initial research and planning led them to develop a framework that fosters two-way communication between the council and its publics/stakeholders and importantly is flexible enough to accommodate change and to adapt to new technologies.

## Guiding principles and standards

Councils often keep a set of guiding principles or standards alongside as they develop their communication strategy.

For example, Principles in paragraph four of the 2011 Code of Recommended Practice on Local Authority Publicity state that:

Publicity by local authorities should:

- be lawful
- be cost-effective
- be objective
- be even-handed
- be appropriate
- have regard to equality and diversity
- be issued with care during periods of heightened sensitivity.

Additional communication standards are often added:

- accurate information;
- deliver key messages;
- accessible to all;
- plain language used;
- appropriate timing;
- appropriate quality of design and production;
- appropriate branding used;
- review and evaluate;
- feedback.

Or with a little more detail:

- encouraging and enabling a two-way flow of information;
- open and transparent – about the purpose of what is being communicated and what will be done with feedback: 'we asked, you said, we did';
- accessible to all – supporting equality and diversity;
- accountable – adhering to corporate policies and guidelines;
- consistent, regular and ongoing – communication is an all year round activity;
- honest, accurate, trustworthy – never knowingly misleading or misinforming;
- monitored and evaluated – identify what is and is not successful, build on what works, learn from poor practice and adjust accordingly;
- good value for money.

### *Monitoring, measurement and evaluation*

All planning models lay emphasis on evaluation – not something that is added at the end but is integral to the entire strategy and, as indicated earlier, key to the initial objectives

North Ayrshire outlines its approach:

> The Communications Team have established more robust methods for capturing baseline performance management information over the past year and have also conducted several surveys and studies which will allow us to determine benchmarking standards against which we can measure our performance and set realistic targets and goals for improving the Communications service and communications across the Council...
>
> By establishing our benchmark position with various target audiences, we have identified the key proposals which require to be implemented in order to achieve our vision of ensuring that our key stakeholders – our customers, our workforce and our partners – have a much clearer, shared understanding and appreciation of the council's operations, our priorities, our core objectives, our ambitions, our values and our challenges.
>
> We will continue to monitor and evaluate the implementation of these proposals through various methods... An annual report will be presented to the Council's Executive on the implementation of the Communications Strategy and the progress being achieved.
>
> (North Ayrshire Council, 2012)

### *Action plan*

To make the strategy real, particularly for those delivering it, an action plan is essential. Nothing too complicated: a straightforward grid or table setting out the activities, targets, deadlines and resources needed to implement each element of the strategy. It will also identify lead officers responsible for each action, and indicate how the success of each action will be monitored and evaluated.

# The practicalities

As stated earlier it is helpful to develop a strategy with a team – whether a communications, management or operations team, involving target audience representatives. To gain ownership, it needs to involve the key players to help frame objectives and key messages. The following case studies involve, consult and engage elected members, managers, staff, partners, public, journalists, other local authority/public sector PR/communications practitioners.

## Case studies

The following two case studies demonstrate the process of developing a communication strategy. Both strategies are available online and readers are encouraged to view them.

Stevenage Borough Council's Corporate Communications Strategy 2011–14 is entitled 'Let's Talk'. The strategy and the associated summary action plan were approved by the Council's executive.

Recommendations include: that the strategy is implemented in order to provide a framework for all communication between the Council and its stakeholders.

In developing the new strategy, consultation was carried out with: the leader of the council, strategic management board, heads of service, partner organisations from the public, private, voluntary and community sectors and members of the public.

The strategy defines:

- the aims of the council's communications activities;
- the council's stakeholders;
- the methods by which the council communicates;
- the information that the council exchanges with stakeholders;
- who within the council is responsible for communicating.

Let's Talk is available on the website addressed 'to you' (residents, partners, etc) and is introduced by the leader of the council, who is also the portfolio holder for communications. From the outset there is a sense of two-way communication – seeking to ensure that people know how to share ideas and opinions with the council. The tone is reassuring making it clear that flexibility is built in, recognising the importance of new media 'without compromising our use of traditional communication methods'.

Stevenage's approach echoes many of the issues discussed in this chapter and one particularly important element to highlight is their claim that communication is the responsibility of all and their intention to embed the strategy's principles into all council activities facilitated by the communications team working with staff and councillors.

**CASE STUDY**  Stevenage explain their process

Published in 2011, Let's Talk replaced an earlier communications strategy, which covered the previous three-year period and was due for renewal. Stevenage Borough Council's corporate communications team started planning and research for the new strategy in the summer of 2009 – around 18 months before its publication.

**FIGURE 3.4**    'Let's Talk': Stevenage Borough Council's Corporate Communications Strategy 2011–14

Stevenage Borough Council
Corporate Communications Strategy
2011 to 2014

Ste**V**enage
BOROUGH COUNCIL

In developing the new strategy, consultation was carried out with the council's strategic management board, heads of service (department managers), the council's key partners, and members of the public.

During the planning stages, the main function of Let's Talk was agreed. In a change to previous strategies, which had set out to plan the council's communications work, the new version was to serve as an outline for the council's approach to communicating and set out a framework for two-way communication between the council and its stakeholders.

The council decided not to detail individual issues in the document because they had no way of knowing exactly which issues could or would arise over the next four years. Similarly, because target audiences will alter over time, any tactics outlined would have to accommodate potential changes, and demonstrate the flexibility to accommodate changes and adapt to new technologies.

The results of the consultation and research led the team to define the purpose of the new communications strategy as: 'To establish and maintain clear and relevant two-way channels of communication in order to create a positive, informed and recognisable profile for Stevenage Borough Council and for the town.'

It is important to the council and its stakeholders that it has a clear strategy that sets out how, why and what it is communicating and to whom.

There is extensive evidence to show that the better informed people are about council services, the more satisfied they feel. Stevenage Borough Council has a good record of successful communication. In its 2009 residents' survey (conducted by Opinion Research Services) nearly four-fifths of respondents (79 per cent) said that they felt well informed about the services and benefits provided by Stevenage Borough Council. While this indicates a high satisfaction level, it also demonstrates that there is room for improvement.

Let's Talk doesn't discuss individual subjects, issues, or projects to communicate. It is impossible to predict everything that will arise over the coming three years but the strategy has been made both flexible and robust enough to accommodate changes, developments and unexpected events.

It defines the aims of the council's communications activities, its stakeholders, the methods by which the council communicates, and the information that the council exchanges with stakeholders.

It also defines who within the council is responsible for communicating and is quite clear that communication is everyone's responsibility. Throughout the lifetime of the strategy, the aim is to embed its principles into all the council's services and activities. To help achieve this, the Communication team works on a programme of awareness and training with staff and councillors.

An appended action plan indicates the work that will be carried out to meet the strategy's objectives. There is also a more detailed action plan that forms a plan of work for the corporate communications team.

Let's Talk was published in May 2011. It is on Stevenage Borough Council's website, was distributed to partners and stakeholders, and is made available for public access: **www.stevenage.gov.uk/content/comms/chronicle-dwnlds/24227**.

**FIGURE 3.5** Page from strategy: communication methods

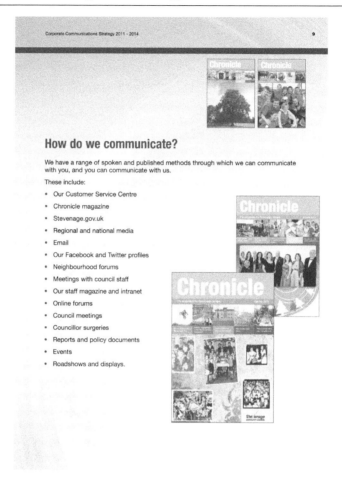

**Let's Talk Corporate Communications Strategy 2011–14**

Summary Action Plan: in addition, a more detailed action plan forms a plan of work for the Corporate Communications team.

**TABLE 3.1**   Activities to achieve strategy aims

| What | Why |
|---|---|
| *Media relations* | Keep Stevenage residents well informed |
| | Manage the council's reputation among all its stakeholders |
| | Address negative or potentially damaging portrayals of the council, its brand and its work |
| | Raise Stevenage's national profile |
| *Community engagement* | Keep Stevenage residents well informed |
| | Reach all sections of the community |
| | Promote respect and trust between the council and its stakeholders |
| *Council publications: Chronicle* | Keep Stevenage residents well informed |
| | Manage the council's reputation among all its stakeholders |
| | Raise awareness of the council's vision |
| | Address negative or potentially damaging portrayals of the council, its brand and its work |
| | Reach all sections of the community |
| | Promote respect and trust between the council and its stakeholders |
| *Reports* | Keep Stevenage residents well informed |
| | Raise awareness of the council's vision |
| | Reach all sections of the community |
| | Keep abreast of technological developments and embrace them where feasible |
| | Promote respect and trust between the council and its stakeholders |
| *Leaflets and posters* | Keep Stevenage residents well informed |
| | Manage the council's reputation among all its stakeholders |
| | Raise awareness of the council's vision |
| | Address negative or potentially damaging portrayals of the council, its brand and its work |
| | Reach all sections of the community |
| | Promote respect and trust between the council and its stakeholders |

**TABLE 3.1** *continued*

| What | Why |
|------|-----|
| *Social media* | Keep Stevenage residents well informed |
| | Manage the council's reputation among all its stakeholders |
| | Address negative or potentially damaging portrayals of the council, its brand and its work |
| | Support council staff in their roles as ambassadors for the organisation |
| | Reach all sections of the community |
| | Keep abreast of technological developments and embrace them where feasible |
| | Promote respect and trust between the council and its stakeholders |
| *Publicity and awareness campaigns* | Keep Stevenage residents well informed |
| | Manage the council's reputation among all its stakeholders |
| | Raise awareness of the council's vision |
| | Support council staff in their roles as ambassadors for the organisation |
| | Reach all sections of the community |
| | Keep abreast of technological developments and embrace them where feasible |
| | Promote respect and trust between the council and its stakeholders |
| *Internal communications* | Manage the council's reputation among all its stakeholders |
| | Raise awareness of the council's vision |
| | Address negative or potentially damaging portrayals of the council, its brand and its work |
| | Support council staff in their roles as ambassadors for the organisation |
| | Promote the council as an employer of choice |
| | Support elected members in their role as community leaders |
| | Keep abreast of technological developments and embrace them where feasible |
| | Promote respect and trust between the council and its stakeholders |

**TABLE 3.1** *continued*

| What | Why |
|------|-----|
| *Corporate identity and branding* | Keep Stevenage residents well informed |
| | Manage the council's reputation among all its stakeholders |
| | Promote respect and trust between the council and its stakeholders |
| *Customer Focus Engagement Strategy* | |
| *Website* | Keep Stevenage residents well informed |
| | Raise awareness of the council's vision |
| | Promote the council as an employer of choice |
| | Support elected members in their role as community leaders |
| | Reach all sections of the community |
| | Keep abreast of technological developments and embrace them where feasible |
| | Promote respect and trust between the council and its stakeholders |
| *Neighbourhood working* | Keep Stevenage residents well informed |
| | Support elected members in their role as community leaders |
| | Reach all sections of the community |
| | Raise awareness of council services in order to maximise access to them |
| | Improve quality of life for communities throughout the town |
| | Promote opportunities for residents, community groups and other stakeholders to engage with the council – partnership working |

# North Ayrshire's Communications Strategy 2012–15

**FIGURE 3.6** North Ayrshire's Communications Strategy 2012–15

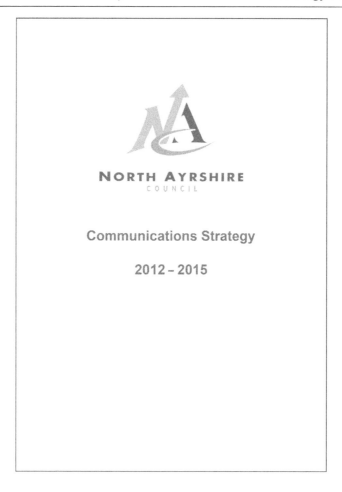

North Ayrshire also presented their strategy to the Council's Executive for approval. Recommendation: That the Executive agrees to:

(a) approve the Communications Strategy 2012/15 and the associated Strategic Action Plan at Appendix A;

(b) receive a future report setting out a Social Media Strategy and Social Media Policy; and

(c) receive an annual report on the implementation of the Communications Strategy and the progress being achieved.

North Ayrshire take a truly strategic approach in aiming to incorporate communications into the Council's business planning process, introducing core communication standards across the Council and recognising the importance of an integrated approach to internal and external communications. And note the use of the word *with* – a small word but with enormous significance in the following statement.

How we will talk with – not at – residents and employees by engaging staff and customers in 'conversations' rather than simply broadcasting information to them, and by actively encouraging feedback from our audiences to help shape future service development and improve service delivery.

**CASE STUDY** North Ayrshire explain their process

Communications was identified as a recurring issue for improvement in the vast majority of service areas across North Ayrshire Council for several years and was deemed crucial to ensuring that the Council's operations and objectives could be better understood by all stakeholders – both internal and external – especially during a period of change and financial challenge.

In 2010, following the appointment of a new communications manager, the Council adopted an Interim Communications Strategy, which provided an overview of the communications service and operations at that time, along with proposals on how the service would evolve and improve over the following year.

The Interim Strategy recognised that engaging with the workforce and securing their trust, loyalty and commitment is crucial – both to building and maintaining healthy and productive employee relations and to improving public understanding and perception of the Council.

It committed the Council to consulting with – and involving staff in – the development of a full Communications Strategy and that commitment was fulfilled through a wide range of in-depth research undertaken over the year.

The final Communications Strategy was developed and revised as a result of input from elected members and the workforce along with discussions with external parties such as local and national journalists, other local authority communications managers and public sector communications professionals. These included:

- Workforce survey conducted on the Council's intranet (Navigate) with hard copy forms distributed to non-office-based staff.
- Series of staff focus groups on internal communications involving office-based and non-office-based staff.
- Series of manager focus groups on internal communications.
- Series of staff workshops on developing internal communications channels (involving office-based and non-office-based staff).
- Customer satisfaction survey conducted with elected members.
- Customer satisfaction survey conducted with senior managers within the Council, and electronic survey of the communications services at other Scottish Councils.

The Communications Strategy 2012–15 identifies the Council's key stakeholders – and key target audiences – as:

- The residents and services users of North Ayrshire
- The workforce
- Partner bodies/organisations – local and national
- Business community and potential investors
- Opinion formers and key influencers – local and national, and
- External scrutineers/funders

It references the Vision Statement within the North Ayrshire Council Plan and states that a crucial element of achieving that vision will be ensuring that key stakeholders have a much clearer, shared understanding and appreciation of the Council's operations, its priorities, its core objectives, its values, its ambitions and its challenges.

The Strategy details how the Council will achieve a more cohesive approach to getting its messages over in an open and honest, clear, concise, consistent, relevant, timely, simple and accessible manner by:

- adopting an integrated approach to combining internal and external communications;
- introducing core communications standards across the Council; and
- incorporating communications into the Council's business planning process.

The full strategy is available online: **www.north-ayrshire.gov.uk/CouncilAndGovernment/ CouncilInformationPerformanceAndStatistics/NorthAyrshirePerforms/ CommunicationsStrategy.aspx**

**FIGURE 3.7**   Screen shot of website

**FIGURE 3.8**    Council's new communication strategy covered in local press

# the3towns ARCHIVE

## Ardrossan - Saltcoats - Stevenston

SATURDAY. 10 DECEMBER 2011

## Council's new Communications Strategy

Ms Elma Murray, North Ayrshire Council's Chief Executive, will this week tell councillors on the ruling Labour Executive that a new Communications Strategy, spanning 2012-2015, will set-out how the local authority intends to "talk with – not at - residents and employees".

A document produced by Ms Murray explains that the Council's Action Plan 2011/12 commits the organisation to developing and implementing a revised external and internal Communications Strategy to support the Council's ambitions, and that "Communications has been identified as a recurring issue for improvement in the vast majority of Service Areas across the Council in recent years and is crucial to ensuring that the Council's operations and objectives are better understood by all our stakeholders – both internal and external - especially during this period of change and financial challenge."

In introducing the new communications strategy, Ms Murray sets out NAC's 'Vision Statement' as: "North Ayrshire offers a better life, better services and better opportunities than ever before. We want to see North Ayrshire and its people thrive, building on our achievements of recent years.

"We recognise that the recent economic downturn creates some significant challenges for us in achieving this vision and we will face a substantial reduction in our finances over the three years of this plan.

"We'll meet this challenge by finding smart solutions so that we become a leaner, more innovative and flexible organisation."

The Chief Executive states, "A key element of achieving that vision will be ensuring our key stakeholders have a much clearer, shared understanding and appreciation of the Council's operations, our priorities, our core objectives, our values, our ambitions and our challenges - especially during this period of change and financial challenge."

Key stakeholders are defined as, "the residents and service-users of North Ayrshire, our workforce, partner bodies/organisations – local and national, business community and potential investors, opinion formers and key influencers – local and national, and external scrutineers/funders."

Said Ms Murray, "Just as we will require to make smarter and more innovative use of our more limited resources in future, we will also require to take our customers, workforce and partners with us on that journey by consulting and communicating with them throughout the process and encouraging them to help shape future service development and improve service delivery."

The Chief Executive's report indicates the Council's new Communications Strategy has been developed and revised as a result of input from councillors, the local authority's workforce and from discussions with external parties, such as local and national journalists, other local authority Communications Managers and public sector Communications professionals.

In conclusion, Ms Murray says, "The Communications Strategy examines how we will adopt an integrated approach to combining our internal and external communications; introduce core communications standards across the Council and incorporate communications into the Council's business planning process."

# All communications should be strategic

In most council communication teams (see Chapter 2) there tends to be a delineation of roles so that different team members work on a particular function often geared to a particular department or specialism within the council's various responsibilities ranging across in-house journal; newsletter/magazine to all households; waste and recycling campaign; fostering recruitment campaign; development framework consultation; community safety campaign; staff intranet; council website, to name but a few.

There is, however, a tendency for communication strategies to be about council communications or large-scale campaigns. They tend to be high level and overarching, with a host of products listed separately and can sometimes be seen as an end in themselves. A communications strategy should be a living document – not something satisfyingly put on the shelf until it is time to review or revise, but something to go back to again and again. Have we addressed every public/stakeholder? Is it accessible to all? Is every element properly branded? What feedback have we had and how are we responding? What changes need to be made?

There are two crucial elements for taking forward strategic communications:

1 Nurturing, involving and developing the communicators themselves so that they see the importance of what they do in contributing to the big picture and delivering the council's objectives. There are PR/communication officers who have never set eyes on the corporate plan nor know when the board meets, let alone how to influence it or to get a communication item on the agenda.

2 PR practitioners must build strong relationships with service departments, and gain a real understanding of their business and of the work of front-line staff. They need to speak the same language, to be facilitators, to inspire, to gain trust and confidence in the added value that strategic communication can bring to every aspect of the council's activities. They must gain buy-in from senior managers, elected members and staff throughout the council. Too often pockets of a council develop their own communications (and logo!) because they perceive the professional communicators to be unhelpful, blocking, lacking in understanding or concentrating only on corporate projects.

Anything 'strategic' may sound dry and stuffy and no amount of templates or guidelines will take away from the passion, flair and creativity that can be brought to a project through a face-to-face planning session. It is important to think strategically whatever the communication, large or small. If it doesn't deliver an element of the council goals and objectives, it begs the question 'why are we doing this'? On the other hand, a strategic approach to all communications will deliver the expectations of the majority of chief executives and give PR/communications professionals recognition rather than being seen as just delivering a set of technical functions (LGcommunications, 2008).

Communications strategies, strategic communications and a strategic approach to all communications are inextricably linked.

## Checklist

- Engage the communications team.

- Engage senior and chief officers and elected members.

- Demonstrate the importance of communications underpinning council strategies.

- Consult internally and externally when developing strategy.

- Undertake a communication audit as an important starting point.

- Communicate more effectively, openly and honestly with residents.

- Listen to residents' views, and then, crucially, be seen to act on the views obtained.

- Focus all communications on council priorities.

- Target all communications to the right people at the right time.

- Foster two-way communication, ensuring people know how to share ideas and opinions with the council.

- Develop an action plan showing the work that will be carried out to meet the strategy's objectives.

- Think strategically whatever the communication, large or small.

## KEY WORDS

Strategy; strategic; planning; research; consultation; framework; two-way communication; involving; engaging; customer focused; honest; transparent; trust; listening; residents' views; evaluation; reputation; dialogue; conversation; feedback; management function; stakeholders; publics; public relations; audit; open; accessible; consistent; value for money; action plan; staff; partners; public; councillors; flexibility; shared understanding; nurturing; involving; developing passion; flair; creativity.

# 04
# Communicating and engaging with citizens

*Local public sector communication is ever changing. We are moving from broadcasting messages to creating conversations and engaging citizens. The use of digital communications is making this much more possible.*

ASHLEY SCOTT-WILCOX, CHAIR CIPR LOCAL PUBLIC SERVICES GROUP 2009–11

*Authorities have a duty to support their residents. I don't have a problem with councils that want to put up council tax if they have a good reason – to fund local opportunities. But I do have an issue if they don't ask permission first. They have to man up. Be straight with people. Take them into their confidence. If the public believes you've got a sensible case they might well listen. But councils should also stop treating residents with contempt.*

ERIC PICKLES MP, SECRETARY OF STATE FOR COMMUNITIES AND LOCAL GOVERNMENT, JANUARY 2013

Councils and public services organisations now talk a lot about engaging with the public. 'Engage' and 'engagement' are relatively new buzz words and they consistently pepper almost every policy report of government, councils, police and health services. Prime Minister David Cameron's much heralded 'big society' is about unleashing community engagement. The new Cabinet Office *Consultation Principles – Guidance* (2012) talk about 'achieving real engagement rather than following bureaucratic processes' with a 'greater focus on robust evidence, transparency and engaging with key groups earlier in the process'.

Such engagement, according to Matt Tee (2009), 'increases public confidence in government activity, provides evidence on which to base decisions, helps give a voice to wide sections of society, including those that have previously been marginalised, and ensures that resources are targeted more effectively'. Engagement, says Tee, should not be confused with the ongoing communication that is part of the everyday business between government, councils and other public bodies and their citizens.

The International Association for Public Participation (2007) has a simple 'spectrum of public participation' – inform, consult, involve, collaborate and empower – with a promise to the public for each stage. The Central Office for Information's 2009 guide to effective public engagement has similarly charted the different levels of engagement and the associated techniques or recommended methods – information giving, information gathering, consultation, involvement and partnership.

Citizens are voters. But when it comes to local council elections most choose to opt out and abstain, despite efforts by the Electoral Commission and many local councils to increase voter registration and voting. At the 2012 English local elections, fewer than one in three citizens (31 per cent) exercised their right to vote for councillors. The 2012 turnout was better in Wales (39 per cent) and in Scotland (40 per cent), but notably the lowest ever recorded on a local elections day. It was significantly higher (54 per cent) in Northern Ireland, when the elections to councils and the Assembly were held on the same day in 2011. In November 2012, turnout was dismally low for the elections for the 41 new police and crime commissioners in England and Wales (average 15 per cent) and for elected mayor in Bristol (28 per cent).

Such low turnouts make citizen engagement on issues between elections more – rather than less – important. Engagement does not replace voting, but fulfils a role, perhaps fills a gap, in the democratic process. There are two current drivers for embracing engagement.

First, citizens are increasingly using the internet, social media and local e-networks and are forcing public services to embrace engagement. Because of these e-channels it is now more possible than ever before for councils and local public services to engage with, listen to and interact with their publics: 'The use of new web technologies has a hugely valuable role to play in helping councils engage with and deliver to local communities' (Sawyer, 2009). E-engagement is easier for the citizen to embrace, than for a council or public services organisation. To date, councils have mainly concentrated their online activity on information giving and transactions (paying council tax, booking a bulk rubbish uplift, making an appointment etc). Council online forums, for example 'Ideas Barnet' and 'Ask Bristol', offer new ways

**FIGURE 4.1** Types of engagement and recommended methods

| Information-giving | Information-gathering | Consultation | Involvement | Partnership |
|---|---|---|---|---|
| Provides balanced and objective information on specific issue(s). | Collecting detailed information on attitudes, opinions and preferences. | Obtaining specific and detailed feedback on analysis, alternative policy options and / or decisions. | Involvement of participants in the decision-making process. | Direct involvement in decision making, including the development of alternatives and identification of a preferred solution. |
| **Techniques** | **Techniques** | **Techniques** | **Techniques** | **Techniques** |
| • Blogs <br> • Direct marketing (e-mail and post) <br> • Factsheets, newsletters & leaflets <br> • Media advertising <br> • Exhibitions <br> • Public notices <br> • Public meetings <br> • Websites <br> • Council newspaper / magazine | • Blogs <br> • Citizens' panels and user groups <br> • Surveys / opinion polls (quantitative research) <br> • Public meetings <br> • Focus groups / interviews (quantitative research) <br> • Online forums <br> • Petitions <br> • Surgeries <br> • Webchats | • Formal written consultation <br> • Online consultation <br> • Outreach <br> • Public meetings <br> • Surgeries | • Citizens' advisory panel / committee <br> • Citizens' (deliberative) forums <br> • Citizens' juries <br> • Citizens' (deliberative) summits <br> • Community toolkits <br> • Online forums <br> • Webchats <br> • Wikis <br> • Workshops | • Citizens' advisory panel / committee <br> • Citizens' (deliberative) forums <br> • Citizens' juries <br> • Citizens' (deliberative) summits <br> • Online forums <br> • Workshops |

Adapted from *Effective Public Engagement: A guide for policy makers and communications professionals*, COI, June 2009 of dialogue with local citizens on issues that matter to them. All public services organisations should develop tools for effective online engagement now and in the future.

> It will become redundant to talk about 'using the web' as these techniques and tools become fully integrated into the way in which councils work. But it's vital to mainstream the mindset as well as the technology and ensure that the best aspects of the web – open, collaborative, non hierarchical and thus, ultimately, democratic – are central to all our activities online and off.
>
> (LGIU, 2009)

Dale (2012) argues that the 'new radical bottom-up tools of communication' through social media will in time solve the problem of voter apathy: 'Social media offers the right prescription for the disease of disengagement because these new spaces are home to more and more people and where more and more people are spending more and more of their time.' Councils have to increasingly take local democracy out of the town hall and 'put it where their residents' eyeballs are, both on- and offline'. But research by Mundy and Umer (2012) into the current use of Twitter by councils 'demonstrates a lack of true engagement with social media spaces'. Twitter, they found, is used by councils primarily as a 'broadcast mechanism' (for announcements about events, recycling, winter road conditions, etc) rather than engaging to obtain a better understanding of citizens' concerns.

Second, with severe financial pressures on public services budgets, engagement is seen as a way of both informing and involving the public in the difficult decisions the council or organisation has to make. In the last few years, many councils have 'consulted' on their budget priorities, seeking views on where cuts could or should be made or on how services (or the council itself) can be reconfigured to save money. Much of this engagement is top-down, at the 'information-giving' level at best with single options and no real dialogue. Such an approach is tokenism, a cynical way of assuming 'buy in' or public legitimacy for a pre-determined decision or course of action. Engagement should inform decision making, not justify it. Ultimately decision makers (whether an elected council or appointed board or quango) have to accept responsibility for their decision: but engagement, if undertaken openly and reported back honestly and objectively, can shape that decision and make it more in tune with the feelings and views of their publics. It can lead to new partnerships with citizens.

Engagement is also critical for both the decision makers and the managers of public services. It provides an 'insightful understanding' of the circumstances and thinking of various stakeholders, according to Jones and Gammell (2009). Crucially, an ability to listen to what they are saying, so that actions can be taken:

> Losing the confidence of key parts of the stakeholder base will, in future, be as fatal for leaders as a failure of performance... and consequently astute chairmen and chief executives will pay at least as much attention to their public engagement programmes as to other aspects of their jobs.
>
> (Jones and Gammell, 2009)

But who are the publics – the stakeholders – for a council or public services organisation? These are either individuals or organisations and groups. Organisations will include other public services partners, parish or community councils, businesses and business groups, community groups, local charities and voluntary organisations, pressure, special interest or self-help groups, and the local media. Individuals come to the council or its services under different persona as a 'client', 'customer' or 'citizen'. There needs to be clarity on what basis they are being communicated, consulted and engaged. Or certainly a recognition of the plurality of the individual's roles.

Pasquier and Villeneuve (2012) identify four different roles: the administered, the user, the consumer and the citizen-partner. These different roles of the individual interacting with public services can cause 'schizophrenia', leading to confused organisations and confused citizens. Confusion is, in part, caused by differences in approach between the new public management agenda (positioning the citizen as a client or consumer) and the democratic governance agenda (where the citizen is a co-producer of policies and services): 'Citizens are not just customers of the public services, their expectations are wider... a citizen interacting with a public organization, no matter how transactional the relationship, will retain part of their political and even electoral nature.' The citizen is not an 'atomized consumer', but a member of the collective body politic. As such, they must be seen not only as the recipient of services, but as one who has a role in determining and shaping these very services.

Engagement and communication go together: some councils and public services bring these two responsibilities under one umbrella section or unit. Others have engagement staff working in different departments. Public services management teams should have an oversight of all engagement for their organisation. This chapter is primarily about the citizen – promoting better dialogue with citizens. It looks at three specific areas of how this can be achieved, through councils and elected councillors, better public consultations and local referendums.

# Councils and councillors

Councils and our local public services are much better at 'information giving' than 'information gathering' when it comes to citizens. This is understandable given that there has been a statutory requirement on councils for decades to provide information about services. Councils, in the past, depended much on the commercial press and broadcast media to get their messages across to citizens, through advertising or news and feature stories. With developments in both print and digital media, this has changed in recent years, with a greater emphasis on direct communications from the council to citizens.

Regular ongoing communication through the council's newspaper or magazine or through council websites and social media channels makes engagement on specific issues easier. In 2005, the LGA reputation campaign encouraged all councils – if they did not already – to publish a newspaper or magazine, as a core communication action. These are professionally designed and produced and are a key way for councils to provide information to citizens and local businesses. They are cost-effective (a delivered copy is usually less than the price of a second class stamp) and most are door-to-door delivered to every household. Most are also published on the council's website.

The Newspaper Society has argued council publications are threatening the viability of local papers, competing on style and on advertising revenue. Tony Watson (2010), managing director of the Press Association, told the Commons Select Committee looking into local media that 'local authorities have a perfect right and indeed an obligation to talk to their council tax payers, but I think it is a world of difference between that and seeking to set yourself up as a bona fide newspaper competing with local titles'. The committee reported that most council publications 'are legitimate communications from a council to its citizens', but recommended that all should state clearly 'not only on the front page, but throughout, that they are a local authority publication'.

The 2011 Publicity Code (see Appendix 1, paragraph 28) now limits council publications to quarterly, although interestingly parish councils are allowed to publish monthly. It states councils 'should not publish... in hard copy or on any website, newsletters, newssheets or similar communications which seek to emulate commercial newspapers in style or content'. This central government edict appears to fly in the face of localism. It also implies that council publications should be of a different or lower standard and style from that available in the marketplace. Due more to current financial restrictions than the code, most councils have opted for quarterly or even less frequent citizen publications; this reduced frequency will seriously impact on communications with citizens, especially at times of service changes and cuts.

Several councils have considered the implications of the code on the future of their citizen communications, and have agreed to breach the code. For example, Tower Hamlets is continuing its weekly newspaper *East End News* because it is both popular and cost-effective and Hackney's award-winning newspaper *Hackney Today* still goes out fortnightly to its 90,000 residents. Westminster City Council have agreed flexibility in the publication of its residents' magazine *Westminster Reporter* – up to eight issues a year 'as circumstances, local need and budget dictate'. The use of the magazine format is now more common among councils; magazines compared to newspapers tend to be retained longer in the home, especially so if key information is included, for example listing local services and out-of-hours contact details, councillor surgeries, local events, public and school holiday dates.

**FIGURE 4.2**   Preferred channels for receiving information about council cuts

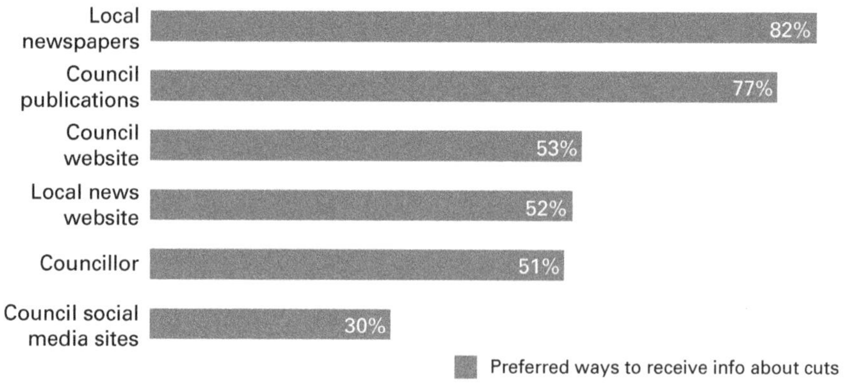

| Channel | Percentage |
|---|---|
| Local newspapers | 82% |
| Council publications | 77% |
| Council website | 53% |
| Local news website | 52% |
| Councillor | 51% |
| Council social media sites | 30% |

Preferred ways to receive info about cuts

**SOURCE:** LGinsight/Populus 28–30 January 2011. 1,002 GB adults 18+ interviewed by telephone

In a Populus/LG Insight poll (2011) asking about council cuts and the preferred methods of communication, local newspapers came out top (82 per cent), but only just. Council publications came a close second (77 per cent). Those polled pointed to the council's duty to tell their citizens directly about any spending cuts, especially impacting on services. Their preferred ways of obtaining such information was through council publications, the council's website and social media channels and local councillors (see Figure 4.2).

A viable local media, both on and offline, can report on and question decisions, providing scrutiny of councils and local public bodies. But the 'scrutiny gap' referred to in the Commons Committee Report (2010) will not be bridged by relying solely on the local commercial media. In fact, fewer local journalists report on or even attend council meetings. The local media can no longer be relied on to cover local councils or local services' decisions. This places an even bigger onus on the council itself to communicate council information to citizens, for example on cuts, service changes or budget options, so that the public themselves can be citizen scrutineers, not replacing the local press or local bloggers, but in addition to it. There are volumes of, often undigested, council information now available on the web – policy reports, minutes, items of council spending over £500 and all that listed under the council's publication scheme – already open to public scrutiny. Council communicators have a responsibility to help citizens find it and make sense of it through more accessible web management, blogs, web summaries and council publications. The easy part is informing people about services.

Several councils have joined in '24-hour Twitterthons' to explain what the council does. Others have tried to make their council meetings more accessible by web streaming live, and having the video available later on archive for anyone interested. This has had mixed success. Hampshire

County Council spent £220,000 on broadcasting their meetings, but had few viewers; the verdict was that long council debates were terribly boring. Stoke on Trent spent £120,000 on a webcasting service to 'boost transparency' and 'engage people in the decisions that affect their lives'. But live viewing figures varied from 25 to 180 in 2012; the council found changing the times of council meeting to the evening increased numbers in the public gallery, but fewer watching on the web.

Bristol City Council records higher viewing by only webcasting election counts, council and cabinet meetings with 'high public interest'. The development control committee dealing with a supermarket planning application was watched live by over 6,100 people. Belfast City Council's webcasting costs £20,000 a year and its first 'live' council meeting webcast in December 2011 was watched by 2,679 people and a further 2,146 later on its archive feed. Viewing figures were much lower for live webcasts during 2012, varying from 91 to 969 viewers. But in December 2012 web viewing peaked (3,536 live and 4,295 later) when the council debated to fly the union flag on designated days, rather than every day, on Belfast City Hall.

Other councils have opened up their council in different ways. Westminster, for example, allows the public to film, record, tweet and blog from committee meetings. And Monmouthshire has an official live blog reporting minute-by-minute on the county council's proceedings. In 2012, the local government minister wrote to English councils saying that citizen journalists and bloggers should have the same access to council committees as mainstream media. Such efforts to demystify and open up councils should be welcomed.

Councils are less good at 'information gathering' about citizens' concerns and views. Complaints and comments could, in many councils, be better monitored and quantified. Citizen petitions to councils did not really take off. Citizens' panels – a representative cross-section of usually around 800–1,000 residents in the council's area – have been the most successful, providing quantitative information for the council. Bristol City Council (2012b) says its citizens' panel of 2,000 is the city's 'biggest think tank'; the panel is surveyed at least three times a year. It is 'invaluable' in finding out how local people feel on issues and is a 'sounding board for future policies and decisions'. In summer 2012, the Bristol panel was asked about the priorities for the city's new elected mayor.

Citizens' panels have to be regularly refreshed, as people leave or opt out. But panels do offer an ongoing sounding board for councils, compared to the one-off poll. It is important that panel members are kept informed; Bristol publishes a regular feedback newsletter. Having a committed panel makes it possible, and easier, to bring together small groups of citizens as focus groups or for deliberative events to look in more depth at specific issues. In January 2012, for example, Barnet Council (2012) brought 74 of its panel members together for a deliberative event to examine the council's draft corporate plan. The panel's recommendations resulted in a redraft so objectives are 'more specific'; a new objective to tackle youth unemployment and a call to improve communications 'more dialogue with residents about the deal between citizens and the council' and 'create spaces, digital and face to face, for citizens to scrutinize council performance in a constructive way with councillors and officers'.

While face-to-face engagement is still important, texting and online communications open up new possibilities for local councils and local public services. Social media platforms and local microsites are available to engage with groups of citizens, take part in two-way conversations and multilogues about issues affecting the council, public services and the neighbourhood. Through these online discussions, and using web surveys and web analytics, councils can get a better picture – a real time picture – of the views and concerns of local citizens. But not everyone is on social media, as Councillor Ed Davie (2012) of Lambeth says:

> Social media can be useful but a lot of my older, poorer and already most disenfranchised constituents don't use it. I tweet and have a website but in the end you cannot actually beat knocking on doors, going to events and delivering well-honed leaflets. My shoe bill would be a lot lower if I thought I could get away with doing it all on a computer but I can't.

Councillors have a key role in any engagement. They are in the front line as local elected representatives. Councils – through their communication team and their democratic services or members' units – should be giving ward councillors more support in their job of informing and engaging at ward and neighbourhood level. This is the essence of local democracy. Some might argue that it is up to councillors to promote themselves; in part they already have done much of that through being elected. But once elected they should be actively supported by the council in their ward role. That means communications support to publicise their work and surgeries, training to use social media effectively and to deal with the media. Most councillors – especially those without portfolios – feel unsupported when it comes to public relations.

The 1988 and 2001 publicity codes of recommended practice unnecessarily limited how councillors could be promoted by the council. Unless the councillor was leader, cabinet member or held a committee chair or vice-chair post, all that could be publicised was 'contact details' and any 'personalisation of issues or personal image making should be avoided' (see Appendix 1a, paragraph 39). Times have moved on: social media is personal and councillors are the council's front-line. The 2011 code for England has made a significant change. Without an election or referendum period, it is now:

- Acceptable for local authorities to publicise the work done by individual members of the authority, and to present the views of those individuals on local issues. This might be appropriate, for example, when one councillor has been the 'face' of a particular campaign. If views expressed by or attributed to individual councillors do not reflect the views of the local authority itself, such publicity should make this fact clear.

- Acceptable for local authorities to host publicity prepared by third parties – for example an authority may host a blog authored by members of the authority (ie councillors) or a public forum on which members of the public may leave comments.

These changes should be embraced by councils. The local work that ward councillors do can be promoted by the council, although not in a party political way. Council websites, too, can provide more links to ward councillors, for example to their blogs, Twitter account, Facebook or LinkedIn. At present, most avoid any mentions of councillors' social media presence. But even more could be done locally. Councillor Michael Payne (2012), deputy leader at Gedling, has advocated: producing council newsletters and e-newsletters 'focused on the ward or housing estate rather than the entire authority area. This is how effective communications can ensure councils are truly rooted in the community and working for people within their boundaries'. In multi-member wards, this will involve two or three councillors, often from different political parties, working together. From 2013 every Welsh council has a new statutory duty to publish an annual report for each elected member (Local Government (Wales) Measure 2011, paragraph 5). This Welsh initiative should be taken up across the UK.

# Public consultations

Consultation is a frequently used method of engagement with individuals or groups of citizens and organisations. Local consultations are required by law in a number of areas – education, health and planning – where public bodies are proposing significant changes, for example, to schooling or hospitals. Other consultations are optional, for example on closing libraries, but underlying them is a moral obligation, sometimes a promise, by the council or public body to consult the public before any decision is taken.

Whether they are 'statutory' or 'voluntary', organising a consultation is a major exercise, requiring pre-planning and considerable preparation in bringing together and publishing all the necessary information about the issue and the development of any options, or preferred option, under consideration. Consultation is not about rubber stamping a decision that has already been made. Genuine consultation must be informed, open and transparent and must be seen to effectively influence any final decision. This requires stakeholder mapping, communicating accessibly to all stakeholders and potential consultees, and deploying a range of appropriate methods for eliciting views.

Some public bodies will have staff experienced in running consultations, others will bring in external consultants, usually working with the consultor's staff from the relevant service area, the policy team and from communications. The task is a multidisciplinary one, with some 70 identified skills and capabilities involving 'a touch of market research, a significant dollop of public relations, with politics and psychology thrown in for good measure' (Jones and Gammell, 2009). For the consultor, such staff have a critical role, both enabling and being objective. They will have to assess public and stakeholder opinion and 'find ways to probe, prompt and capture often difficult messages' and then have the responsibility to report them fully to the decision makers.

Much of the work on consultations in the United Kingdom has been undertaken by the Consultation Institute, set up in 2001. The Institute's definition of a consultation is 'a dynamic process of dialogue between individuals or groups, based upon a genuine exchange of views, with the clear objective of influencing decisions, policies or programmes of action'. The Institute's Consultation Charter (2010) sets out seven best practice principles. These are, in summary:

1 *Integrity.* The consultor must be willing to listen to the views advanced by consultees and be prepared to be influenced when making subsequent decisions. [If decisions have already been taken, such a consultation is a 'fraud' and 'purposeless exercise'.]

2 *Visibility.* All those who have a justifiable right to participate should be reasonably made aware of the exercise.

3 *Accessibility.* Methods of informing and consulting must be 'appropriate for the intended audience'.

4 *Transparency.* Stakeholder invitation lists, consultee responses (with consent) and consultation results should be published.

5 *Disclosure.* Consultors are under a duty to disclose information, including financial details, which could materially influence the nature and extent of consultees' responses.

6 *Fair interpretation.* Responses to the consultation have to be collated and assessed objectively. If weighting methods were used to assist this assessment, these must be disclosed.

7 *Publication.* There is a 'proper expectation' that the output and outcome of the consultation will be published within a reasonable time.

Since 1999, the UK government has issued various guidance on public consultations. In 2008, the most comprehensive code on consultations was published (BIS, 2008). However, it has now been superseded by a three-page guidance paper from the Cabinet Office (2012) on consultation principles. The latest guidance applies to all government departments and other public bodies, including English councils, health services, police and fire authorities. The Consultation Institute has produced a useful annotated briefing paper on the new guidance (Jones, 2012).

The new guidance states that 'the objectives of any consultation should be clear' and 'policy makers should think carefully about who needs to be consulted and ensure the consultation captures the full range of stakeholders affected'. Consultations should not be launched during election periods and timeframes should be 'proportionate and realistic' to allow stakeholders and groups sufficient time to provide a considered response. A typical consultation timeframe may now be between 2 and 12 weeks (previously a minimum of 12 weeks was recommended). It adds:

> Information provided to stakeholders should be easy to comprehend – it should be in an easily understandable format, use plain language and clarify the key issues, particularly where the consultation deals with complex subject matter. Consideration should be given to more informal ways of engaging that may be appropriate – for example, email or web-based forums, public meetings, working groups, focus groups, and surveys – rather than always reverting to a written consultation. The medium should be appropriate for the subject and those being consulted.
>
> (Cabinet Office, 2012)

All consultations are governed by both formal guidance and the law: both should be considered before undertaking any consultation. Several local councils and other public bodies have their own separate guidance. The NHS in both Scotland and in Wales has published guidance for health services consultations. Bristol City Council, which has had a consultation strategy for 10 years, publishes on its website its own code and separately a consultation toolkit (Bristol, 2012b). This includes the council's seven – very practical – consultation principles (see case study). All public consultations must be inclusive: ensure all groups affected are included, especially the 'seldom heard', 'hard to reach' or the 'easy to forget' because they are too difficult to include. This means that communications with these groups about the consultation issue – and the channels used – must be appropriate and accessible, so their genuine views are retrieved.

**CASE STUDY** Bristol City Council: Seven consultation principles

### 1. Time consultations well and allow sufficient time to respond.

- Consultations should be timed to allow the results to influence policy/proposal development.
- Wide scale public consultations, such as citywide or large parts of it, should run for a minimum period of six weeks.
- The timing of consultations should consider the availability of target groups.
- Consultations that are primarily focused on the voluntary and community sector should run for a minimum period of 12 weeks.

### 2. Clearly present relevant information and encourage informed opinion.

- The consultation should clearly state: the proposal, why we are consulting and how we will use the findings.

- The consultation should provide enough information to enable consultees to give an informed opinion and not simply an instant reaction. This information should be written in plain English.

### 3. Be well targeted and reach out to seldom heard groups.

- The views of those people/areas most affected by the proposal should be sought.

- Attempts should be made to listen to the views of non-users, especially when service changes are being consulted on.

- Attempts should be made to include the views of groups frequently excluded or overlooked.

- Consultations should consider the needs of people with impaired sight or hearing or people whose first language is not English.

### 4. Offer genuine options and ask objective questions.

- Where options are offered, they should be realistic and deliverable.

- Surveys and questions should be written in an objective way allowing people to express their views.

### 5. Be well planned, managed and coordinated.

- The council's consultation toolkit contains step-by-step instructions to enable managers to effectively manage consultations and avoid unnecessary duplication.

### 6. Be listed on consultation finder and be well communicated.

- We will publicize consultations and make attempts to let people know they are happening.

- Consultation Finder (on the council's website) lists all our consultations in one place.

- Major consultations eg citywide or affecting a large number of people will be publicized by press release and in council publications such as the council's magazine 'Our City'.

### 7. Provide fair, accessible feedback.

- We will publish the findings of consultations and later how they have been used.

- The findings will be reported in a balanced way.

Over recent years, there have been several legal challenges to consultations, mostly through judicial review. The courts have found that some major council and health service consultations have been flawed because they have not followed due process or failed to take into account equalities legislation. For example, consultations on library closures (by Somerset and

Gloucestershire councils in 2012) and on provision and eligibility of social care services (by Birmingham and Isle of Wight councils in 2011). In the Birmingham case, Mr Justice Walker stated in his judgment:

> a consultation process must provide consultees with sufficient reasons in support of particular proposals to allow an intelligent response to be made and must ensure that the responses are conscientiously taken into account when the ultimate decision is taken. My conclusion as to failure to comply with section 49A [of the Disability Discrimination Act 1995] inevitably carries with it a conclusion that the consultation was inadequate.
>
> (R (ex parte W etc) v Birmingham City Council (2011) EWHC 1147 (Admin))

In 1985, a judicial review on school amalgamations in Brent set out four requirements for consultations. These have been subsequently called the 'Gunning principles'. They are: i) proposals to consult must be at a formative stage; ii) sufficient reasons should be given to permit intelligent consideration; iii) adequate time for consideration and response; and iv) responses must be conscientiously taken into account in decision making [R v London Borough of Brent ex parte Gunning, 1985]. These requirements have been restated in subsequent judgments:

> it is common ground that whether or not consultation of interested parties in the public is a legal requirement, if it is embarked upon it must be carried out properly. To be proper, consultation must be undertaken at a time when the proposals were still at a formative stage; it must include sufficient reasons for particular proposals to allow those consulted to give intelligent consideration and an intelligent response; adequate time must be given for this purpose; and the product of consultation must be conscientiously taken into account when the ultimate decision is taken.
>
> (Lord Woolf MR in R v North and East Devon Health Authority Ex Parte Couglan [ 2001] QB 213, paragraph 108)

> Information contained in a consultation document should not be so inaccurate or incomplete as to mislead potential consultees in their responses. Inaccurate or incomplete information may preclude an informed and intelligent response, which may in turn operate to the disadvantage of a party that may be affected by the decision to which the consultation is directed and in consequence render the consultation process so unfair as to be unlawful.
>
> (Royal Brompton Hospital Judicial Review [ 2011] paragraph 25)

There is now a growing body of legal judgments on consultations, setting precedents. The four 'Gunning principles' apply; and councils are accountable to their electorates for the merits of their policies and decisions but they are accountable in law for their actions when they undertake consultations. However, in April 2012 the Court of Appeal, in ruling that the consultation affecting the London Royal Brompton Hospital was lawful, said that courts should only be involved if there is some 'irretrievable flaw in the consultation process'.

Jones and Gammell (2009) have argued that insufficient thought and resource is given to what happens after a consultation. This, they say, is the 'critical point of the consultation'. There are two tasks – analysing what the consultation data says and interpreting what the data means. Those organising consultations are often unclear whether or not it is their job to report and also to make recommendations. There is also a 'dearth of feedback' to both consultees and decision makers. Councillors and boards rely heavily on officers to provide objective feedback; officers must not simply tell councillors or other decision makers what they want to hear, but be rigorous in both enquiring and reporting to them.

One of the most effective recent consultations was in Warwickshire over changes to their library service, a controversial issue nationally where hundreds of public libraries are at risk of closing because of spending cuts (*Independent*, 2012).

In 2011, the council ran 34 libraries in towns and villages across the county. With reducing council funding in the future, the library service had to save £2.2 million by 2014. A business review of all 34 libraries was undertaken and the council identified 16 libraries that were 'unsustainable' in their current form. All 16 were initially listed for closure, but the council decided to open up the consultation for the community to consider other options for running them. The consultation ran for 12 weeks from March to June 2011.

Key to the consultation was the involvement of a senior councillor, the portfolio holder for libraries, who was the main spokesperson and fronted the consultation along with council staff, not just from the library service, but also head of property, the corporate officer for equalities, and legal officer. The library service in Warwickshire had its own communications and publicity staff and having both communications and engagement staffs working together aided the consultation process. Much of the information and dialogue with the public was provided through the libraries website, a printed consultation document, letters, a supporting roadshow around the county and local public meetings about each library. The Consultation Institute, as an external adviser, reviewed the progress of the consultation at five key stages (see case study).

## CASE STUDY  Warwickshire library services consultation 2011

### Intervention 1 – scope (February 2011)

Clarified and confirmed the precise scope of the consultation. There was much debate as to the extent to which the list of 16 potential closures could be influenced by consultation. Council willing to consider proposals for alternative ways of sustaining the service.

### Intervention 2 – project plan (March 2011)

After discussion a detailed project plan was signed off. All key stakeholders identified and assessed through a stakeholder mapping exercise.

## Intervention 3 – mid-consultation review (May 2011)

Council officers met Consultation Institute to review early responses. Levels of interest and participation were seen to be weak in key parts of the county and actions agreed to stimulate greater interest in schools and among hard-to-reach groups.

## Intervention 4 – closing date review (June 2011)

Responses were considered from 4,977 questionnaire respondents, over 500 emails/letters, 1,671 roadshow attendees, 763 public meeting attendees and petitions with a total of 10,041 signatures. Analysis methodology agreed.

## Intervention 5 – final report (July 2011)

The council's communities overview and scrutiny committee received the final report and recommendations. The consultation process and report was endorsed by the Consultation Institute.

(based on information from the Consultation Institute)

A lot has happened since the Warwickshire consultation. A year later, 14 of the 16 unsustainable libraries have opened as community libraries, using a roster of local volunteers and in some cases funding from the Big Society Fund. The consultation enabled these 14 communities to be both realistic and positive about embracing change and new ways of running their libraries. But there was understandable disenchantment with the consultation in the two communities where they were unable to secure a future for their local library.

For the council this very public exercise – which received considerable local media coverage – was seen as an engagement success, leading to new local partnerships. It was not challenged in the courts, like other council-run library consultations. That was partly because the consultation was both extensive and exhaustive and the council took independent advice at critical points. Significantly, the council was open about the funding problems it faced and genuine in seeking a solution for its libraries through engaging with local communities.

Budget consultations are more complex than single issue consultations and much more difficult to manage and make sense of. Most councillors, as ultimate decision makers, will readily admit that they find finance and budgets difficult to grapple with, especially when they are presented with conflicting funding priorities and hard decisions on cuts. Lopata, Jones and Headland (2011) identify the structural and financial complexities of council budgets as a 'major barrier' to consulting the public and stakeholders; local councils are constrained by statutory commitments and the choices they can make, and this means some aspects of the budget are 'set in stone' before any consultation. They also add that if there is no genuine political will to listen to local citizens, such budget consultations are 'worthless and in actual fact damaging to any future attempts at engagement'.

Despite this, many councils have embarked on budget consultations to both inform and involve their citizens on the critical funding dilemmas they face. Some councils, like Thurrock and Redbridge, have as well as outlining possible areas of savings, openly sought ideas from their residents. Others, including Redbridge, have developed online calculators setting out the budget options and asking the public to register their choices for cuts and spending. Across councils, the most common budget consultation methods used were online surveys, citizens' panels, deliberative events, public meetings, written submissions, online budget calculator and discussion groups (Headland, 2012). Participative budgeting was hardly used; this more detailed approach is more appropriate for local ward or community budgeting.

Headland's 2012 survey of 45 English council budget consultations found that in about half the councils, citizens had very little or no influence on the budget decision making. In six councils the consultation was 'very influential' and in a further 18 it was 'influential on a limited number of issues'. These findings raise questions about the real value of such consultations. A rethink is needed into how citizens and stakeholders can be more meaningfully involved and make a contribution to a council's budget exercise.

Headland (2012) recommends that both councillors and managers clarify from the outset the scope of the consultation and exactly what citizens can influence. He warns of the dangers of 'jumping to the methods' of consultation without considering first the objectives and possible outcomes. Given the complexity of budget consultations, more thought should be given to deliberative methods that require a dialogue with citizens.

A deliberative approach 'offers opportunities to more fully explore why people feel the way they do and allows the time to develop ideas, options and priorities with the public' (Involve/NCC, 2009). Such an approach takes time and preparation; it involves the public in decision making through, for example, citizens' juries, workshops, forums and events, where participants first find out more about the issue, consider and discuss the relevant evidence before presenting their view. It offers more informed decision making, and greater insight into an issue, exploring the wider options available. There are many different deliberative consultation methods; some 44 of these, with examples, are outlined in the Participation Compass website: **www.participationcompass.org**.

Consultations by councils, health services and other public bodies can generate considerable media coverage. Often the focus of media coverage is about the assumed impact of the consultation – a row over proposals to close a school or hospital or cut a service, with local interest groups up in arms about what they fear will happen. Such campaigning groups, whether formally or informally organised, can set the agenda, using both social media and the local press, TV and radio to increase public support for their stance and thus influence the outcome of the consultation. They will be willing to be quoted and interviewed and they will offer personalised case studies of what would happen if the school, hospital or service closes. For the media, this makes easy headlines and strong local stories, which can go national. It puts the consultor – the council or public body – on the back foot.

Jones and Ashton (2006) in their paper on 'Consultation and the Media' have highlighted the differing interests of consultor, consultees and journalists and broadcasters and have identified 10 points in a consultation lifecycle where communicators should be alert to possible media interest. They advise all consultors to involve their communications and media specialists in developing the consultation project and, in particular, the use of appropriate media channels to promote the consultation, encourage public participation, respond to developments and criticism during the process and publish accurate feedback.

The onus initially is on the consultor with the announcement and launch of the consultation; this is often the first opportunity to tell the public about the proposals or options and the scope of the consultation. Serious consultors will seek publicity so that everyone affected (in addition to the identified stakeholders and known consultees) is aware of the consultation and has a chance to contribute. A communications plan should be prepared in tandem with the consultation plan and diary for every consultation and it should cover the lifecycle of the consultation. Consultation documents, together with any media releases or supporting printed or online summaries, must present the information in an understandable and accessible way so that the public, stakeholders – and the media – can easily assimilate the issues at stake. All the data used, including costings, must be robust, as these will be open to scrutiny.

While individuals and interested groups may make their views known publicly and even oppose specific proposals or options under consultation, it is important the consultor – the council, its councillors, its directors, senior managers and staff – do not make any statements or remarks that could give the impression decisions have already been taken. To do so would compromise the consultation and lead to accusations and media reports of a 'sham consultation'. Consultation exercises are open to freedom of information requests or, as we have seen, expensive court challenges; these can provide additional stories for the media and call into question the trust and reputation of the consultor.

> It is in the interest of everyone who cares about open, transparent public debate to observe best practice. Poor consultations benefit no one in the long term even though the media can enjoy short term disputes or rows whilst blame is allocated. At its best the media has the potential to play an important part in holding public bodies accountable for the quality and integrity of their attempts to consult the public.
>
> (Jones and Ashton, 2006)

# Local referendums

In England, the Localism Act 2011 has introduced specific powers for councils to hold local referendums on neighbourhood planning issues and on council tax increases above a government-set maximum. All UK councils already have some discretionary powers to conduct local referendums related to their functions and services or in pursuit of general wellbeing of the area; the outcome is advisory and does not mandate the council.

The new powers in the Localism Act are not discretionary, but obligatory on councils. Local citizens in England through such referendum votes can actively have a say about their neighbourhood plan and subsequent planning permissions or stop or support an 'excessive' council tax increase proposed by their council. For the 2012/13 financial year, English councils were told that any increases of 2 per cent or above were excessive and would require a referendum. But because of loopholes, some councils will be billing increases of over 3 per cent without a referendum. Secretary of State Eric Pickles (2013) has described such councils as 'democracy dodgers' who are 'cheating the taxpayers'. He promises to close any loopholes, lower the threshold and force councils to go down the referendum route for any increase. It will be interesting to see how many councils opt to put their tax increase to a public vote.

Local referendums are not new, but have not been a significant feature of British democratic life, as in Switzerland or in some states in America. Last century, until the licensing laws changed, most local referendums were about alcohol; these were votes on whether or not to allow pubs or off-licences in areas of Scotland or Sunday drinking in the Welsh counties.

Since 1972, English parish councils had powers to hold a parish poll on any community issue if requested by local electors. But only a handful did so, perhaps because the cost had to be borne by the parish council and there was no certainty the vote would change things. Recent parish polls include a vote to increase council tax to fund a local swimming pool set to close in Wotton-under-Edge and to oppose a low-level radioactive waste site in East Northants without success. In May 2011, local people voted almost unanimously (98 per cent) in Menston, near Bradford, against plans to build 300 homes in the greenbelt village. The result, although not binding, was delivered to the planning authority, Bradford City Council. The initiator of the parish referendum, a local lawyer, Paul Schofield was quoted in *The Guardian* (2011): 'This is a democratic weapon which has largely been forgotten... It shows that the new ideas of localism have been enshrined in legislation for 40 years, albeit buried from view.'

In the last two decades, many of the local referendums held have been related to council governance matters – in the 1990s citizens were asked to vote on whether or not they wished to be part of a bigger 'unitary council' or since 2000 for a directly elected mayor, as advocated by successive governments to strengthen local democracy.

Just over 50 local mayoral referendums have taken place between 2001–12 in England. Only one-third of the ballots voted 'yes'. Most areas rejected the idea, often overwhelmingly. The mayoral referendum turnouts ranged from a high 64 per cent in Berwick upon Tweed 2001 ('no' vote) to a very low 10 per cent in Sunderland and Ealing (both 'no' votes). In May 2012 Bristol voted 'yes' for a mayor on a turnout of 24 per cent and Manchester 'no', turnout 47 per cent. Overall, the mayoral referendums – and the subsequent mayoral elections for areas voting 'yes' – have not increased citizen participation, with turnouts around or below that of a local council election.

The controversial issue of congestion charges has prompted local referendums in Edinburgh City in 2005 and in the 10 councils in the Greater Manchester area in 2008. Edinburgh and eight of the Greater Manchester councils generally supported congestion charging, because it would both raise money and lever in funds from government for local roads and public transport improvements. But the councils knew the public were less enthusiastic, so they took the referendum route and put the case to the people. The charges became the focus, rather than the much-needed investments. Edinburgh, in a postal referendum, voted 74 per cent against the 'preferred strategy', charging and new transport infrastructure. The city's council leader at the time said 'the charging issue is now dead and buried'. Similarly the voters in Greater Manchester rejected charging, 72 per cent in Manchester City to 84 per cent in Salford. In so doing, they lost £3 billion capital from the government's transport innovation fund.

Despite the Mayor of London's success in bringing in the congestion charge without any referendum, the Edinburgh and Manchester referendums have wider implications. Fearing a similar citizen reaction, other UK cities and towns have put on hold, at least for the time being, any congestion charging plans. Edinburgh lost the debate because most citizens didn't know what 'preferred strategy' meant, and saw it solely in terms of congestion charges. Policy makers and communicators can learn many lessons from the Edinburgh and Manchester experience.

The biggest local referendum ever held in the United Kingdom was run by Strathclyde Regional Council in 1994, during the lengthy parliamentary committee stages of the bill to reorganise local government in Scotland. It was over the future of the regional council's water and sewerage services; the council warned that the proposed legislation to establish a West of Scotland water quango could lead to the ultimate privatisation of the service, as was happening in England and Wales. There were concerns about possible legal challenges to the council – these centred around the referendum's cost and politics (a Labour council against a Conservative government). There was angst among officials over whether a region-wide opinion poll, at a proportion of a referendum cost, would be a more cost-effective option for the purposes of the council.

Costs, which totalled £650,000 in 1994, were minimised by opting for a postal ballot. To publicise the ballot and encourage voting, the council took advertising in local newspapers and on local commercial radio. The agreed radio ad was simply a call to action, to vote and post back the ballot paper; there were no radio (or press) ads promoting either 'for' or 'against' as these would be seen as political. Council spokespersons had to be 'neutral' during the referendum.

The postal ballot took place over a three-week period in March 1994. Some 1.7 million electors in the 33 parliamentary constituencies within Strathclyde received ballot papers. Over 1.2 million voted, 71.5 per cent of the electorate, one of the highest turnouts for either a national or local referendum. Over 97 per cent said 'no'. Less than 3 per cent supported the government's plan. Although Strathclyde was abolished and water and sewerage services were transferred initially to three area water quangos (now merged into one, Scottish Water), the Strathclyde water referendum vote had significantly more impact than an opinion poll. It has ensured to date that water services in Scotland have not been privatised and still remain under public ownership, albeit overseen by Scottish Ministers and the elected Scottish Parliament rather than councils. But notably water and sewerage services are still included in council tax bills north of the border.

Aberdeen's referendum in March 2012 on its £140-million city garden project development raised questions about the 'political' nature of local referendums. With only just over half the electors voting – by post, phone and online – the project was narrowly backed by 52 per cent of voters, with 48 per cent opting to retain the existing Union Terrace Gardens. The council subsequently voted down the development. But a series of radio adverts, taken out separately during the referendum on behalf of some business campaigners supporting and an individual opposing the development, were found to breach the Section 321 of the Communications Act 2003 and Section 7 of the Code of Broadcast Advertising.

Ofcom's ruling (2012) is important for all concerned with local referendums, including council communicators:

> Ofcom considers local polls to constitute referendums for the purposes of s321(3)(a). Therefore all of the advertisements under consideration plainly sought to influence opinion in respect of a referendum... the ban of political matter in broadcast advertising extends to campaigning, supporting a point of view in an election or referendum and seeking to influence public opinion on controversial matters.
>
> (Ofcom, 2012 – see online resources for full Ofcom judgement
> **http://www.koganpage.com/PRGov**).

It was the broadcasters – local radio stations, Northsound 1 and 2 and Original 106 – not Aberdeen City Council who breached the Communications Act 2003. All 'controversial' broadcast adverts should have been referred for national clearance; this did not happen because the broadcasters wrongly believed they were dealing with a local interest issue – not a political matter – when they accepted and transmitted the ads for and against the project.

This Ofcom ruling underlines that local referendums, as well as elections, are also governed by the UK's broadcasting legislation. Section 321 of the 2003 Act bans all TV and radio adverts that could influence the outcome of referendums, the policies and decisions of local government or public opinion on a matter that is one of public controversy. This does not preclude taking adverts advising citizens about a local referendum vote.

For the new neighbourhood planning and council tax referendums in England, there are specific statutory regulations (2012) on the conduct of the ballots, the wording of the questions, and rules on the information to be provided, including costs and use of council website. Additionally, there are legal restrictions publishing any promotional material during the referendum period. Press notices during the referendum must contain 'factual information where the sole purpose of the publication is to refute or correct any inaccuracy in material published'. Council communicators involved in local referendums have to be wary of the wide interpretation of 'publish or make available to the public or a section of the public', as this will include the use of social media and the council's own websites.

---

## Checklist

- Include social media as part of any citizen engagement or consultation.
- Develop e-tools for engagement, appropriate for different publics.
- Recognise the plurality of roles – citizen, customer and client.
- Provide clear, honest information directly on cuts and service changes.
- Ensure communications are frequent, accessible and cost-effective.
- Review best ways council meetings can reach wider audiences.
- Councillors are in the front line and should get official public relations support.
- Public consultations – follow the four 'Gunning principles' and guidance.
- Develop media plan for the lifecycle of any consultation.
- Local referendums – check publicity code, 2012 regs, broadcasting legislation.

---

## KEY WORDS

Engagement; consultation principles; turnout; e-engagement; stakeholders; citizens; customers and clients; information-giving; information-gathering; council magazines; council newspapers; citizen scrutineers; web streaming; citizens' panel; complaints; e-petitions; statutory and voluntary consultation; consultation charter; judicial review; Gunning principles; consultor; consultees; referendums.

# 05
# Communicating with the council customer

*This council believes that communications between itself and the citizens of Sunderland is vital if it is to provide the best services it can to the people of Sunderland. The more local people are involved in the planning and design of Council services the more they will be able to influence and improve them and ensure that they are relevant to their wants and needs.*

**SUNDERLAND CITY COUNCIL**

Chapter 4 made clear the difference between citizens and customers. Citizens are voters. They are part of the democratic process and through the ballot box and consultations citizens have the opportunity to have their say. They are not just customers or recipients of public services but have a role in determining and shaping those very services and priorities.

Customers are receivers and consumers of public sector services without necessarily exercising their democratic say in how they are delivered – nonetheless there is a duty of care, to inform, to engage, to ascertain their needs, wants and expectations. Studies indicate that public services should be provided in a way that is fair and equitable, but that also meet good quality standards of customer service (2020 Public Services Trust, 2010).

Local councils are responsible for a wide range of services for local people, ranging through checking food safety, economic development, education, environmental health, housing, libraries, parking, pavement maintenance, planning, schools, social care, sports facilities, street cleaning, trading standards, roads, waste collection and disposal – and local councils either provide services directly or arrange for other organisations to do so.

Everyone is a council customer through the host of services a council provides. Most councils will have three distinct groups: citizens and families who live in the area; businesses based in the area; and tourists or visitors to the area (SOCITM Consulting, 2012).

Using examples of good communication, this chapter highlights the need for a very focused and clear communication for every service; how best to promote existing services, underused services, new services or changing services, dealing with expectations, meeting different communication needs and exploring the possibilities of two-way communication. It is worth noting that in times of recession demand may increase for certain services, such as housing benefit, homelessness, debt counselling and money advice, and there can also be an increased demand and a greater recognition of the importance of 'free' leisure services, such as museums, libraries, galleries, sports pitches, playing fields, skateboard and BMX parks, playgrounds, public parks and open spaces. It is often a time when customers voice their views about how they value certain services – for example in their opposition about proposals to close libraries (eg *Hands Off Old Trafford Library*, 2012) or to sell off Country Parks (*Suffolk Free Press*, 2011).

There are 433 councils in the United Kingdom: 353 in England, 22 in Wales, 32 in Scotland and 26 in Northern Ireland (LGIDa, nd). It is important that local people, who are the customers of those services, know what services are available and how to access them. Local government public relations has played a considerable part in the development of public relations overall (see Chapter 1). Local councils have long given consideration to communicating with the council customer, for example via 'the information centre' which Lewis described as far back as 1973 as a key means to afford face-to-face contact between the council and the customer. Libraries were seen as key information points providing direct contact with council customers and places to obtain information not just about clubs and societies but about council services more generally. Over time different methods of direct contact developed: one-stop shops, information kiosks, mobile centres, contact centres, call centres, websites and social media.

There was a sense that in the early days PR/communications was one way: local councils sought to publicise their services; customers had little choice and there was a take-it-or-leave-it attitude.

It's not just UK research that provides us with evidence about the importance of customer communications. Ipsos MORI indicate that in dozens of studies they have conducted, their findings highlight the central importance of communications in determining how people rate central and local government: 'Public services that are better at keeping people informed are better rated by local citizens' (Ipsos MORI, 2010).

Their research also indicates the importance of information provision:

> Significant minorities do want to be more actively engaged, but most people would prefer to just receive information about what services are doing. This does

not imply that concentrating on capacity building and encouraging involvement among those who want to be engaged will be a waste of time – just that improving communications for the wider majority should also be a priority.

That's not to negate the importance of encouraging greater involvement and engagement through two-way communication but it does highlight the importance of asking customers what they want.

Communicating with the customer may be geared to signposting, making clear who deals with what; making information readily available and accessible. And not just about services available but about council decisions, policies, planning proposals, town centre developments, community safety. Such communications echo Grunig and Hunt's (1984) public information model of public relations, demonstrating a one-way method of communication but also aiming to give clear and factual information.

Until relatively recently councils have been ambivalent about using the word 'customer' – it conveyed a sense of 'selling' but when linked to other words such as care or services it gradually gained recognition and is now in fairly common usage. It gives a greater sense of empowerment to the customer, rather than being a passive recipient, and has led councils to make clear what customers should expect of services, of communications and of standards, often through customer charters.

Chapter 4 covers in greater detail engaging citizens. This chapter provides a broad overview of communications with customers but the key word here is *with*. There will be occasions when communications will be of the public information kind but as can be seen from the examples here, councils work hard at ensuring their customers have the opportunity to feed back their views not just about services but about communications. SOCITM Consulting (2012) point to the importance of knowing 'who the council's customers are, and what their needs are, using well-thought-out customer surveys; listening to what customers have to say'. What is important is to ensure that all channels are open and that feedback is utilised, recorded and resulting outcomes are reported back to customers as and when appropriate. Customers need to have ease of access regardless of whether they use phone, e-mail, web or text.

# My council, total place, customer insight, reputation guide

Successive initiatives put customers at their heart and provide important vehicles for effective public relations/communications.

Following an initiative by Northamptonshire County Council, the My Council campaign was launched by the Local Government Association (LGA) at its Annual Conference in 2008 to encourage councils, through a series of posters, to tell people about the vast range of services that their council tax pays for (LGID, 2008).

The hard-hitting images and messages were not met with universal acclaim (Corrigan, 2008) but were important nonetheless in encouraging councils to promote their services. Stockport Council, for example, ran a poster campaign showcasing some of the 600 services it provides to local people. The campaign, part of the Stockport Pride initiative, featured people who help provide and use some of the services.

Various studies indicate that people are vague as to the services that are provided by local councils: 'The leisure centre you keep fit in, the collection of your household rubbish, the school you or your children go to, the care of those who are disadvantaged, the hygiene standards in your local restaurants and shops, the range of reference materials in your local library – all of these things are the council's responsibility, plus many more besides' (LGA, nd).

Where does the problem lie? From the beginnings of local government PR (see Chapter 1), a key aim of PR/communication teams has been to inform, to tell local residents what services are available, what people are entitled to, what their payment of council tax (or its predecessors) covers.

A further approach has been Total Place – a government initiative (HM Treasury, 2010) focusing on the 'whole area' with which local customers identify (rather than who provides services). The intention was to avoid duplication and overlap between different service providers and to work with local communities in order to develop services that meet local needs, improve outcomes and deliver better value for money.

This initiative has led local councils to work with partners (see Chapter 7) across a range of services, including:

- safeguarding children;
- caring for vulnerable adults;
- tackling unemployment;
- dealing with crime and anti-social behaviour;
- minimising flood risks;
- dealing with climate change. (LGIDb, nd)

Customer insight is a programme that seeks customers' views to help local councils have a better understanding of their customers and their needs and to use that insight to develop more effective and efficient services.

Ideally local council PR practitioners are involved throughout initiatives of this kind and not just co-ordinating the communication of messages. Many of the recommended tools and techniques have been applied by local council PR practitioners for years, including customer consultation exercises and surveys, focus groups, customer feedback including complaints, compliments and comments, mystery shopping exercises and the experience and intelligence of front-line staff and elected members (IDeA, 2010).

LGA guidance also makes it clear that various council skills should be harnessed including consultation and customer service. Results should be communicated in a way that makes an impact on customers, and also enthuses others and engages effectively with staff throughout the council (LGA, 2010).

A case study from East Riding of Yorkshire (LGID, 2011) indicates public relations and communication as key elements.

The project envisaged that bespoke customer segmentation would tell them:

- what type of customers lived in the area;
- where the different types were located;
- how they preferred to interact with local services;
- how best to communicate with specific customer groups;
- which customer groups had a low or high demand for certain services.

## Original Reputation Guide

As a result of research undertaken by MORI and drawing on the knowledge and expertise of local council PR practitioners, the LGA developed its *Original Reputation Guide* (LGA, 2006), which identified five core communications, two of which were important in informing customers about services available to them. The guidelines for producing an A–Z of services and a council magazine/newspaper stand the test of time in providing pointers as to how to produce, and these guidelines apply as well to online information.

**1. To provide an A–Z guide to council services** with idealistic aims that can be applied to all customer communications:

- a clear layout and brief explanation of services
- include information for other local strategy partners such as police and health
- organise information in alphabetical order, not according to council structure
- use plain language and avoid council jargon
- refer to services from customer's point of view, eg bins not refuse, schools not lifelong learning or children's services
- deliver directly to every household and business
- use door-to-door delivery service or mail it out with your council tax bills
- offer a range of access points (phone, email, post, personal contact etc) and cross-reference to your website
- produce in an 'easy to use and keep' format so that people will want to keep it by the phone.

**2. To publish a regular council magazine/newspaper to inform residents**

- easy to read, jargon and acronym free
- available in accessible formats
- arresting headlines and interesting features
- entertaining, with crosswords, competitions and columnists
- useful, with service information, contacts, and 'what's on' listings
- credible, honest and reliable

- politically neutral and objective
- well designed with a clear format and quality photographs
- published at least four times a year and distributed directly to every household
- produced in partnership with key stakeholders
- focused on the community and its priorities, reporting the views of community groups and having features on particular parts of your locality
- clear in demonstrating the value for money provided by the council a quality product.

(LGA, 2006)

Essex Communications gold winner in the CIPR East Anglia PRide Awards Outstanding In-House Public Relations Team (2011/12) demonstrates a clear commitment in its mission statement to inform its customers about its services:

> Essex Communications exists to promote the work of Essex County Council; to enhance and protect its reputation; to win resources for the organisation and county; to attract and retain quality members of staff; to increase access to and awareness of services; to increase residents' satisfaction and to promote the wider county of Essex as an unrivalled place to live, invest, learn and visit.
>
> (CIPR PRide Awards, 2011)

# Why are you communicating?

It seems an obvious starting point but there have to be clear reasons for communicating:

- Think about the purpose of the communication.
- Are you merely providing information?
- Is it related or part of a wider communication strategy or campaign?
- Are you seeking involvement or a response?
- Is it to encourage take-up of service?
- Is it to reduce expectations and/or better target services?

# Using all channels

Many of the examples described here could be seen as one-way communication but councils seek feedback, have letters pages, ask people their views via citizens' panels and focus groups and invariably seek views as to the best way to communicate. What is key is reaching the right people with the right information at the right time, using the right communication channels and recognising the different ways that information can be communicated (Ipsos MORI, 2009).

# Sharing best practice

Local councils have a good track record of sharing best practice with each other – not least through excellence awards organised by the CIPR local public services group and LGcommunications. They also prove themselves when competing with other sectors in, for example, the CIPR PRide and PRWeek awards. Through the years there have been some councils which have stood out and whose examples are worth emulating. They include Camden Council, Derbyshire County Council, Edinburgh City Council, London Borough of Hackney, Norfolk County Council, Northamptonshire County Council, Stockport Metropolitan Borough Council, Waltham Forest Council and Westminster City Council.

Much of their information can be found online including, for example, Stockport's overview of its customer focus:

> Communication and engagement with local people continues to be developed, helping to ensure that they are informed, involved and listened to. A range of public information campaigns during the year have helped the Council communicate some of the changes being made in how services are delivered, such as increased access to services via the website, changes to waste collection arrangements and a planned approach to road maintenance...

Developing the communication and engagement with local people, to ensure that they are **informed, involved and listened** to:

> Throughout the year, a range of public information programmes have focused on communicating the Council's strategic business objectives. A Channel Shift programme has focused on ensuring the Council uses the most effective channels for the provision of information, while the 'Right Thing, Right Bin' public information programme helped to deliver real benefits in increasing recycling levels and avoiding landfill charges with £5.2 million now saved. Improved online communications on waste and recycling have made it easier for residents to find the information they need first time and reduce the cost of transactions with the Council. This has resulted in significant savings from reduced calls, complaints and contamination levels. Reflecting the growing importance to residents of road maintenance, the Council launched the Streets Ahead Public information programme. This demonstrated the Council's planned and coordinated approach to road repairs, street lighting repairs and winter gritting through a dedicated and more accessible website that helped to promote online reporting of faults and queries. Twitter and Facebook were also used as an effective tool to inform the public about gritting during the winter period.

> A full consultation programme was delivered as part of the Transformation Project, whilst the recommendations from the council-wide communications Scrutiny Review continue to be implemented. Results of research into how the Council communicates with residents and the ways that residents like to make contact with the Council are being reported back to appropriate Scrutiny panels and used as part of programme development in 2012/13.
>
> (Stockport Council, Portfolio Performance and Resource Annual Report 2011/12)

**FIGURE 5.1**  Bridgend 'recycle for victory' posters

Recycling is an issue that affects all council customers and has proved tricky to communicate, not least because it requires one of the most difficult of PR outcomes – a change in the way people behave.

Councils have risen to the challenge, including Bridgend who won gold in the CIPR Cymru/Wales PRide Awards 2011 to encourage more Bridgend residents to recycle. Their initiatives included direct mail to residents and a series of newspaper and radio adverts on the theme of 'recycle for victory', to help households understand the best way to recycle, and why this is important. Their efforts moved Bridgend from being one of the worst performing authorities for recycling in Wales to one of the best.

The PRide gold award was just one in a series of awards for Bridgend's recycling scheme. It also won a public vote to top the Local Authority Partnership category of Cylch's Wales Recycling Awards; a Green Apple Award; the final of the APSE Awards, and was shortlisted for the EDIE Awards for Environmental Excellence.

The key outcome in terms of customer response is: 'The performance is credited to the way residents have embraced the weekly recycling and understand the wide range of materials which can now be recycled at the kerbside.'

# Customer charters

Most councils make clear to their customers what they should expect from their services and their communications often through a pledge or promise that outlines their standards. Pembrokeshire County Council makes clear its commitment to customers: 'One of our key principles is putting customers first, our customers are the focus of everything we do and the way in which we work' (Pembrokeshire County Council, 2012).

---

### Our Customer Charter

Pembrokeshire County Council provides a wide range of services for its customers. Schools, social care, libraries, road maintenance and leisure centres are just some of our many services. One of our key principles is putting customers first, our customers are the focus of everything we do and the way in which we work.

No matter which service or part of the Council you are dealing with, you can expect to receive a consistently high level of service.

We intend to make dealing with the Council as easy as possible, delivering services in ways that are convenient for you.

We will:

- be polite, helpful, open and honest

- listen to you and take notice of what you have to say

- do our best to advise you

- do what we say we will do

- respect your confidentiality and privacy

- provide clear information, using plain language and in a format to suit you

- treat customers fairly and equally

The Charter then goes on to explain the different ways in which people can contact them – by phone, in person, in writing or online – what they can expect 'from all Council services at any time' and the availability of Welsh speakers.

It ends with:

*Help Us to Help You*

We are always keen to hear your views about our services. If you would like to make a comment, complaint, compliment or suggestion about any Council service, ask a member of staff for a leaflet, or call our Contact Centre on xxxx. Or go online **www.xxx**

Thank you

Stockport Council also states that its Customer Charter sets the standard for improving customer experience (Stockport Council, nd).

## Stockport Council Customer Charter

What is the Customer Charter?
The Customer Charter is our commitment to customers and residents and outlines the standards of service you can expect when dealing with Stockport Council.

You said you wanted us to:

- Respond to your enquiry promptly, accurately and in a polite manner
- Explain clearly and concisely
- Refer you to someone who can help if we are unable to assist you
- Let you know what will happen next with your enquiry
- Offer services that are easy to access in a variety of different ways
- Follow up on comments and complaints and learn from them

You can help us by:

- Telling us if you have difficulty accessing our services
- Advising us if you have any special requirements
- Telling us about any relevant changes in your circumstances as soon as you can
- Asking us to explain anything you are unsure of
- Giving us all the information we need to help you
- Being considerate and polite to our employees and other people using our services

### Measuring our Performance

We receive feedback from:

- Customer Surveys
- Customer Consultation & Focus Groups
- Individual feedback
- Information on the performance of Council Services can be found on the Council website

If you have any comment to make regarding the Charter please contact Customer Services: followed by telephone, fax and minicom numbers and email address.

# Customer services

Councils increasingly address themselves to customer services and link customer services directly to their public relations/communications function. Cumbria County Council is one example of a council that has developed a Customer Services Strategy putting customers at its core:

> To create the conditions for Cumbria's communities to thrive by putting customers at the heart of everything we do and work with others to deliver excellent services for those who need us most.
> (Cumbria County Council, nd; Customer Services Strategy 2011–14)

Hartlepool Borough Council has developed a framework to ensure that communication is open and effective and describes on its website its four key overlapping strategies (each with its own action plan). These are: communications; customer service; consultation; and complaints and comments.

The Customer Service Strategy has very clear objectives:

- to provide services that are easy to access and meet customers' needs;
- to make sure that all customers have equal access to the services they need;
- to respond to all enquiries and requests effectively and efficiently, within the agreed timescales;
- to maintain and promote the Council image to all of our customers and partners;
- to appoint a Councillor Customer Service Champion and an Officer Customer Service Champion in each department to drive change.

Norfolk County Council has a combined customer service and communications unit and since 2008 has had an integrated Customer Service Strategy, which sets a framework for providing good customer service:

> We help people who live, work, visit or do business in the county to understand and access council services they need. We also provide information to help people understand what the County Council does, how it uses its resources and the policies and decisions it makes. In addition we help the council better understand the needs and views of local people through research and consultation and make services more responsive by ensuring that people are able to have their say in shaping and developing them.

Norfolk County Council's Customer Service Strategy 2011–14 (Norfolk County Council, 2011) builds on its previous 2008 strategy, and importantly was approved by full Council. It embraces offline and online channels. The report to council raises some important issues and underlines the importance of constantly keeping up to date:

The growth of social networks, coupled with increasing sophistication and accessibility of technology – these allow people to share their satisfaction, or lack of it, faster and more prolifically than ever before. Customers are behaving in new ways, have higher expectations and frequently make decisions using their own trusted sources or references. This makes it important we consult, engage and build relationships with our customers effectively, actively asking them for their views, comments and suggestions on what we can do to improve and demonstrating we are using those views.

The strategy report also indicates that customers' expectations are changing with many now expecting an instant response to their queries and 'often try a variety of access channels simultaneously to get results. This means, queries are often more complex when they hit contact centre or back office staff because the customer has already tried and failed to sort out the query for themselves. It is critical that our access channels are up to the challenge presented by these fast-paced changes.'

Complaints handling is a vital part of customer services, whether corporately or departmentally managed. It has a crucial impact on the reputation of the council and public services. The public always has an ultimate recourse to the Ombudsman, but it is best for organisations to take time and sort out complaints internally, sensitively and in a timely manner. A complaint is an opportunity to review practice. This requires a culture within the organisation that values complaints, rather than dismissing them or demonising the complainant, and a management that actively assimilates the information and intelligence from complaints or comments on how services are delivered or not delivered. Norfolk's desired strategic outcomes highlight the importance of such customer insight.

Brennan and Simmons (2013) argue that complaints handling can be used to transform services, what they call a 'complaints-led innovation'. Internet platforms and new smartphone apps can 'create shorter lines of feedback' and 'a near frictionless experience' that can capture dissatisfaction and issues that need attention. Complaints can help 'broaden and deepen discussion' between service users and providers:

> Knowledge derived from complaints can be crucial in supporting a new relational model of public services that can better meet people's needs and aspirations. Complaints help raise awareness of service failures and illustrate areas for improvement. They can also provide valuable insight into citizens' perspectives on complex issues, engaging with complaints can be a fertile approach for innovation. If used effectively, complaints can help drive the transformation required to produce sustainable, equitable and person-centred public services.
>
> (Brennan and Simmons, 2013)

---

**Desired strategic outcomes**

- Easy access to our services for all who need them.

- Improved customer satisfaction with our services and the County Council overall.

- Access channels that are efficient; represent excellent value for money, and are responsive to changing customer needs, experiences and expectations.

- Consistent use of customer information/insight to help continually improve the quality and efficiency of the Authority's services and better support and enable the delivery of the Council's service transformation and efficiency programmes.

- A culture of good practice in customer services in the Authority where staff and customers are clear about the standards of customer service they can be expected to deliver or receive, and the Authority consistently meets or exceeds them.

Note the words 'strategic' and 'outcomes' – both significant aspects of public relations/communication activity. Transparency is another important public relations term admirably shown by Norfolk County Council not only in making its strategy available online but also its six-month progress update.

(Norfolk County Council, 2012)

---

# The council tax leaflet

Central government requires local councils to supply information to accompany the annual council tax bill. Councils vary in their approach – some keep the information short and to the point with straightforward messages about council budget and spending, explaining how the money is spent, where the money comes from and how much comes from council tax. Others take the opportunity to include additional information about services.

Derbyshire County Council, for example, includes a clear explanation on its website: the council tax leaflet is published every year in March: 'It is sent out with your council tax bill. It explains how we spend the money we get, where this money comes from and how much comes from council tax.'

The actual leaflet makes clear that the amount of council tax paid 'helps meet the cost of all council services – not just the ones you use':

It pays for the services we all rely on like roads, schools, buses, waste disposal and libraries. But it does so much more than that – it pays for those services that few of us use. But we need them – our communities need them. Services such as:

- protection for children who are at risk of harm;
- home support and residential care for the elderly;
- special education for children with learning difficulties;
- consumer and benefits advice.

Even if you don't need every service we provide, someone in your family or living near to you does. And you might need them too at some point in your life.

(Derbyshire County Council, Your Council Tax 2012/13)

Brighton and Hove City Council take the opportunity to include information about other services in their *Residents Guide to Brighton and Hove Services*, which covers essential council and NHS contact details plus 'Your council, Your city, Your guide to Council Tax and where it goes 2012/13; your Easter and bank holidays 2012 and recycling and refuse collection dates' (Brighton and Hove City Council, 2012–13). Glasgow City Council issues its council tax bill and information in a white envelope overprinted with the message 'Pay up for Glasgow', listing the services the council provides.

# Council publications and A–Z guides

Council newspapers and magazines, although subject to political restriction (see Chapter 9) continue to provide important channels to inform council customers.

The CIPR LPSG excellence awards outline, regarding the category 'Council newspaper/magazine' continues to state: 'Recognised as one of the most effective ways to reach residents but does yours look good, read well and importantly what do the residents say?'

Councils use their newspaper or magazine in different ways but invariably refer to them as a means to signpost to services and how to get in touch. They often use real people's stories to help illustrate the services they provide and may also feature real staff to inform about the range and nature of services – the park ranger, the swimming pool attendant, the home carer, the teaching assistant. Several councils also provide information jointly with health and other partners (see Chapter 7).

A small number of councils have stopped producing as part of their cost cutting and others have gone completely online. In both cases it removes the opportunity to reach every household and business with hard copy that can be kept to refer to when needed, especially when including the Council's A–Z of services. Councils need to monitor carefully how their online versions are accessed and whether or not they meet council customer needs.

**FIGURE 5.2** Derbyshire County Council, Your Council Tax 2012/13

DERBYSHIRE COUNTY COUNCIL
**TOUGH** DECISIONS
**FAIR** SERVICES
**EFFICIENT** COUNCIL

# 0%
## AGAIN
no increase in our share of Council Tax

YOUR COUNCIL TAX
## 2012/2013

**DERBYSHIRE** County Council
Improving life for local people

---

### HELPING YOU
### HELP YOURSELF

Across Derbyshire thousands of people volunteer their time and skills to make a difference to local life. They see what needs doing and are happy to get involved to do their bit. And they make life better for us all.

You and your neighbours know best what needs doing close to your home. It's our job at Derbyshire County Council to support you and your community so you can get on and do it. We can't do it all – and we may not be the best at doing it.

That's why we are investing in our communities, local organisations and volunteers. We've set aside cash to help support and extend the work they do. We're working with them and paying some of them to deliver services on our behalf. We're offering:

**Big Society Grants** – cash to contribute to big community projects.
Visit www.derbyshire.gov.uk/bigsocietygrants

**Community Action Grants** – up to £1,000 for small groups with big ideas.
Visit www.derbyshire.gov.uk/cag

**Sports Action Grants** – up to £1,000 for groups and clubs to get more people taking part.
Visit www.derbyshire.gov.uk/sportsactiongrant

**Derbyshire Volunteer Passport** – free training for adults who want to work with children.
Visit www.derbyshire.gov.uk/passport

**Derbyshire Directory** – a one-stop shop of information with more than 2,700 local groups and not-for-profit services listed.
Visit www.derbyshire.gov.uk/directory

Big Society is not new in Derbyshire but this is Big Society in action.

Published by Derbyshire County Council, County Hall, Matlock DE4 3AG

---

### TOUGH DECISIONS.
### FAIR SERVICES.
### EFFICIENT COUNCIL

We've frozen our share of your council tax for the second year running – so we don't add to the cost of your bills.

We know how hard it is for many of you to make ends meet. We know tax rises are tough. And we know your council tax is one of the biggest bills you get each year. We don't want to add to your burden.

Like councils across the country – we're facing up to some really difficult choices. We have to – they can't be left for another day.

We cannot continue to spend, spend, spend. That would mean asking you to dig even deeper to pay for your council services. We know you don't want that and we're not prepared to ask you to.

We need to reduce our spending by £25 million over the next 12 months – that's on top of the £45 million we have saved over the last two years. It also means a further 600 county council jobs will go as part of a planned reduction of 2,000 jobs over four years.

We are doing our best to protect front-line services. We are cutting more from our back-office budgets. But – inevitably – there will be reductions and changes to some services. And we will continue to cut waste, red tape and bureaucracy as well as finding better and cheaper ways of working.

Importantly, we are making sure your services are delivered fairly – across the whole of Derbyshire. Above all we will work hard to make your council tax go further so you get even better value for money.

---

### TOUGH DECISIONS.
### FAIR SERVICES.
### EFFICIENT COUNCIL

Your council tax is based on the value of your property. The amount you pay helps meet the cost of all council services – not just the ones you use.

It pays for the services we all rely on like roads, schools, buses, waste disposal and libraries. But it does so much more than that – it pays for those services that few of us use. But we need them – our communities need them too. Services such as:

- protection for children who are at risk of harm
- home support and residential care for the elderly
- special education for children with learning difficulties
- consumer and benefits advice.

Even if you don't need every service we provide – someone in your family or living near to you does. And you might need them too at some point in your life.

What we promise is that you get:
- good value for your money
- high quality, flexible services that meet your needs
- help to improve your community, your health and your life.

We are taking tough decisions. But – above all – we will be a fair and efficient council.

You can see more about our plans at www.derbyshire.gov.uk

**For more information about our budget contact:**
Paul Stone on 01629 539239.
Email: paul.stone3@derbyshire.gov.uk
Write to: Derbyshire County Council, County Hall, Matlock DE4 3AG

Or Call Derbyshire on
0845 058 058 or 01629 533190.

**FIGURE 5.3**    Brighton and Hove City Council Residents Guide to Services

**CASE STUDY**    Belfast City Council's *City Matters* (winner of six CIPR PRide Awards) and Gold winner in the CIPR Northern Ireland PRide Awards 2011 in the external newspaper/magazine category

Judges' comments: Fantastic-looking and informative publication. Sets a good example for all local authority newspapers. *City Matters* sets a high standard for reader engagement with an impressive amount of feedback from customers for every edition. Too many local authority publications get mired in political priorities and pitfalls but *City Matters* steers clearly through that tricky ground to provide an informative and engaging publication for everyone in the city of Belfast.

*City Matters* is a regular free magazine for Belfast City Council residents which has been running successfully since 2002.

Typical content includes:

- information on council activities and city news;
- an A–Z guide of key council services;
- an events calendar; and
- regular features such as a seniors section, consumer advice and celebrated citizen.

The main objectives of *City Matters* are to be:

- relevant;
- appealing;
- informative;
- two-way;
- diverse;
- cost effective;
- honest, balanced and fair;
- accessible; and
- reputable.

## CASE STUDY

*Dacorum Digest* was the best newspaper gold winner in the CIPR Thames and Chiltern PRide Awards in 2010. The judges were impressed with the look and feel of the publication, as well as the overall positive attitude towards the publication from stakeholders. The *Dacorum Digest* is a community newspaper that is targeted at all residents, distributed to 59,000 households across diverse communities and age groups. The judges felt that the content of the publication was well targeted and engaging, and that research showed the target audience found the publication to be useful. The judges were particularly impressed with the range of local stories, essential information and overall accessibility of the publication. The *Dacorum Digest* explains services, and how to access them, in a straightforward clear way (CIPR PRide Awards, 2010a).

The *Digest* is also online in an e-zine format with live links direct to online services. The spring 2012 edition includes 'Dealing with debt' – support and advice available; advice on recycling – signposting to guide as to 'what goes where' and parking charges.

The award-winning *Hertsmere News* (CIPR PRide Awards, 2010b), produced by Hertsmere Borough Council, is a quarterly magazine delivered to every home in the Borough. The primary audience is residents but *Hertsmere News* is also distributed to the local press, community groups, partners and

**FIGURE 5.4**   *Dacorum Digest* online

also 'to key stakeholders and those who have influence in our community, such as focus groups, friends' groups, Neighbourhood Watch coordinators, police/fire services and parish and community newsletters.

*Hertsmere News* plays a key part in delivering the wider Corporate Communications strategy, including informing residents about Council-led services and where and how they can access them and the quality of service they can expect. The award-winning entry makes reference to previous content: registering to vote; providing help in the recession; the introduction of fines for littering and dog fouling; making the most of recycling facilities; police priorities; and service provision during cold weather. Supplements to support other communication campaigns are included when appropriate such as the annual A–Z guide and regular waste and recycling collection calendar.

# The council website and online information

James Grunig (2009) warns that history shows that when new media are introduced, communicators tend to use them in the same way that they used the old media: 'In the same way, public relations practitioners first used online media as an information dump, in the same way that they used traditional media, newsletters, and publications.'

That may ring true for many councils when they look back to their original use of websites, perhaps putting leaflets online and expecting users to scroll down through pages of information.

Websites increasingly provide comprehensive information on all services, and make the information easy to find and relevant to customers, such as including bus times, country parks, libraries, registration offices, school directories, recycling centres.

Particularly important is information that usually comes under the heading of 'Education and learning', which covers childcare and family services, schools, secondary schools admissions, adult learning, term dates and school holidays:

> We provide opportunities for learning at all stages in your life. Here's the information on everything you need to know about education and childcare in Derbyshire.
>
> (Derbyshire County Council website)

Local Councils' websites give an indication of the wide range of services for which they are responsible, and to help the customer they often divide topics into general services and highlight the most regularly visited topics and tasks, as in the Staffordshire example below. The most popular topics shown

**FIGURE 5.5**    Staffordshire County Council website

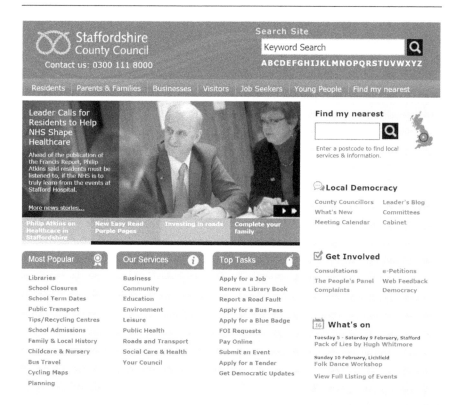

**FIGURE 5.6**    Wigan Life Centre

## Bill payments
Information about how to pay a council bill.

## Bills, Money and Debt

## Birth Certificates - Historical Searches
Requesting Certificates for Family History Purposes

## Black Bins
Your black bin is collected every two weeks.

## Blocked drains
This page tells you what to do if you have a problem with your drains.

## Blue Badge Scheme
The Blue Badge Scheme is a national scheme that provides parking concessions for individuals who qualify.

## Book Request Service (Wigan Leisure and Culture Trust)

## Boomtown Project (Wigan Leisure and Culture Trust)

are libraries, school term dates, public transport, tips/recycling centres, school admissions, family and local history, child care, school closures, bus travel, cycling maps and planning – these give PR practitioners a really good barometer of key customer interests at any one time. The top tasks are interesting in terms of interactivity online – apply for a job, renew a library book, report a road fault, apply for a blue badge, FoI requests, pay online, submit an event, apply for a tender, get democratic updates.

Others will have an A–Z of services either on their home page or clearly and quickly accessed from it, as in the Wigan example on page 115. What is then key is to ensure that the terms used within an A–Z are those that the customer would use, eg do customers refer to 'refuse collection' or to 'bins'?

# Equality in communication

Accessibility of information to all, clarity and user-friendliness for the various audiences, consideration of languages and two-way communication are principles to maximise equality in communication.

(Leicestershire County Council, 2009)

Councils can be bewildering places from the outside, especially in two-tier authority areas where joint information provision is good practice. Think about:

- Where do people get their information?
- Where do they find that telephone number?
- How easy is it to find information on the website?
- What other ways do you use to reach your customers?
- Are libraries, leisure centres, council reception areas, CABx, partners, local radio helplines, local businesses regularly kept up to date?
- When is it really useful to produce a leaflet?
- Are people assured of quick and helpful responses to e-mails, telephone calls, personal visits?
- When is it appropriate to consider house-to-house distribution or a mail drop?

One response to the questions above is to ask your customers where they expect to find information (what are their preferred channels?) and test with them print and website information before and after publishing. However good your information, if it is not easily accessible in style and language it has failed as a communication.

Local councils have a good track record of seeking to make sure that their communications are accessible using large print, accessible formats and alternative languages on request. Most also produce style guides or toolkits that indicate how and when accessible formats should be used.

## *Dacorum Digest*

The newspaper meets accessibility standards using clear, readable type and colour schemes that offer good contrast. Audio cassette versions are available and there is also an online version, an interactive version with live links direct to online services and other related information. This also gives readers the option to subscribe to the publication and to be notified as soon as a new issue is published (Dacorum Borough Council, 2010).

## *Hertsmere News*

Hertsmere Borough Council's quarterly magazine is also available on the Council's website and as an audio package, and can be provided in different language formats which follow RNIB guidelines:

> We aim to follow RNIB guidelines as far as possible such as avoiding capital letters to help those with visual impairments to read it more easily and have a contrast between the text and background. We also avoid using certain colours together that colour-blind people would not be able to tell apart.

Many councils such as Bradford refer to their commitment to the Five Principles for Producing Better Information for Disabled People. They also refer to holding regular meetings with disability groups to discuss their needs and how they can be met by the Council's newsletter *Community Pride* (City of Bradford Metropolitan Council website). *Community Pride* is delivered to every household in the district and includes information about Council services and policies in a clear, simple and jargon-free way that residents can easily understand. Every edition of *Community Pride* is scrutinised by the Plain English Campaign and carries their 'Approved by' logo for plain English.

The publication is also available in audio formats, Braille or as a large print Word document. The publication conforms to high standards of accessible design – including the font size and colours used – which support the Council's commitment to the Five Principles for Producing Better Information for Disabled People. Regular meetings with disability groups are held to discuss their needs and how they can be met by the publication. The publication is also available as a downloadable pdf from the Council's website (CIPR PRide Awards, 2010c).

Like Bradford, councils frequently refer to the five principles that are available in the very useful *Improving Information for Disabled People* produced by the Office for Disability Issues (2007):

> Five key information principles
> The following five core information principles have been developed from the findings of the ODI's review. They are essential to underpinning good service and information design and delivery.
> **1** Ensure that disabled people are involved from the start
> **2** Provide information through a range of channels and formats

**3** Ensure your information meets users' needs

**4** Clearly signpost other services

**5** Always define responsibility for information provision

The five principles interrelate to reinforce each other, so ideally they should be approached as a package rather than in isolation. They can be applied to:

- large-scale projects such as service designs, rebranding, positioning exercises and public consultations; and
- smaller information initiatives such as the design of leaflets, posters, advertisements, films, events, websites or newsletters.

Websites are rich sources of information. They demonstrate accessibility with the ability to increase the size of words on screen, leaflets can be downloaded and short video clips are being introduced with people discussing their experiences. Easy-read websites (see the Blackburn with Darwen example below) are emerging, aimed mainly at people with learning disabilities, but frequently appreciated by other groups.

**FIGURE 5.7** Blackburn with Darwen Learning Disability Partnership Board easy-read website

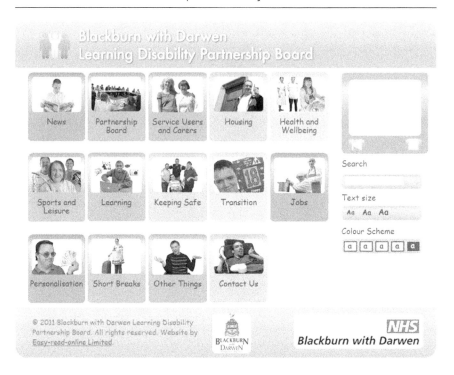

**FIGURE 5.8** Inclusive Communication Essex (ICE)

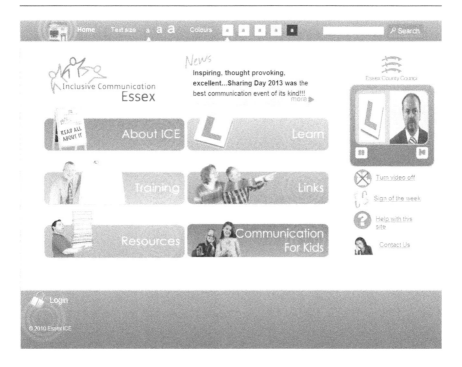

There are some pioneering endeavours such as Inclusive Communication Essex (ICE), which seeks to share information and to communicate in a way that everybody can understand. They provide valuable insights into improving communications for local public services.

# Can there ever be too much information?

There was a time when there seemed to be a council leaflet (and often an accompanying poster!) on every conceivable topic. Customers themselves referred to too much information; preferring instead to have signposting only when needed. This can be summed up by an interview participant in a Joseph Rowntree Foundation study:

> You don't know what you don't know until you need to know it!

> We are awash with information and good advice, but most of the time it is like water off a duck's back... until you need that piece of information or advice. That's when you should be able to find it but can't!

> (Dunning, 2005: 20)

The message here is to achieve the right balance about signposting customers to information. Avoid overloading them with information but equally avoid continually referring them elsewhere to get the information they want (ODI, 2008).

## Two-way communication and the all important feedback

> One simple thing local and municipal government can do to improve quality of life is to ask citizens what matters to them... By asking citizens what they want, delivering it and keeping citizens informed, municipal authorities can both improve citizens' quality of life and raise perceptions of their own performance.
>
> (Ipsos MORI, 2010)

Over time there has been a considerable change with a far greater concentration on establishing relationships with customers: consulting, listening, engaging, involving. Harvey (1995) as cited in Wakeman (2012) not only emphasises the importance of keeping customers informed about the activities of an organisation but also the need to educate colleagues about the value of communicating with customer groups and 'the importance of being responsive to customer needs and opinions' (see Chapter 4 regarding consultation and engagement).

Accessibility of information to all, clarity and user-friendliness for the various publics, consideration of language and two-way communication are principles to maximise equality in communication.

## Monitoring and evaluation

This is an oft-repeated message of this book but inevitably one of the most important – that of showing that your work is properly evaluated. Whatever the PR aims and objectives, it is vital to be clear about how outcomes will be measured – how to know:

- whether or not your work has been successful;
- what difference it will make to your customers – whether residents or businesses;
- how it will support council priorities and deliver council objectives.

---

### Checklist

- Make sure communication for every service is focused and clear.

- Meet different communication needs.

- Help local people know what services are available and how to access them.

- Signpost.

- Make clear who deals with what.

- Make information readily available and accessible to all.

- Consult, listen, engage and involve.

- Make clear what customers should expect of services, of communications and of standards.

- Make sure customers have the opportunity to feed back their views not just about services but about communications.

- Reach the right people with the right information and use the right communication channels, recognising the different ways that information can be communicated.

- Link customer services directly to the public relations/communications function.

- Ask your customers where they expect to find information; what are their preferred channels; and test with them print and website information before and after publishing.

---

## KEY WORDS

Total place; customer insight; customer charters; customer services; contact centres; information; channels; council tax leaflet; council newspapers or magazines; council website and online information; signposting; accessibility; two-way communication; ask; consult; listen; engage; involve; monitor; evaluate.

# 06
# Communicating with employees

*Effective communication is not a task for communications specialists alone; everyone involved in, and connected with, the Council has a role to play – through what they say or do and how they say or do it. Good communication requires a commitment from members, chief officers and staff, and is a two-way process; communication is about listening as well as informing.*

**ALLERDALE BOROUGH COUNCIL**

## Defining communications with employees

There seems to be a constant debate about terms and definitions and the theme of this chapter might be understood as any of the following:

- internal communication;
- internal relations;
- employee engagement;
- employee communication;
- employee relations;
- internal communications and engagement.

Definitions do differ from those who take a top-down approach focusing on influencing rather than engaging employees: 'The planned use of communication actions to systematically influence the knowledge, attitudes and behaviours of current employees' (Strauss and Hoffmann, 2000) to those such as Cornelissen (2004) who regard it as 'all methods used by a firm to communicate with its employees', to Yeomans (2006) who takes a pragmatic view describing internal communication as the term 'used in the UK and elsewhere to describe an organisation's managed communication system where employees are regarded as a public or stakeholder group'.

This chapter will tend towards 'internal communication', which seems to be the prevailing term in local councils. The key words to note in the definitions above are 'planned' and 'managed'.

The importance of communicating strategically was covered in detail in Chapter 3 and applies equally to internal communication. Some councils will include internal communication in their overarching communication strategy – others will have it as a separate strategy but within the overall communication umbrella.

According to Fitzpatrick (2012) there are five main reasons for good communication within an organisation, and these are:

1 Meeting legal obligations to communicate
2 Building the community
3 Helping get the job done
4 Promoting advocacy
5 Supporting change

**FIGURE 6.1**  Five main reasons for good communication within an organisation

Based on Fitzpatrick 2012

Local Government Improvement and Development have useful pointers for councils on their website and echo the value of good internal communication and what it can achieve. For example, it can:

- help create a 'can-do' culture and build a committed and high-performing workforce focused on achieving the council's goals;
- boost morale and motivation;
- encourage staff to be your ambassadors;
- provide a better customer service – informed front-line and other staff will be up to speed on what's happening in the council and why.

From the staff notice board to Yammer, via text messaging, best practice in internal communications is all about knowing what works for your council (Groves, 2011).

Every Council is unique with its own culture and its own way of doing things. 'Internal communications used to mean a staff newsletter and the occasional bulletin sent to managers' (O'Dea, 2011) but in recent years, and with impetus from various comprehensive inspection regimes, Investors in People and the LGA's Reputation Campaign, councils have increasingly recognised the value of communicating with employees.

Internal communication might rely on the Core Briefing cascading once a month, top down, through the council's staff, or the staff newsletter/in-house journal, or the intranet or the chief executive's blog – or a combination of all four or more. Too often in the past they were information tools – delivering information in one direction only, what Bernstein (1989) described as the pea-shooter model of communication. Just because the information has been sent does not mean that it has been received, understood and, if required, acted upon.

Yeomans (2006) takes this a step further by focusing on staff and their communication needs. She suggests that what they need is:

- general information about the organisation;
- specific information to help them to do their jobs;
- clarity about their roles;
- a clear company/organisational vision;
- information on workplace practices;
- opportunities to be involved and consulted;
- feedback on performance;
- access to training and development;
- access to communication channels.

O'Dea (2011) takes a similar view relating specifically to local councils:

Good internal communication builds a committed and high-performing workforce that is focused on achieving the council's goals. Informed, engaged employees are less likely to leave, more innovative and work harder for the organisation. Staff who understand what the council is doing and why can advocate on its behalf.

# Identifying internal publics

Communicating with council staff is exceedingly complex and to talk about staff communications is something of a misnomer. Increasingly, services may be delivered through a diverse workforce who may be made up of a mix of council staff and outsourced service providers, through partnerships and shared services. It is also important to recognise that many staff do not have access to e-mail and internet; they may work shifts, work out of depots, in people's homes, in schools, in call centres; are field workers, homeworkers, on sick leave, maternity or impairment leave. Trade unions too are important internal publics.

It is therefore crucial to ensure that 'the tried and tested methods are really well done – for example, the staff briefings by managers. Ultimately, the type of channel being used doesn't matter if your information isn't timely, accurate, honest and "discussable"' (Caveney, 2011).

Staff need to understand the council's vision and values so that they can see how their own work and individual services or projects fit into the bigger picture.

Elected members should not be forgotten in internal communications plans and strategies – they may have direct involvement in the communication process, they may need to be kept informed of the progress of an internal communication programme or they will be responsible for the final approval. Internal communication is ongoing and should be happening all the time in a planned and sustained way.

There will, however, be times when a particular issue necessitates a specific communication campaign to run parallel when the need is to be 'open in your communication, and involve and engage staff in any large scale change programme that might be taking place' (Briggs, 2011), as demonstrated in the later case studies from Edinburgh and Norfolk.

Often it is at a time of change that the importance and value of internal communication is at its greatest. Restructuring, transformation, pay and service reviews, and budget reductions can all understandably create great fear and anxiety. Councils who already have sound internal communication strategies where staff feel involved, consulted and listened to, will be better placed to deal with change and will recognise that communication is a crucially important component of any change programme.

As you think about the role communication will need to play in supporting the change programme, also use the following overarching principles to guide your planning:

- Be respectful of the past and present whilst focusing on the future
- Be timely with your communication – when you've got something to share, share it
- Be honest and open and communicate the facts (and don't hide the negatives!)

- Use a variety of channels (face to face, electronic, print, workplace) to engage people
- Listen, listen, listen – ensure feedback mechanisms are included and use research to understand what your audience is thinking, feeling and doing
- Bang the drum for change – communicate progress and celebrate successes
- Champion the changes in actions as well as words – get leaders and managers to demonstrate the behaviours you are seeking in others
- Enlist the support of the influencers inside your organisation – recruit highly connected people at all levels to shape the programme, champion it and spread the word

(Smith, nd)

Virtually all of the above points apply equally to all communications with employees – not just at a time of change. It is also important to be honest and transparent – communication is not about 'spin' and only telling good news. Staff need to trust the credibility and authority of the information that comes to them even if the messages are difficult. Feedback from different councils also underlines the importance of communications being timely and relevant – staff may not give full attention to issues that don't seem to affect them directly. The Edinburgh and Norfolk case studies are good examples of internal communication programmes taking account of staff being affected in different ways at different times.

Inevitably all staff do not respond to communication in the same way. Quirke (2008) identified different degrees to which staff are willing to engage and participate from 'unguided missiles' or 'hot shots' to 'slow burners' and 'refuseniks'. What is important to recognise is that they all have communication needs – particularly during a time of change, where staff need to be kept informed of unfolding events. Staff also indicate that their preference is to be given regular updates even if there is nothing new to report – a gap in communication will lead to it being filled by rumour.

**FIGURE 6.2**  Different degrees to which staff are willing to engage and participate

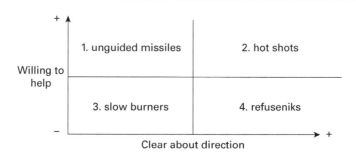

SOURCE 'The different degrees of employees' clarity and willingness Quirke 2000'

# Voice: staff at the heart of internal communication strategies

Sean Trainor, previous Chair of CIPR Inside, the specialist group for Chartered Institute of Public Relations members with an interest in employee communications and engagement, is quoted (Groves, 2011) as saying that 'employees need to be at the heart of all internal communication strategies' and that the communication channels used are merely tools.

> One of the keys to successful engagement is ensuring your people understand the overall strategy and how they can best contribute towards it. It's also clear that this has to be a two-way relationship. Gaining employee trust and commitment also means seeking your people's views and feedback, understanding any issues and seeking to address them.
>
> (Investors in People)

# Voice: hearing what staff have to say

As mentioned in Chapter 3, employees are often referred to as important PR ambassadors (Oliver, 2007) yet all too often staff complain that they first see something about their council in the media. There may be enormous activity in communicating outwards about a change in service delivery so that residents are well prepared and informed, but communications with staff are overlooked. A large proportion of council staff are 'front-line' in touch with local residents on a regular basis. Not only is it important for staff to be informed but the way they feel about their work and the council will affect the way they speak of it when outside work. It has to be remembered that many council staff are also residents and voters in their council area and they have friends, relatives, neighbours who are likely to trust what they hear from someone with direct personal contact. And again, two-way communication is vital – recognising that they provide a vital source of ideas and information.

## CASE STUDY

Torbay Council, in their employee engagement campaign, aimed at developing 'an internal communications programme to ensure that staff morale is improved across the council and they are kept up to date on key corporate objectives' ably demonstrated through consultation on the kinds of issues that concern staff:

- 'I receive far too many all staff e-mails and most of the time they are not relevant to me.'

- 'It would be beneficial to get a better understanding of what other teams do.'

- 'Team meetings are not very informative and often do not happen at all.'

- 'The notice boards are a mess and most of them are out of date.'

- 'The staff newsletter needs modernising and could be sent electronically rather than hard copy.'

Not only did they consult but they listened to staff and acted upon their feedback, putting into effect 'we asked, you said, we did'. These are some of the actions taken:

- A 'daily news' all staff e-mail detailing 'need to know' information that is relevant to all staff. Any other news is placed on the news page of the intranet.

- Shadowing days set up to allow staff time in other departments.

- Monthly Team Talks are now compulsory and Team Talk briefing packs are sent to all managers each month containing corporate information ensuring that all staff receive a consistent message.

- Each team is encouraged to feedback on recent successes, comments or questions.

- Notice boards were revamped with a new banner 'Keeping staff informed'. Designated Key Communicators have been assigned to each board and they are sent regular e-mails containing consistent and relevant information for the boards. Each board also contains a sounding board allowing staff to anonymously post questions/comments if they wish.

- The staff newsletter has been modernised and now contains a mix of need to know and nice to know features including Meet the Team, staff announcements, share success, updates from Senior Management Team and a guest editor. It is sent electronically to all staff and a hard copy is available on notice boards for those people who do not have access to a pc. MP3 audio transcripts and large print, text-only versions of each edition are available.

## Outcomes

An internal communications survey was carried out in January 2011. Despite the difficult economic climate and budget reductions, the survey showed a remarkable increase in staff morale – from 11 per cent to 68 per cent.

The percentage of staff who felt they knew what was going on in the council as a whole also increased from 37 per cent to 78 per cent.

Other comments from the survey included: 'I think internal comms have vastly improved over the last six months. News is in one place, it's consistent, it looks good. Well done Comms Team.'

(Torbay Council, 2011)

# Voice: internet gives opportunities

If staff don't feel they have a voice the internet now gives them the opportunity to air their views demonstrated by the widely publicised 'Watching Lincolnshire County Council blog' (now deleted by the authors), a whistle-blowing site giving disgruntled staff the opportunity to anonymously air gripes, grievances, gossip and occasionally confidential information (Briggs, 2011). Ideally, honest and transparent internal communication makes this kind of activity unnecessary and it's no surprise that increasingly councils refer to 'conversation, dialogue, engage, consult', resulting in adapting and adopting different approaches to communication based on staff views and opinions. The latter fits with Grunig's model, which suggested that by adopting two-way symmetrical communication then 'open, trusting, and credible relationships with strategic employee constituencies will follow' (Grunig, 1992). Grunig's excellence study (2008) showed 'that a symmetrical system of internal communication increased employees' satisfaction with their jobs and with the organisation'.

> Face-to-face communication: By distributing information in the belief that they are communicating, organisations are deluding themselves. They are confusing information with communication. The sharing and distribution of information is the first, but not the last, step in the communication process. Information can travel over wires. Communication happens between the ears.'
>
> (Quirke, 2008)

# The crucial role that managers play

Surveys repeatedly find that staff prefer face-to-face communication and that in particular they want information to come from their immediate supervisor or manager (Yeomans, 2006; Communicators in Business/Ipsos MORI, 2003). They regard line managers as the most trusted source of information, and the second preferred channel is the team briefing. This points to the need for PR practitioners to ensure that they support managers so that they are fully briefed not only to impart information but to answer their team members' questions and to act as a communication channel up, down and across the council. Inevitably there will be some managers who find this role harder than others and so there need to be mechanisms in place that prompt staff to expect certain information coming from their managers 'at their next team meeting' or show that there are other ways for staff to feed back directly if they feel there is any blocking at the manager level.

Management relationships with employees are key to engagement and creating a positive organisational culture, where the style is less about command and control and more about empowerment and appreciation, feedback and involvement (LGA Reputation Campaign).

Digital can't, and shouldn't, replace team meetings, but it can help to make sure managers are equipped with the right information when they go into these meetings, and can feed back afterwards.

(O'Dea, 2011)

Managers at every level should take responsibility for their part in communicating effectively with employees, and are key players in the PR practitioners' communication network.

# Channels of internal communication

Different channels of communication have been referred to in this chapter. Each council will use ways that are most relevant to its size and spread. What is important is to use several methods, with messages reinforcing each other. It is also important to hear from staff about what works best for them. Some council communications teams have staff panels or focus groups or champions who are in a position to feed back views about internal communication.

The following list of possible internal communication channels is adapted from a list compiled by students in a CIPR Diploma work group in 2012.

## Face to face (method preferred and valued by employees)

1:1 briefings; HQ staff meeting with chief executive/head of communication; department/corporate/regional/local staff meetings; all staff meetings; management meeting; team meetings; team brief; lunchtime staff briefings; drop in surgeries; cascade; monthly core briefing; meetings with line managers; shop floor talks; roadshows; work councils; workshops; focus groups; staff conferences; clubs and societies; 'back to the floor' programmes.

## Print (reference document to keep; reach those not online)

Weekly/monthly internal newsletter; staff magazine; head office newsletter; extraordinary newsletter; annual report; annual report for employees; letter to all staff from chief executive; FAQs; leaflet; pay slip messages; poster; posters on toilet doors; surveys for those not online.

## Broadcast

Website; video in all team meetings (consistency); video on staff intranet eg message from chief executive/leader; video of examples of good practice;

DVDs, podcasts; webchats – live with eg chief executive/head of human resources; intranets/internet, e-newsletters, e-bulletins, webinars, text messages, plasma screens, business TV; information forums, news; online polls and suggestion box; chief executive's blogs, staff blogs, microblogs; Web 2.0 and Enterprise 2.0: texting, social media, instant messaging, Facebook, Twitter; FAQs.

## Digital

E-mail; all staff e-mail; by group; e text; intranet (news and dedicated section); Facebook group message; housekeeping bulletins/updates; web chats; webinars; digital e-petition; surveys; twitter; e-newsletter; e-zines; website – download guides; PowerPoint presentations to use in team briefings.

## Events

Training sessions; roadshows; presentations; annual awards; 'local heroes'; celebrations; visits; exhibitions.

## Corporate Social Responsibility (CSR)

Engaging staff; part of organisational culture.

## Media

Local radio/debate/phone in; local newspaper(s); local broadcast media; Chief Executive quoted in media – credible/authoritative source for staff too – often more believable because is in media.

Staff need to know what is happening before going public/external.

## Other

- Suggestion schemes.
- Training and secondments.
- One method reinforcing another; linking; saying same things in different ways.
- Messages get blocked – going up and down – how to overcome/circumnavigate?
- Ongoing programme – underpinning business objectives/ideally part of corporate communications plan.
- Separate projects – often related to structural/organisational change.
- Celebrate achievements.

# Engaging staff and employee surveys

Councils conduct periodic employee surveys seeking employees' views not just regarding job satisfaction but on how well informed they feel about the council and its priorities and how they prefer to be communicated with.

Results are valuable in identifying groups that may feel disengaged, ensuring managers are equipped with knowledge and communication skills to engage with their own team, recognising the importance of internal communication during a time of change or restructuring, ensuring staff are genuinely engaged and feel involved, understanding how their job contributes to the entire council – not just the area they work in. Results of employee surveys may also point to a need for greater visibility of chief and senior officers and provide insights into what should be included in induction programmes and reward and recognition schemes.

Employee surveys are important barometers of the mood of staff at any one time and provide important comparisons with previous surveys. As indicated previously, what goes on inside the organisation affects the world outside and vice versa, and poor results are likely to be published externally as was shown in the cases of Glasgow City Council and Cumbria County Council in 2012. 'Morale hits rock bottom' was a too oft repeated headline in 2012. Glasgow City Council commissioned Ipsos MORI Scotland to conduct qualitative and quantitative research to identify and explore the issues important to staff and the impact of these on their working lives:

> Analysis included putting results in the context of the views of all working people across the UK, the views of staff in other local authorities and previous Glasgow City Council staff surveys conducted in 2007 and 2009. The analysis also included key driver analysis to explore the drivers behind feelings of pride, job satisfaction and advocacy of the Council as a place to work.

Reporting included production of a special edition staff newsletter and 50 service and department level presentations.

The qualitative phase of the research involved a series of discussion groups with staff and in-depth interviews with senior managers. The aim of this phase was to provide interim management information on the status of staff opinion and to consult with staff on the development of the 2012 survey. This was followed by a survey of all employees in 2012. All 19,500 staff were sent either an e-mail invitation to an online version of the questionnaire, a paper self-completion questionnaire to be returned in a reply-paid envelope, or they were invited to participate by completing an abbreviated questionnaire at a self-completion session. A total of 6,545 staff returned a completed questionnaire between 2 February and 23 March 2012. This represented a response rate of 34 per cent. The response in 2007 and 2009 was 27 per cent.

Findings reported by Braiden (2012) in *The Herald* included:

- Of 6,545 staff who took part in the survey, 62 per cent said their jobs had got worse over the past three years.
- Almost a quarter said they considered the council to be one of the worst employers around.
- A third of the staff reported that stress from work impinged on their personal lives.
- More than half said they had been subjected to abuse from the public.
- 30 per cent said they had been bullied by a colleague or superior.
- Glasgow, like many councils, have been hit by cost-cutting measures.
- In recent years, the authority has shed more than 3,000 jobs as they try to find tens of millions of pounds of savings.
- But other councils surveyed attained better results in the staff survey.

Similarly the *North West Evening Mail* and the *Cumberland News* carried the headline along the lines of 'Morale among Cumbria council staff at rock bottom'.

- This time 46 per cent were 'satisfied' with their job, down from 61 per cent in 2009.
- The proportion 'dissatisfied' almost doubled from 22 to 40 per cent.
- Complaints included the poor morale of colleagues, lack of opportunity to progress, inadequate pay and worries about job security, while 59 per cent did not 'feel valued'.
- Workers were generally happy with their line managers but not with senior bosses.
- More than half thought the senior management team did not listen to feedback, failed to act openly and honestly and did not keep promises to staff.
- Mrs Stannard [CEO] said: 'Staff felt we weren't listening because we couldn't give them what they were asking for. People don't want change. Many had a change of line manager and they saw that as being done by the senior management team.'
- Arguably the most worrying finding was the continued rise in bullying.

Such headlines are worrying but more so the survey results that councils need to listen to and take appropriate action, which a robust internal communication programme will do much to assist.

What is clear is that one size does not fit all. Many council staff will be non-office-based – without work access to a computer or to the council's intranet. Internal communication has to be constantly improving, meeting different needs, being creative in seeking ways to reach staff without electronic access while keeping up to date with improved digital communications.

Research conducted by Ruck and Trainor (2011) reflects on the importance of strategic internal communications – not merely 'plugging gaps' with newsletters, briefings, posters and videos, but developing more holistic systems of communication incorporating information and dialogue. The employee survey will provide PR practitioners and communicators with the opportunity to ensure that they ask some pertinent questions about communications and the results overall will provide important insights as to ways forward in developing employee communications.

> Information must be communicated to staff and councillors that is relevant to them doing their job and providing the best service they can. In addition, transparent, equitable and consistent access to information about wider council business will increase knowledge about key issues and developments and enable staff to become more involved in policy and service planning.
>
> (Allerdale Borough Council)

Many councils recognised the importance of engaging staff in preparation for the Audit Commission's Comprehensive Performance Assessment (CPA) including Rushcliffe Borough Council who won the Chartered Institute of Public Relations' (CIPR) Local Government Group Excellence in Communications 'Best internal communications' Award 2008. Rushcliffe ran a series of staff events including 'tea and biscuit' sessions and regular use of intranet and e-bulletins. Following their success in gaining an 'excellent' CPA rating they continued to focus on their staff.

In March 2012 the East Midlands Improvement and Efficiency Partnership featured Rushcliffe as a good practice case study highlighting their passion for communicating:

Rushcliffe is passionate about communicating. Everyone understands what the Council has done, is trying to do, its successes and what needs to be done to improve. The Council communicates in plain English – and gives people the right information, at the right time, in the right way – so everyone knows what they are doing and why. An innovative approach is Rushcliffe's 'Find Out Fridays'.

Find Out Friday: is a monthly event where different services showcase their work to other colleagues. These sessions have proven to be a fantastic way for staff and Members to network, forge relations and build team spirit. This transparent approach to communication extends outwards to the community as well and has delivered some inspiring results – residents read what they write, listen to what they say and get involved when asked for feedback.'

Find Out Fridays have run their course but Rushcliffe continues to develop internal communications with face to face continuing to be the preferred method for communicating important news. The intranet has been updated, a weekly staff magazine and members magazine are produced; case studies are posted on internal walls highlighting good work/success and are changed frequently. 'We have an annual very popular staff award scheme/celebration where we nominate colleagues in various categories including innovation, going the extra mile and hidden gem'. This demonstrates the importance of the constant need for flexibility, for review and ensuring that internal communication channels and methods continue to meet the needs of internal publics.

## Inside out and outside in

The Rushcliffe mini case study ends with a crucial point – wherever responsibility for internal communication is located – whether in the corporate communication or human resources team – it is vital that the inter-dependence between internal and external communications is recognised. Staff feel valued if important council news is relayed to them as soon as is possible and certainly before it appears in the local media. Staff also prefer to be told that 'there's nothing to report' rather than there be silences in communication. As indicated earlier rumour will quickly fill any communication vacuum.

PR practitioners are often described as 'barometers' able to sense the moods of external publics and relay these back into the organisation. This is equally true of internal communication within councils – but even more so: PR practitioners also provide the 'bridge' between departments and services; between elected members and staff; between chief officers and staff. And they provide bridges up, down and across the council as well as taking account of the world outside.

## Creativity

Creativity is often not mentioned in strategic plans but from a communication perspective it is a crucial element. Topics to be communicated may at first sight seem dull and unexciting, and staff already feel bombarded with e-mails and other communications. So, internal communications need to be interesting, focused and capable of attracting attention – the two case studies that follow demonstrate how two particular councils made difficult subjects interesting.

# Evaluation

The importance of evaluation cannot be overstated – not just at the end of any internal communication programme but in setting measurable objectives and ongoing monitoring to ensure that the programme is operating effectively across the council and adjusting appropriately if needed. Regular feedback and evaluation is important to make sure the communication needs of staff and the objectives of the internal communication strategy are being achieved through related outcomes.

# Case studies

Rather than look at individual internal communications such as newsletters and intranets, the following two case studies are exemplars in dealing with difficult topics in creative and comprehensive ways covering many of the issues already discussed. These include: identifying internal stakeholders and publics, finding the most appropriate way to communicate with different staff groups; recognising the importance of managers; providing support to managers and head teachers; identifying ambassadors; ensuring communications are available and accessible; using a variety of methods to communicate; recognising that many staff are 'hard to reach' but need to reach; translating complex (legal) information into plain English; developing communications to meet staff needs.

Extended case studies are included in the online resource for this chapter at **http://www.koganpage.com/PRGov**

## CASE STUDY

In April 2010 Norfolk County Council implemented its Modern Reward Strategy, the culmination of a four-year project supported from the outset by a comprehensive internal communication strategy. Their aim was to introduce a new pay structure and revised terms and conditions for 16,000 employees. Many people would experience a reduction in pay, so to make these changes trade union members had to vote 'Yes' when balloted on the proposal. From the outset, aims and objectives were clearly thought out – to raise awareness about the project's aims; to make sure employees understood the potential impact on them; to reduce uncertainty; to reach other stakeholders including elected members, school governing bodies and employee support organisations; to provide opportunities for employees and managers to feed back any concerns/issues; to prepare employees and managers for implementation of the changes.

**FIGURE 6.3**    Modern Reward explained: cover of Information
Pack in 'travel brochure style' with colour
co-ordinated side index tabs

Key to the success of the strategy was reaching all affected staff, 75 per cent of whom did not have regular access to a computer at work. Whatever their role and wherever they were located, their need for easy access to information and support was recognised, and a vital element was briefing and supporting managers and head teachers to equip them to lead and support their teams. A range of channels was used encompassing face to face, print and online, and encouraging feedback, views and comments throughout. In the full case study, note the word *conversation*: 'An ongoing conversation was developed with employees...' The extensive range of communication is covered in the full case study but an innovative approach to note is that they developed an internet (rather than intranet) site allowing access to information 24/7 from work, home and local library.

### Welcome to the Modern Rewards Information site

Every member of staff is receiving an individual letter explaining how the proposals affect them and detailed information about the full package of terms and conditions.

All letters will be sent on xx/xx so please allow time for them to arrive before contacting us.

We have set up this site especially to answer any questions you may have or you can check them out with your manager.

We will update the site regularly adding the answers to the most asked questions. There's plenty of time but make sure you have your say before the end of the consultation period on xx/xx.

**4 weeks left to have your say!**
*Find out more…*
*Career development for staff on MRS protected salaries*
*The bigger picture*

Lunchtime webchats gained the highest participant figures when compared with webchats on other matters, and roadshows were always 'sell out' events with extra dates often added. The final outcome was that they succeeded in reaching all 16,000 employees using print, online and verbal methods of communication – producing regular newsletters in collaboration with the trade unions ensured employees had greater confidence in the process.

*Norfolk County Council won gold for internal communication in the CIPR East Anglia PRide Awards 2010.*

## CASE STUDY

The City of Edinburgh also faced the challenge of communicating Modernising Pay proposals. Following lengthy negotiations with three trades unions, they didn't agree to the proposals and the Council entered a legal process of voluntary sign-up followed by dismissal and re-engagement in order to make the changes. Challenges were identified at the outset and the strategy was based on sound research to ensure that the mix of communications, including face to face, met staff needs and managers were fully briefed and supported. An excellent and engaging design of 'images of staff' was used throughout.

**FIGURE 6.4**   'Images of staff' design

Objectives included raising awareness of changes to 16,000 staff ensuring they were informed about the proposals, why they were needed, how individuals would be affected and what they needed to do; protecting the programme's and Council's reputation and brand; encouraging sign-up voluntarily to the changes.

Initial research helped to point the way to a focused strategy to fully inform and engage staff on a scale that had not been attempted before. Some points to note are their highly visual people-focused Modernising Pay brand; supporting managers who were key to cascading information and delivering difficult messages; close working with HR, legal and other colleagues to ensure communications were appropriate and consistent.

The campaign was run in two phases: 1) to raise awareness; and 2) a call to action to encourage staff to sign up voluntarily within a three-week period.

Messages were appropriate to the stage of the campaign:

- It's time to think.
- It's time to change.
- It's time to sign.

**FIGURE 6.5** Banner messages appropriate to stage of campaign

For full details of the range of tools and channels used, visit the online resource for this chapter at **http://www.koganpage.com/PRGov**. Again face-to-face sessions proved to be key 'to delivering these important changes and we used signing stations/surgeries in offices, information sessions/roadshows'.

Their evaluation demonstrated the effectiveness of the campaign with the judges including in their comments: 'A comprehensive and effective campaign carefully thought through; well executed; delivered under budget and on time; objectives were surpassed and evaluated; staff feedback demonstrated they felt informed and engaged.'

*The City of Edinburgh Council won gold for internal communication campaign at the CIPR Local Public Services Excellence Awards 2011.*

## Checklist

- Know what works for your council.

- Help staff understand the council's vision and values so that they can see how their work fits into the bigger picture.

- Do not forget elected members when planning internal communications and strategies.

- Make sure internal communications are honest, transparent, timely and relevant.

- Remember that employees have different communication needs.

- Remember that employees prefer face-to-face communication.

- Remember that employees want information to come from their immediate supervisor or manager.

- Support and train managers to communicate effectively.

- Make sure managers take responsibility for their part in communicating effectively with employees.

- Use several methods of communication with messages reinforcing each other.

- Ask employees what works best for them – seek regular feedback.

- Recognise the inter-dependence between internal and external communications.

- Monitor, review, evaluate.

## KEY WORDS

Strategic; two-way; planned; research; commitment; relationship; conversation; dialogue; engaging; involved; listened to; face-to-face; honest; open; transparent; timely; relevant; trust; credibility; authority; valued; creativity; consultation; feedback; evaluation.

# 07
# Communicating as partners

*The boundaries between local public service providers are breaking down. Councils are sharing services and Council communications teams are taking on health and other public service communications roles. Our new challenge is to communicate joined up messages about 'place' and access to services whilst protecting and enhancing the individual reputations of the organisations which make up local public services PLC.*

MIKE BROWNE, CHAIR 2008–09 TRANSITION FROM CIPR LOCAL
GOVERNMENT GROUP TO CIPR LOCAL PUBLIC SERVICES GROUP

In a local authority, sharing information and co-ordinating service delivery with local agencies is widely recognised as part of its licence to operate (LGID, nd). For many service areas, provision is distributed between organisations, so that at an operational and at a strategic level partnership work is a necessity. The range and impact of these partnerships reflect the diversity of local public services. Child safe-guarding has received much media attention in recent years, with high-profile cases such as Victoria Climbie and Baby Peter bringing partnership work under the spotlight.

Joint working and collaboration have been at the heart of local public services for several decades, driven by the aims of improving service delivery and pooling resources to provide good value for money. Under the Labour Government, informal partnerships were institutionalised through Local Strategic Partnerships (LSPs) and partnership work was encouraged in order to attract central government funding (Tizard, 2010). Joint strategic commissioning between the NHS and local authorities and crime and community safety partnerships featured in the government's vision of 'Total Place'. The formal reporting mechanisms of the Comprehensive Area Assessment, Public Service Agreements and Local Area Agreements monitored and rewarded partnership activity.

It was in this climate that the Chartered Institute of Public Relations' (CIPR) Local Government Group (LGG) expanded its membership base to include practitioners from housing, fire, police, health and education in order to 'promote the benefits of partnership working' (CIPR, nd). In 2009, the rebranded CIPR Local Public Services Group (LPSG) added a Partnership Award to its annual Excellence Awards in recognition of the level of partnership activity that local authority PR practitioners were engaged in.

Although the coalition government has since abolished some of the formalised partnership arrangements and the associated grants they once awarded, partnership and collaborative working continue to play a central role. The Localism and Devolution agenda, the Big Society, Health and Policing reforms, Local Enterprise Partnerships and Community Budgets all encourage partnership working (LGID, 2010). In this landscape, 'nimble' partnerships are emerging, which are results driven and mobilise around an issue or service, rather than the static, formalised partnerships of the past.

The second shift in partnership working is an increased emphasis on productivity necessitated by central government's reduction in council funding by around 26 per cent over a four-year period (HM Treasury, 2010). The coalition government has made it clear that public services should 'consider fundamental changes to the way in which they provide services' (HM Treasury, 2010: 51). Ensuring value for money is a top priority. Shared services, strategic integration and joint strategic commissioning, such as the Westminster and Hammersmith & Fulham, and Kensington and Chelsea 'super councils', are just some examples of the radical approaches considered (LGID, 2010). It is in this setting that local authorities would work not just *with* partners but crucially *as* partners. Several pilots up and down the United Kingdom have highlighted the extreme challenges of working in these ways and several pilots have been abandoned.

While changes to central government may therefore rewire and influence the way local authorities operate, joint working and collaboration are consistently encouraged by consecutive governments. Local authorities are not only publically accountable for service provision but as is evident through the full political and economic cycles, providing 'value for money' is also a priority. Partnership work across local public services is now widely recognised as central to ensuring good outcomes and best value (LGID, nd).

The CIPR defines public relations as 'the planned and sustained effort to establish and maintain goodwill and mutual understanding between an organization and its publics' (CIPR, nd). The potential role of public relations in building relationships between partnership bodies and the stakeholders they engage with is explicit. The form that this may take, however, is the subject of much debate, with communicators expressing fear that a shared communication resource could become 'a lightning conductor during times of conflict between those partners' (Wakeman, 2010).

This chapter will examine these tensions and the potential role of the local authority PR practitioner working in partnership across local public services and beyond at regional and national levels with a range of organisations.

# Local partnerships

At a local level, the range of potential partners working with local government is extensive and includes fire, police, health, business, charities, voluntary groups and those commissioned to deliver services.

Partnership work with fire and police is a necessity around issues such as emergency planning and community safety. The local government PR practitioner should develop relations with these services through planning meetings and informal networking, ahead of any crises, which will demand co-ordinated communication. Polly Cziok, Head of Communication and Consultation, London Borough of Hackney (2011): 'Having established relationships with the Police and Fire PR teams meant that we had already built up levels of trust and agreed protocols of joint working, before the riots in 2011 took place, which helped enormously in working together through the confusion.'

Similarly, close working relations with PR practitioners in health, should be developed ahead of the spotlight of child protection. With the return of public health to local government, those that did this will have been able to draw on practical support from the NHS when this service was transferred. In some areas, a close working relationship with the NHS had already been established by a demographic that demanded that public health was also a priority for the local authority. Blackburn with Darwen Council had a track record in jointly funding public health campaigns with the NHS because of the levels of obesity within the borough, which impacted significantly upon council services. A joint campaign, which led to a 20 per cent rise in the number of active adults within the borough between 2007–10, paved the way for the launch of the Care Trust Plus in 2010, which created a fully integrated senior management team across the NHS and council. The merger brought together the communication of health and social care issues under one roof. This outcome demonstrates the potential of successful partnership working when priorities are shared and budgets tight.

Service delivery at a local level is increasingly complex, involving a diverse range of organisations with different levels of contribution. Partnership work is no longer confined to public services but now includes a range of private sector organisations, arm's length management or external organisations (ALMOs or ALEOs) and voluntary groups. Agreement should be reached on the branding for partnership activity and protocols put in place for media relations, identifying issues and dealing with crises. These can be set out in a Principles of Joint Working document, which outlines the key principles and includes the signatures of agreement from each of the partner organisations. These principles identify the organisation in charge of co-ordinating communication activity – usually this is the local authority. They also state a commitment to the collective sign-off of media and other communication materials in advance of distribution. This should prevent one partner organisation taking the credit for joint working. It is also important to agree that representatives carrying out informal discussion/interviews with the media should advise all partners in advance and that any media coverage generated should be reported to the lead communication officer. The principles may also include an intent to minimise duplication and to undertake activities that reflect the agreed vision for the partnership. Detailed communication arrangements will also be drawn up on a project-by-project basis and crisis communication will be accounted for in emergency planning documents.

In local partnerships, it is usually councils that lead communications, drafting press releases, publicity material and providing spokespeople. This can be interpreted by partners as an attempt to control the messaging, rather than as an offer resulting from better resources and infrastructure. Talbot (2012) recommends local authority PR practitioners be open and honest with partners such as housing associations, who have less bureaucracy and are not accountable to officers and politicians. This dialogue may diffuse their frustrations in the protracted length of decision making and sign off within councils.

Local authorities are also being encouraged to work with local communities as partners rather than recipients. Talbot (2012) suggests that local authorities are generally still seen as remote, while organisations who have higher profiles within communities have achieved this through face-to-face interaction. Local authorities have the opportunity to develop relationships with voluntary groups and the community by building on existing networks fostered by front-line staff across the organisation. If PR teams are to engage with community groups, they must first of all have strong relationships with departments internally, supporting, where necessary, their outreach work and informally exchanging knowledge and information. The Green Dog Walkers Group was a 'bottom up' initiative of volunteers from the Community Green Initiative (CGI) who approached Falkirk Council for advice and support in developing a project to tackle dog fouling in the area. The CGI knew who to approach as the council had delivered 'community conversation' campaigns each year to generate dialogue about the issues that mattered to people most. This meant that they were the CGI's first port of call to take their initiative forward. Delivering community conversation campaigns are a good way to build relationships with local residents.

While the range of potential partners at a local level is extensive, all of these relationships depend on the proactive approach of the PR practitioner both internally and externally, whether borne out of necessity, crisis, good practice or a mix.

# Regional partnerships

Providing good value is at the heart of local government service delivery and this has been a key driver of PR practice. In and out of times of recession, PR practitioners must continually strive to do more with less and working in partnership with both the public and private sector is one way to work towards achieving this. Reduced budgets often remove the opportunity to commission bespoke research for individual campaigns. Increased partnership work and developing networks with other organisations, provide opportunities to obtain information that can be used to inform local planning. Regional organisations, such as waste authorities, undertake research, which can be used to complement local benchmarking data. Stockport Council use regional recycling statistics generated by the Greater Manchester Waste Authority to inform their planning. Research commissioned by other local authorities with a similar demographic can also be useful. Hackney Council included research commissioned by Lambeth Council when planning their approach and key messages for their award-winning Census Campaign (CIPR, 2011).

At a regional level, some local authorities are working even closer, with some achieving strategic integration. Worthing and Adur were among the first to develop this, with a merger across most service areas and a single communication team. In Cornwall, which has recently become a unitary authority, regional working has become a reality, with a single communication team working across the county.

Regional partnership work has become a necessity for those PR practitioners working in organisations that have merged, while for others collaboration and information sharing makes good business sense.

# National partnerships

Many local authorities have extended their partnership work to a national level utilising the principles they have put into practice at a local and regional level. Working with partners, in delivering government-funded behaviour change campaigns, such as Recycle Now, enables local authorities to benefit from national awareness-raising activity.

Partnering with national private sector organisations can also be beneficial. Stockport Council partnered with the Energy Saving Trust (EST) in their campaign to tackle the borough's carbon footprint, having been rated as the third most energy obese area in the United Kingdom. EST offered residents loft and cavity wall insulation at a reduced cost, provided a free phone helpline and joined the council at awareness-raising events.

In Cornwall, the local and regional partnership work of Newquay Safe was extended to a national level. The Home Office Minister was invited to meet the partnership, who have as a result, been asked to contribute to forthcoming licensing legislation, while the Home Office is now providing training for officers and councillors on licensing regulations. The British Red Cross have also joined the partnership, educating young people in Newquay on how to use first aid in a crisis.

At a national level there is clearly value in working with both private and public sector bodies in both exchanging information, tackling issues at a local level and in working with central government in both a lobbying capacity and in demonstrating the local contribution towards the national agenda.

Partnerships are usually established through necessity and soldered during a crisis. Some authorities operate beyond this and initiate relationships where they can add value. Although there is no single model applicable to every local authority, there are common principles of working together, which are consistent across the full range of partnership communication work, which will be examined in the next section.

# Partnership work: the challenges and opportunities

## *Developing a shared vision*

Identifying the culture of an organisation is key to building any relationship. For organisations that are working towards strategic integration, understanding the cultural differences and similarities is a crucial element of PR planning. For those organisations working closely with the NHS, there are fundamental differences, which have been identified by local authority practitioners. Schmid (2011) highlights the impact of the differences in accountability, with councils serving their local communities, while the NHS, reporting to the Secretary of State, has a national focus. Communicating the impact of the new Care Trust Plus in Blackburn with Darwen at a local level was therefore one of the key messages for NHS staff through the merger to rewire their thinking. For organisations undergoing a strategic merger, the expectations from both leadership teams for the shared service must be agreed and communicated. This should include a clear financial benefits statement.

For local authorities working with local public service partners, an overall vision for the area may have been created through the local strategic partnerships of the past. More recently, a partnership vision is more likely to be created around a particular project to capture the aspirations of joint working.

## The role of internal communication

Internal communication is important to any partnership work in keeping employees briefed on progress and engaging them in dialogue to shape practice. Internal communication campaigns should aim to improve understanding among staff of any changes, clarifying if necessary the new organisational structure. It should also set out the impact of those changes, which may include redundancies. Gregory (2010) recommends enlisting the help of those who are supportive and who could work as champions across the organisation. Good practice would also involve dialogue and making the necessary organisational adjustments in response to feedback from staff. Communication should highlight evidence of willingness to change and learn. When introducing new working practices to support partnership working, internal communication objectives should take a platformed approach aiming to:

- create awareness;
- promote understanding;
- inform;
- develop knowledge. (Gregory, 2010)

Networking is essential for successful partnership working and for those organisations becoming integrated, it is critical in building knowledge, contacts and credibility. The communication team in Blackburn with Darwen worked across the local authority and NHS sites to reduce perceptions of a local authority takeover. Agreement on the governance of the future organisation, including where it will be hosted and who people will be working for should be communicated clearly to staff. The benefits of the new ways of working should be prioritised in the key messages and regular updates should be provided for staff and elected members.

Internal communication tools should include established and trusted channels such as e-zines and opportunities for engagement through social media and events, which enable the chief executive to directly answer questions from staff.

## Strategic decision making

In organisations that are developing strategic integration and for those delivering more traditional models of partnership work, the role of the PR practitioner should involve strategic decision making. Acharya (1985) suggests that dynamic environments provide opportunity for such practitioners to operate as managers: planning PR programmes, making communication policy decisions, diagnosing public relations problems, counselling management and acting as a catalyst for management decisions. Strategic integration and partnership work are dynamics requiring research and issues management.

At Blackburn with Darwen, the communication team secured regular access to the senior management team and a forward-planning PR grid was established to identify and plan for risk. There was a protocol agreed to tackle differences of opinion that could emerge between the NHS and local authority. Potential conflict was reduced by having a single chief executive on a joint management team who could balance the views of both organisations and align their messages. Where a difference of opinion still existed there was an agreement that two separate statements could be issued by the PR team.

The extensive partnership of Newquay Safe had a single communication plan and media strategy and a communication lead, which aimed to prevent conflicting and confusing messages externally. It was the lead communication officer's access to senior management across the partnership that supported negotiation towards reaching agreement.

## Providing value for money

Working with less budget and staff, local authority PR practitioners are increasingly required to do more, whether that is communicating across a newly integrated organisation or communicating on behalf of partners. Establishing an annual communications plan enables practitioners to explain why they are unable to take on ad-hoc communications activity, which does not contribute towards the overall business plan. Forward planning also enables partner organisations to co-ordinate campaigns, to share good practice and provide best value.

In Blackburn with Darwen, joint working improved campaign delivery. For the Refresh campaign, which promoted a more active lifestyle, the NHS social marketing approach was crucial to the success of the campaign. A social marketing agency was commissioned to provide insight into the target groups to make leisure services more accessible. Many local authority PR practitioners engaged in partnership communication work have noted that transfer of information is one of the major benefits. Cross-organisational working provides opportunity to facilitate learning.

## Information sharing – co-ordinated and joined up

Partnership work mobilising around an issue builds relationships that often have a life beyond the scope of the initial project. In Newquay, as a result of the Newquay Safe Partnership, a communication network has developed with the common aim of rebuilding the reputation of the town.

Maintaining regular contact is crucial to developing relationships. In Newquay, weekly face-to-face meetings and monthly steering group meetings, which include representation from residents' associations, councillors and regeneration groups and annual evaluative feedback events open to all interested parties, have kept everyone on board.

However, practitioners recognise that it is the informal relationships and the ability to pick up the phone that enables information to be shared successfully between partners, rather than by following agreed protocols. Talbot (2012) highlights the importance of honesty and openness between PR practitioners across partnership bodies. These relationships can enable practitioners to steer their leadership through conflict with partnership bodies and keep lines of communication open.

## Communicating changes to residents

PR practitioners should communicate changes made to service delivery as a result of partnership work honestly and transparently with residents who should be involved in the decision-making process when possible.

Newquay Safe invited residents and the local media to join the Partnership and attend meetings. Information was made freely available. This included the Partnership Media Strategy, which was published on Facebook by a residents' association who criticised the work in the context of budget cuts. The Partnership had the confidence to share information and then engage with the dialogue and online discussion. By inviting external stakeholders to comment, voices were introduced, which were able to vocalise what those at a senior level may not have been able to.

In Blackburn with Darwen, once the level of cuts began to emerge, the communication team began a borough-wide consultation process, which gave residents the opportunity to identify the priorities. Regional and local media were invited to the town hall and briefed on the implications of the reduced budgets, including redundancies and a reduction in services. The communication team highlighted the innovative measures adopted such as a joint management team, shared services and the subsequent reduction in management spend.

The consolidation of campaign work across the newly formed Care Trust Plus focused on providing better value for money under an umbrella theme of 'Having pride in your borough'. Residents were encouraged to play their part in making savings and communication activity demonstrated, for example, that every pound spent on clearing up litter was a pound that could instead be spent on libraries, parks or other popular services. The local community was treated as a partner responsible for making savings.

## Engaging with communities

Front-line staff working in the public services are in direct contact with the local community. Supporting internal staff across the organisation in their outreach and education work may provide PR practitioners with access to the often hard-to-reach groups they would like to engage with. In Falkirk, communication support provided to the Litter Team in the delivery of their community conversation campaigns significantly raised the profile of the council with voluntary groups. As a result, the Green Dog Walkers Group developed as a grass roots initiative, supported by council expertise.

Developing strong relations across departments in the council may also support practitioners in identifying issues that are emerging in the community as well as identifying the 'community live wire' and potential partners in community engagement work.

In Newquay, the 'We Want our Town Back' petition was used as an opportunity to harness residents who were already actively engaged with the issue of tackling anti-social behaviour. They were encouraged to join the Newquay Safe Partnership. Recognised as the 'eyes and ears' at community level, the residents continued to identify problems in the town and contributed towards finding solutions, diffusing criticism of the council as they became part of the decision-making process.

Working in partnership with other public services widens access opportunities for PR practitioners through the collaborative use of established networks and communication channels. Partnership communication activity has the potential to reach a far wider and more diverse audience.

## Widening partnership work

Having established successful partnership activity at a local and regional level, many local authorities then progress to developing their work nationally. In Newquay, strong evaluation provided the platform for the partnership to share their work at a national level with central government and the private sector, as an example of best practice in tackling anti-social behaviour through collaborative working. Diageo and DrinkAware made further contributions to the scheme through their corporate social responsibility policies and the Home Office Minister invited the partnership to contribute towards forthcoming licensing legislation.

The Green Dog Walkers initiative, developed in Falkirk, has been adopted by eight other local authorities, who in the spirit of partnership, have fed back on their own experiences to further develop the project.

## Practitioner behaviour

Research into local government PR roles identifies behaviour as a significant factor in the position of the PR practitioner (LGcomms, 2008). In partnership work this is crucial, with practitioners identifying that without the passion to take partnership work forward, it would have floundered. Beverly Hill, Communications Officer, Cornwall Council and lead communication officer for the Newquay Safe Partnership (2011) commented: 'Goodwill and working above and beyond the day job ensured that this project took off.' A commitment to deliver what was promised and on time was noted by James Brokenshire, Home Office Minister, who in 2010 praised the: 'strong personal and corporate commitment which was second to none.'

## Checklist

- Make contact with partners' lead communication officers and agree expectations and responsibilities.

- Develop a shared vision between partners with a protocol to follow in communicating differences of opinion.

- Use internal communication to engage staff in partnership work.

- Highlight the cost savings of joint working to senior management, across the partnership, to staff and other key stakeholders.

- Build relationships with departments across the council and staff who work in the community.

- Identify the community live wire and follow social media groups to monitor emerging issues.

- Build trust and transparency. Stakeholders should discuss, debate and contribute.

- Select staff able to foster good relations.

- Build and maintain relationships forged during a crisis.

- Extend successful partnership work at local and regional levels to a national level.

## KEY WORDS

Sharing information; co-ordinating service delivery; joint working; collaboration; shared vision; internal communication; staff; dialogue; networking; cost savings; joint working; stakeholders; trust and transparency; shared services; strategic decision making.

## CASE STUDY  Newquay Safe

Joint winner: CIPR Local Public Services Group Partnership Award 2010

A partnership operating at local, regional and national levels.

### Background

In 2009, two teenagers died in cliff falls in Newquay and two others were seriously injured. The father of one boy who died, called for a boycott on Newquay by teenagers. The national media focused on the tragedies and local concern grew around young people's safety and the increasing alcohol-related anti-social behaviour within the town. Residents delivered a petition to Cornwall Council declaring: 'We want our town back.'

A multi-agency team was called together to review the situation following a meeting between Cornwall County Council and Devon and Cornwall Police who made a commitment to pool resources and intelligence. In July 2009, over 12 organisations, including Cornwall Council, the police, Local Safeguarding Children's Board, NHS services, the town council, residents' associations and licensed businesses, formed Newquay Safe. The council leader, recognising the impact of the incidents on the town, allocated £20,000, which partners were able to spread over two years to fund any shortfall that could not be covered by existing resources, sponsorship and the large measures of goodwill that staff contributed from across the multiple agencies.

The partnership is action centred with a focus on making a difference rather than merely being in a partnership because it's mandatory or the right thing to do.

The partnership's objectives were to:

- encourage young people visiting Newquay to be responsible for their own and each other's safety;

- let people know, locally and nationally that the town deals effectively with safety issues associated with unaccompanied teenagers drinking alcohol;

- protect and restore Newquay's reputation as a world-renowned seaside resort.

### Strategy and implementation

The partnership developed an awareness campaign and safeguarding scheme to prevent teenagers from accessing alcohol and to help them if they did drink and became vulnerable.

A council communications officer led the communication for the partnership, agreeing strategies across the organisations and liaising with communication officers in the police, Royal National Lifeboat Institution (RNLI) and NHS so that they could distribute information across their networks. The council assigned 80 per cent of the officer's time to this project but there was also a large amount of goodwill to make this project happen.

The timing was significant: six district councils had just become one unitary council and it was in this dynamic of change that opportunity emerged to break down the silos that had previously existed between the council and its partners. Four council staff from the town centre management and community networks were relocated in police stations to encourage joint working.

From a commitment made by the Chief Superintendent and Director of Communications, a co-ordination group was established covering five different work streams including communications and marketing. The lead communication officer attended all streams to advise and co-ordinate PR and marketing activity across the project.

The partners each led one of the campaigns below, while Cornwall Council's communication team co-ordinated delivery across the parallel campaigns:

- 'Lost': Immediately following the cliff fall incidents, the 'Lost' campaign targeted the areas teenagers frequented, with posters, ads and T-shirts highlighting the dangers of young people losing their friends, their dignity or even their lives while under the influence of alcohol. Local bus companies, clubs and *Boardmasters* surfing magazine all donated or subsidised advertising space.

- Secondary school visits: Treviglas Community College students worked with a local Cornwall councillor and his wife to produce a video about coastal safety. The councillor and his wife personally visited secondary schools in Berkshire, where many teenage tourists come from, giving advice and distributing Coast Safe leaflets.

- Operations Brunel and Touchdown: Police met trains and planes arriving in Newquay and gave guidance on alcohol and behaviour to young people found with alcohol or drugs.

- Accommodation providers' safeguarding guidelines: Over 400 local accommodation providers, especially budget surf lodges, received safeguarding guidelines and parental consent forms to ensure they were aware of their responsibility for unaccompanied teenagers.

- 'Go out – be safe': A credit card sized message for teenagers recognising that they want to have fun, while highlighting the need to be responsible and safe. It included local police and hospital phone numbers. The NewSTART residents' association drove this campaign, emphasising the need for positive Newquay messages.

- Alcohol-free entertainment for teenagers: The national charity Drinkaware ran a 'Got Your Back' café. The police, council and youth service Exodus scheme provided teenagers with free wristbands so they could access alcohol-free, under-18 entertainment and discounts for daytime activities.

- 'No ID, no Newquay': Bars and clubs agreed not to allow young people access without a passport or a driving licence as ID. Hundreds of fake IDs were confiscated.

- 'Follow you home': Local media and schools in teenagers' home areas were targeted with publicity about children having alcohol confiscated and parents having to collect them when they were found drunk and incapable. Local police in those areas visited the families involved in each incident, ensuring what happened in Newquay, didn't stay in Newquay.

Throughout, the partnership worked proactively with local, national and international media to promote the key messages to teenagers and parents to turn the image of the town around. The partnership hosted visits by the One Show, GMTV, Radio One, international TV documentaries and other high-profile media.

Newquay Safe has been praised by local residents' associations and the Home Office as an excellent example of how local authorities should be working with partners and local communities.

## Evaluation

- Since the launch of Newquay Safe there have been no deaths or cliff falls. Twenty people have been prevented from getting into trouble or being injured along the cliffs or coastline.

- Recorded crime at Newquay's Run to the Sun event was 16 per cent lower than the previous year.

- Newquay is now one of 12 Neighbourhood Agreement Pathfinders, as part of a Home Office strategy encouraging agencies to work together to deal with local anti-social behaviour and crime issues.

- Newquay has subsequently been voted the nation's sixth favourite seaside town in a Which? Holiday survey.

- In 2009 every press article about the situation in Newquay was negative. In 2010 every article was positive or acknowledged the partnership's work to keep teenagers safe.

- A local community survey has shown that nearly 58 per cent of respondents have heard of the partnership and its work.

# 08
# Communicating a campaign

*Shortlisting this year was a hard task, as there were more strong entries which demonstrated a strong logical flow linking research, objective setting, strategy and evaluation than ever before... The extra criteria which earned this year's top five entries a place on the shortlist were creativity, great visual design and 'inclusivity', using two-way communication at key points in a campaign to identify issues and guide the best use of tactics as well as involving hard to reach or frequently overlooked publics.*

JUDGES' COMMENTS OF LOCAL GOVERNMENT BEST CAMPAIGN 2011

Local government has a track record in delivering a diverse range of communication campaigns across service areas, from recruiting foster carers to encouraging recycling. Traditionally, these were at the 'public information... end of public relations' (Harrison, 2000: 173). However, more recently councils have moved beyond passive information giving to actively engaging with residents, recognising their accountability and the part that residents must themselves play in shaping the policies and services that they are then encouraged to support (Yeomans, 2009). This shift can in part be attributed to the impact of citizen-led journalism and social media (Wakeman, 2012).

The development from a one-way towards a two-way model of communication is none more evident than in local government campaign work, the best of which are showcased in the annual CIPR Local Public Services Awards.

The judging criteria for 'Campaign of the Year' requires an overview of objectives, strategy and implementation, creativity, budget and evaluation.

When there is increasing pressure on budgets, specific evaluation research may dwindle, demanding that practitioners draw on their creativity and partnership work to measure communication campaigns (Powell, 2010).

Campaign selection will vary depending upon the needs of the locality, and for some areas such as Blackburn with Darwen, with a population characterised by ill health partnership work between the local authority and the NHS tackling activity levels, made good business sense and enabled organisations to share expertise and budgets. With the return of public health to local government, this practice has now been consolidated formally across the United Kingdom.

Tackling social problems has been a key priority for public services in recent years, with local government communication campaigns addressing issues such as obesity and binge drinking, which are a drain on resources and tend to become worse in times of recession.

Stockport Council estimated in 2010 that the related costs of obesity within the borough were £76 million and rising. Their award-winning campaign (CIPR, 2010) used the findings from a citizens' panel to identify that residents' main barrier to exercise was lack of time. The campaign focused on the clear message that the level of exercise adults need to maintain health recommended by the government is only 30 minutes, five times a week. The campaign used cost-effective research to identify the issue and related barriers to change and two specific evaluation methods in addition to those more easily available. Providing good value, whatever the economic climate, should be a key priority for local government PR practitioners. The communications team were able to offset the £25,000 budget and cost per resident of £0.09p against the campaign results, which included 11 per cent of residents making changes in their lives.

NHS Northamptonshire, in their award-winning campaign targeting need to reach groups (CIPR, 2010), were able to secure a £240,000 budget to tackle binge drinking, which through reduced hospital admissions and cost savings to the police has been estimated as saving the county £2.3 million.

National campaigns funded by central government and delivered by representative bodies or by government agencies provide local government PR practitioners with a cost-effective way to inform, raise awareness and bring about behavioural change locally. The Local Government Association (LGA) has launched a series of national campaigns following the Ipsos MORI research they commissioned in 2005, which identified the ongoing need to improve the public image of local government.

The Reputation Campaign (LGA, 2005) recommended core communication actions that local government should deliver including the publication of a council newsletter and an A–Z directory of council services. In 2007, the LGA launched the 'My Council' campaign to raise public awareness of the range of services councils provide. The campaign used posters and images to demonstrate what councils do that affect people's lives.

The LGA has encouraged local authorities across the United Kingdom to deliver this campaign, which is available through downloadable resources and can be tailored to a locality.

The New Reputation Guide (LGcomms, 2010) built on the Reputation Campaign (LGA, 2005) using data from the 2008/09 national Place Survey to analyse the relationship between the reputation of councils and communications activity. The report identifies five rules of reputation that should be considered when designing any local authority communication campaign. These are:

- proving the council provides value for money;
- always inform and engage residents and staff;
- build trust and confidence in what councils do;
- improve key services and show you are doing so;
- focus on changing lives for the better.

(LGcomms, 2010: 28)

Local authorities can also take advantage of the support available from government-funded agencies such as WRAP in their campaign work. The 'recycle now' campaign, which aims to improve recycling performance through effective communication, is recognised by 65 per cent of people in England. The brand and supporting communication materials are available for local authorities, retailers and community groups to adopt. The partners' website provides a range of resources including radio advertising, posters and branding, which can be localised to build on recycling awareness raised at a national level.

Throughout the economic cycle, as a publicly accountable organisation charged with providing best value, it is essential that local government PR delivers results. Campaign delivery should involve partnership work with local and national bodies sharing expertise and resources, and use easily available data to identify issues. Creativity is important in identifying tactics and cost-effective evaluation methods. Robust research and evaluation should lie at the heart of the business case for campaign work. These essential elements of campaign planning will be examined in more detail in the following sections.

# Planning the PR campaign

When there is increasing pressure on budgets, council priorities need to be finely tuned and communication objectives must directly contribute to the overall business objectives. Agreeing projects with senior management that work towards achieving these will enable you to explain to departments why requests to work on projects outside of these parameters, unless they impact reputationally, should be declined. In councils that have not yet achieved the centralisation of communication, departmental officers have the potential to work more closely with the corporate team on campaigns agreed with senior management. Behavioural change campaigns, which enable you to demonstrate real cost savings to the organisation, should be prioritised.

PR campaigns should be identified by an overall communications strategy that establishes how communication can support the corporate and business objectives. This strategy, explored in Chapter 3, should provide the key to any communications work in establishing the role that PR will play in resolving the situation that the organisation faces. This exploratory work involves identifying those stakeholder relationships that are critical in enabling the organisation's objectives to be achieved, and understanding how PR can influence the attitudes, opinions and behaviours of these stakeholders. It is from this overall communications strategy that campaign work springs.

If this approach is adopted, all campaign work will therefore contribute towards the organisation's corporate and business objectives. In doing so, campaigns must be flexible in adjusting to any changes made centrally. Gregory's (2010) PR planning model is generally regarded as best practice in its inclusion of ongoing monitoring, acknowledging that any plan 'should not be a straightjacket' and that there must be flexibility in response to changes in the environment.

At campaign level, the plan will be adjusted in response to the effectiveness of its tactics, and in response to changes made to the communications strategy, which will itself adjust in line with changes made to the overall corporate strategy.

The PR campaign plan should use the Research Action Communication Evaluation process also employed for the overall communications strategy. The cycle of any communications campaign should therefore begin with examination of a particular issue, establishing the role of communications and the desired outcomes and effects; this should be followed by the selection of messages, publics and target audiences through to tactics and channels. The campaign execution will then be followed by evaluation that will feed directly back into the programme, the communications strategy and the corporate and business strategy.

The campaign plan will follow the same model (Gregory, 2010) used in developing the overall communications strategy and outlined in Chapter 3.

## Research – analysing the environment

Research is an essential element in the process of campaign planning. It helps practitioners to analyse the problems, formulate the priorities for action and plan strategies.

The CIPR's five-step Planning Research Evaluation (PRE) cycle is an integrated planning process with research and evaluation at its heart. The first stage of gathering information builds the foundation for the campaign. In the nine steps of strategic public relations (Smith, 2005) phase one includes analysis of the organisation, situation and publics.

Formative research can help to identify key trends in the environment. Local authority PR practitioners should be analysing the success of previous communications programmes and monitoring the strength of stakeholder opinions and attitudes.

This will establish benchmarks in knowledge, attitude and behaviour to measure the success of campaigns against, and will identify a range of scenarios resulting from alternative courses of action.

In the current economic climate, research and evaluation are key to demonstrating the value of your work. Communication is an area traditionally at risk and it is vital that you demonstrate the impact of your work through obtaining benchmarking data that identifies the issue and the potential barriers to change.

Reduced budgets often remove the opportunity to commission bespoke research for individual campaigns. Introducing questions to citizens' panels, which have already been commissioned, is a cost-effective way of gathering feedback. Increased partnership work, developing networks with other public service and umbrella organisations, nationally, regionally and locally, also provide opportunities to obtain data that you may be able to use to inform your work. This could include using the findings from a regional organisation such as a waste authority to complement recycling statistics within your own locality. Similarly, research undertaken by the Local Government Association can be used to inform and direct campaign work.

The first step, therefore, in any PR campaign involves analysis of the situation, the key issues and the organisational and environmental context in which the plan will be required to work. The analysis should identify the internal and external pressures affecting the organisation. This includes examining the key stakeholder relationships that the PR programme will need to influence and the factors affecting their perceptions of the organisation. The nature of past communications activity and the likely scenarios that may result should also be examined. Other external/internal variables that may affect the organisation's plans, such as implementing new legislation, should also be considered.

Analysis techniques that can be used include the EPISTLE and SWOT analysis, stakeholder mapping, issues analysis and scenario building. The EPISTLE and SWOT are useful frameworks in organising and recording the local authority's position and context in relation to its environment. The EPISTLE analysis focuses on the organisation's key stakeholder relationships, examining how economic, political, information, social, technological, legal and environmental factors might impact on them (Gregory, 2010). These categories should be applied to the issue identified by the communications strategy as the focus for campaign work.

Issues are developments, events or trends that are considered to have consequences for the organisation because they have the potential to impact on the organisation's goals. From the perspective of PR, issues arise as a result of the consequences that an organisation's actions have for a particular group. The unit of analysis in identifying PR issues is always that of organisation/stakeholder relationships.

Consideration of funding issues is particularly pertinent when considering the *economic* position. *Politically*, emerging legislation and the relationships with central government and the local political parties should be examined. *Information* is power, and access to and availability of information among the stakeholders, should also be monitored. The impact of *technology* on the local authority, with consideration of how new discoveries could change operational working and a review of the spending allocated for research and development should be undertaken. The *legal* or regulatory aspects of local authority working should also be monitored to identify emerging issues. *Environmental research* includes considering the impact of hot topics such as sustainability and waste disposal on the local authority. This analysis may need to look beyond the present and examine forecasted, ongoing developments and their implications for public relations planning purposes.

The EPISTLE provides a checklist of the key drivers for any organisation, and by monitoring these, PR practitioners will be able to identify the key issues to be addressed through campaign work.

Having identified the relevant headings and information from the EPISTLE, the SWOT is a way of organising this material into strengths and weaknesses, and potential opportunities and threats. The SWOT, as a tool, can be used to draw the overall analysis together before identifying the approach to be taken. The SWOT analysis should identify the five to six most important factors under each heading that are relevant to the issue matching strengths to opportunities and weaknesses to threats.

From the analysis stage, the next step is to identify and evaluate what alternative communication options exist. This may involve examining possible scenarios in terms of how stakeholders might respond to different courses of action. Consideration should be given to how different approaches might be used to promote and enhance the organisation's reputation, how external events outside the organisation's control might develop and influence communication outcomes, and how competitors and the media might respond.

Identifying the different roles that communication might play and how communication might help the organisation achieve its goals/resolve its problems, will enable the PR team to identify the focus and approach of campaign work.

## Identifying the stakeholders

The success of any PR programme depends upon identifying the key stakeholder relationships that are crucial to resolving the situation/problem. In local government, the immediate stakeholders to monitor internally are staff and externally residents, businesses and the media, in addition to those who could be considered to straddle both internal and external such as local councillors.

The active publics should be identified first. These are those stakeholders who are directly affected by the organisation or who can frustrate or facilitate the organisation's goals. Further analysis may be needed to determine the priorities among these publics – those whose support/opposition is most critical to the success of the programme.

In each case a brief rationale should be provided to support the prioritising of the key target publics. A detailed profile of each target public should be drawn up in terms of geo-demographic, attitudes, opinions and behaviour with respect to the organisation and the issues involved in the situation. Such profiles are essential in identifying the most effective tactics to reach the target publics. From this analysis it should be possible to identify a clear set of communication objectives. These should identify the intended outcomes with respect to the key stakeholder relationships. This should include the values the organisation wishes to communicate and the attitudes, opinions and behaviours it wishes to promote towards the organisation.

Social marketing has been widely used by the health sector, and is increasingly being adopted by local public services delivering campaigns in partnership with the NHS or by those aiming to change behaviour with a target group, particularly when more traditional educational initiatives have failed. This approach demands extensive research usually undertaken by an external agency into the attitudes, behaviours and knowledge of stakeholders with the aim of improving their personal welfare and that of their society (Andreasen, 1995). Having a thorough understanding of the target group enables an intervention campaign to be designed, ideally through collaboration, which will ultimately change their behaviour.

South Wales Fire and Rescue Service commissioned Cardiff University to undertake research in Tonypandy with the aim of preventing deliberate grassfires, which cost the Service £7 million annually. The in-depth research revealed that:

- The fire-setters were predominantly young males, but included a wide range of youngsters, not just the obviously disaffected ones.
- Their motivations were boredom, thrill-seeking, attention seeking, peer pressure, natural curiosity and experimentation.
- Fires were perceived as a nuisance, but starting them as relatively 'harmless' and 'risk-free fun'.
- Adults remembered fire-setting in their youth themselves, making it a seasonal tradition and a social norm within Valleys communities.
- People underestimated the costs of the fires and overestimated Fire Service resources.
- Many believed that 'something should be done', but there was little belief that the situation could be changed.

(CIPR, 2011a)

This extensive research into youngsters engaging in anti-social behaviour underpinned a creative campaign that involved them in the creation of a cartoon mascot and a programme of Easter activities. The 46 per cent reduction in grass fires in South Wales, three times its original target, was attributed to the stakeholder research that guided the campaign design.

## Setting objectives

Objectives should be defined as precisely as possible and indicate the intended audience they relate to, the timeframe involved and the measurable response that is to be achieved. Campaign objectives should follow the SMART model and be measurable, achievable, realistic and targeted (Gregory, 2010).

In addition to defining overall objectives for the campaign as a whole, where there are multiple target publics, specific objectives should be identified for each of the key target public/audience strands.

While the ultimate aim will be to try to bring about some change in behaviour of the target publics, in most cases PR programmes can only try to increase the pre-disposition of the target publics to act in a desired manner – public relations cannot force behavioural change on people.

Changing attitudes and ultimately behaviour may in some cases take a relatively long time and hence campaign plans may have both short-term and medium-/long-term objectives.

## The campaign approach

Thaler and Sustein (2008) suggest that it is possible for organisations to nudge target groups towards desired behaviour by employing particular approaches. In 2012, the Cabinet Office Behavioural Insights Team undertook research to identify seven tactics drawn from behavioural science, which were designed to reduce the prevalence of fraud, error and debt. Nudging offers an alternative approach to campaigns that may have in the past focused on communicating the penalties and fines issued by non-compliance.

Insight 1. **Make it easy:** Make it as straightforward as possible for people to behave as desired.

Insight 2. **Highlight key messages:** Draw people's attention to important information or actions required of them.

Insight 3. **Use personal language:** Personalise language so that people understand why a message of process is relevant to them.

Insight 4. **Prompt honesty at key moments:** Ensure that people are prompted to be honest at key moments when filling in a form or answering questions.

Insight 5. **Tell people what others are doing:** Highlight the positive behaviour of others.

Insight 6. **Reward desired behaviour:** Actively incentivise or reward behaviour that saves time or money.

Insight 7. **Highlight the risk and impact of dishonesty:** Emphasise the impact of fraud or late payment on public services as well as the risk of audit and the consequences for those caught.

(Cabinet Office, Behavioural Insights Team, 2012)

Manchester City Council estimated it saved up to £240,000 in council tax discounts due to a trial that nudged residents towards honesty in returning their council tax forms. The forms were easy to complete, key messages and required actions were highlighted, and the risk and consequences of fraud were clearly communicated. The honesty of residents was tested as they were required to actively complete information in order to make a claim.

In Kingston and Merton, the Councils in partnership with B&Q, offered a discount for green products that increased in line with the number of neighbours taking part. It is anticipated that highlighting the positive behaviour of others will boost the overall take-up.

In Preston, the Council offered TVs, DVD players, jewellery and vouchers to residents to encourage them to put their rubbish in the bin. The 'bin it to win it' campaign was designed as an alternative to 'Don't drop it or else' strategies that had failed in the past. They also set up 'gum boards' and offered gum pouches to make it as easy as possible for people to discard their gum. This pilot campaign in 2005, employing nudging techniques, resulted in an 80 per cent reduction in gum litter.

Hackney Council, in their award-winning Census campaign, nudged residents towards completing the form by clearly communicating the benefits to them, their families and their neighbourhood, rather than threatening to issue penalties. This approach resulted in an 85 per cent response rate and 13 per cent increase on the return in 2001.

These approaches demonstrate the impact of nudging techniques employed in local authority behaviour change campaigns.

## Designing the message strategy

The message strategy should indicate the broad themes of the communication campaign, capturing what it aims to convince people to believe, support, or do. The message strategy should not be confused with a summary of 'the copy' to be used in press releases, brochures etc. It should be an umbrella statement from which the key messages will emerge. Stockport Council's overall message for their award-winning campaign tackling obesity (CIPR: 2010), was 'Lack of time is no excuse – just five sessions of 30 minutes of exercise per week is needed to keep adults healthy'. The key messages developed from this and which would be included directly in their communication materials were:

- There are hundreds of ways to get active in Stockport.
- Get involved by walking to work and cycling to school.
- It's easy to fit in $5 \times 30$ minutes of exercise per week.

Social norms can play an important part in the take-up of messages. In research, signs erected by office lifts that stated that most people used the stairs as a good way to exercise increased usage by 7 per cent (Cabinet Office, Behavioural Insights Team, 2011).

## Selecting the tactics

The selection of tactics will be made using the information collated on the target audience in order to identify the best ways of reaching them. The effectiveness of tactics should be constantly monitored and adjusted. The Cabinet Office, Behavioural Insights Team (2011) suggest that testing, learning and adapting is crucial in understanding which nudges may work for a particular audience.

Gregory (2010) suggests that if robust research has been undertaken initially, it will be the tactics, not the overall plan, which will change if the desired objectives are not being met.

The use of printed publications across local government in the United Kingdom is declining with a surge in the use of online media. Partnering with other public service or community organisations will also enable you to deliver more with less. This is further outlined in Chapter 7.

## Budgeting

Any PR programme must take account of the budget available and, where necessary, elements of the plan may need to be adjusted to remain within the allocated spend. Here a project-based approach should enable the essential elements of any plan to be retained while cost savings can be achieved by reducing 'non-essential' elements of the programme.

## Monitoring and evaluation

Monitoring the success of the programme during its implementation and then evaluating the outcome against the objectives is critically important and is often one of the weaknesses in programme management.

In reality, evaluation has often been limited and PR practitioners have tended to rely on relatively unsophisticated evaluation measures. This has been claimed to be because of the costs of pre- and post-testing of audiences, lack of time and lack of research skills (Watson and Noble, 2007).

In local government, traditionally PR has been delivered on a shoe string and practitioners have become armed with ways of undertaking cost-effective evaluation. From the 1990s onwards computer based evaluation services/software packages have become available. Most of these programmes rely on evaluating media coverage, often assigning AVEs. Digital media lends itself to evaluation but measures lower levels of awareness. These techniques are helpful in the mix, but should be blended with methods that identify changes in audience attitude or behaviour.

CIPR LPS judges noted the 'dwindling use of specific evaluation research' (Powell, 2010). Evaluation techniques from award-winning entries (CIPR LPS, 2010; CIPR, 2011b) have included inserting campaign-specific questions into the council's e- and citizen panels, monitoring attendance at events, measuring estimated opportunities to see based on advertising, amount and sentiment of media coverage, recording the number of enquiries made and measuring the uptake of a service following campaign delivery.

Most of these techniques fall within the most commonly used evaluation techniques that record the number of messages sent, accuracy of messages carried, amount of media coverage – column inches, notional financial values based on advertising equivalent and number of people who potentially were exposed to the message.

These methods measure the effectiveness of the process rather than the impact, especially in terms of attitudes or behaviour. Effective evaluation must measure not just the communication output, but the effects on the target publics – in terms of attitudinal or behavioural change. Inserting questions into established citizens' forums or e-panels is a nod in the right direction, but may not provide opportunity to question the specific audience you are targeting and can only provide information on what they claim to be doing or thinking. Similarly, gathering number crunching statistics at the end of a campaign doesn't isolate the effects of the PR programme from the many other influences people have been exposed to.

Ideally, evaluation should include impact measurement as outlined in Macnamara's macro model of PR Evaluation, which is still regarded as the definitive guide to PR measurement (CIPR, 2011b). This model distinguishes between output or process measures and the impact measures of PR results. It also offers practical guidance on planning and managing evaluation approaches for PR campaigns. It is important to adopt measures that focus on the *impact* achieved, ie changes in attitudes and behaviour rather than simply the success of the process of communication, ie measuring media coverage.

The accurate impact measurement of results requires bespoke pre- and post-campaign assessment of changes in attitudes/opinion/behaviour. This would usually be commissioned by an external research company and is expensive. However, if you are able to present the potential cost savings to the organisation from the campaign, such as NHS Northamptonshire were able, it may be possible to secure the budgets required. In their case, £240,000 was allocated for the campaign.

The Barcelona Principles, launched by the International Association for Measurement and Evaluation of Communication (AMEC) in July 2010 presents a global commitment to measurement and goal setting. The principles state that media measurement should assess both quantity and quality and that quantity measures on their own are inadequate. The Principles state that advertising value equivalents (AVEs) cannot measure the value of PR. They suggest that social media can and should be used and that measuring outcomes is preferable to measuring outputs. Launched in the depths of a recession, it will be interesting to see the impact of this guidance. For local government PR practitioners, creativity and using cost-effective evaluation methods available from within the organisation, and where possible securing budgets for specific evaluation through arguing a strong business case, is key.

---

**Checklist**

- Ensure that your campaign contributes to the overall business objectives of the organisation.

- Research is key. Significant time should be spent on formative research (Gregory, 2010).

- Ensure the ongoing monitoring of tactics, which should be adjusted if ineffective.

- Campaign-specific evaluation should be commissioned where possible.

- Use cost-effective research methods available from within the organisation.

- Work in partnership locally, regionally and nationally to obtain data to inform your campaign, enhance your resources and expand your communication channels.

---

## KEY WORDS

Engagement; two-way communication; business objectives; research and evaluation; behaviour change; stakeholders; nudging; partnership working.

---

## CASE STUDY  Hackney Council

Winner CIPR Local Public Services Campaign of the Year 2011

### Background

In 2001, Hackney's census return rate was the second lowest in the country with only 72 per cent of households in the borough returning a form. This meant that the area, already one of the most deprived in the country, potentially lost out on millions of pounds of funding for essential services over the last decade.

In 2011, with the prospect of cuts to the Council's budget alone totalling £44 million, this was potentially the most important census ever for Hackney. As such, a marketing and communications campaign was executed to help support the aim of securing the fairest possible funding for the borough.

### Objectives

#### Overall objective

To increase the percentage of households returning a form by at least 10 per cent and in line with ONS targets for all local authorities.

#### Communications objectives

- Work closely with Hackney-based ONS staff to ensure consistency of message and ensure maximum impact by building on the national campaign.
- Encourage maximum participation (at least 10 per cent higher than 2001 and in line with ONS targets for London) through the development of an integrated communication campaign to support targeted engagement.
- Raise awareness of the link between the census and funding for local services.
- Work closely with partner organisations, including the voluntary and community sector to help convert awareness of the census to return of forms.
- Ensure ONS and local help routes are as widely publicised as possible.

### Creative development

The foundations of the campaign utilised existing focus group research conducted by Lambeth, a London borough with similar demographics to Hackney. This revealed that people were more likely to return their form once they understood the benefits to themselves, their family and their neighbourhood, and once they were reassured that it was completely confidential.

Messages around creating a 'historical archive' or being fined for non-return were less persuasive. In Hackney, resident surveys identified that their key priorities were health, education, housing and work and training opportunities – all key services with funding directly linked to calculations based on census data. Therefore, an approach that combined simple messages highlighting specific services that clearly outlined this link, combined with an emphasis on confidentiality was developed.

Fundamental to the campaign was presenting the key messages in a personal way, putting faces that reflected Hackney's diverse communities to the facts – helping to create a sense of shared responsibility and demonstrating that the census is important for everybody. The 'I'm filling in my census because...' campaign resonated well with pilot groups, helping them to see beyond the official form to the benefits that a high census return could bring to their borough. The form itself became a secondary part of the campaign, and as a result some of the negative perceptions related to it were rendered less of an obstacle to completion.

In order to maximise the impact of communications and to create a visual link with the national campaign, Hackney utilised the same colour palette, included the 2011 Census logo on all artwork and adapted the national strapline.

### Strategy and implementation

#### Phase One: awareness raising

In order to create initial awareness of the census, an information campaign was implemented prior to residents receiving their forms. One of the key risks identified was that people might throw their form away without knowing what it was.

Therefore, the first stage of the campaign used the image of the census envelope itself, building recognition, encouraging people to look out for it and to return it as soon as possible.

The artwork was used on:

- approximately 3,000 posters distributed to public access points across the Borough including libraries, GP surgeries, housing estates, voluntary and community sector groups, leisure centres and job centres;

- 10,000 bookmarks to give to all borrowers in Hackney libraries and students at the community college;

- screensavers on PCs in public access points including the Council's main customer service centre and libraries;

- Council and partner websites, on high traffic pages and those likely to be visited by target audiences;

- Council's social media channels.

In addition:

- footers were added to all outgoing e-mail;

- messages reminding people to look out for their form were added to call holding for incoming calls to the Council and its partners;

- editorial was carried in *Hackney Today* (the Council's publication delivered free to all households) local and ethnic media and partner newsletters.

Approximately, a third of Council employees are also Hackney residents so the full range of internal communications channels were employed, including: screensavers, weekly e-bulletin, managers e-briefing and staff magazine. This also encouraged all staff to talk to residents about the census.

### Phase Two: conversion

Once forms hit doorsteps in mid-March, the second phase of the campaign was implemented using the 'I'm filling in' artwork and messages to help convert awareness into action. This utilised the same channels as phase one with additional impact provided by:

- high visibility lamp post banners, six versions across 150 sites;

- a four-page wrap around in *Hackney Today*;

- flyers included in the annual mailing of Council Tax bills (reaching approximately 100,000 households);

- adverts in specific local ethnic media, complementing the ONS schedule;

- a pack designed specifically for residents attending citizenship ceremonies.

A major push in the local media resulted in excellent coverage, with a reach of over 100,000 (taken from circulation figures). This included a range of local ethnic media including a four-page feature in the *Jewish Tribune*, reaching one of the hardest to count communities in the Borough.

### *Phase Three: signposting help points*

Phase Three supported the door-knocking phase of the ONS programme. This involved using all available communications channels to signpost people to sources of help. Key message cards listing the helpline number, url and key helpdesk locations were given out by frontline staff in organisations across the Borough; click through buttons and banners were placed on high traffic web pages and *Hackney Today* carried a front page feature.

## Engagement

From the outset, it was obvious that the success of the communications campaign would be intrinsically linked with engagement and outreach work. A wide-ranging engagement plan was developed, in consultation with the ONS Area Manager, to complement communications.

Hackney has a strong third sector and these groups ran briefing sessions and completion events, faith and community leaders were encouraged to explain and promote the census, census staff attended events and roadshows and the Council's library staff were trained to help people fill in their forms at dedicated computer terminals. The Council provided templates that could be used to advertise these events in community languages, saving money on extensive translation and encouraging wider ownership of the campaign.

## Evaluation

As part of evaluating the effectiveness of local communications, Hackney undertook an online survey in late March with residents via the council's E-Panel. This showed a strong awareness of the census with 93 per cent of respondents aware of it and 67 per cent reporting that they had already completed their form. Particularly, the results showed that while residents found out about the census primarily from the national campaign, the local campaign made people more likely to complete and return their form, with over 80 per cent reporting that the posters and lamppost banners they had seen made it more likely that they would return.

Spikes in attendance at completion events and visits to library helpdesks correlated with key activities, for example, when residents received issues of *Hackney Today* that highlighted the census.

The Council enjoyed an excellent relationship with the ONS Area Manager who praised the communications campaign as an 'extremely valuable' contribution to the 2011 Census in Hackney.

At the time of the awards submission, Hackney's response rate was 85 per cent, an increase of 13 per cent on 2001 and 5 per cent higher than ONS aspirations for all local areas. While various factors contributed to this success, there is clear evidence that the integrated campaign played a major part.

## Campaign budget

£27,000 including print, distribution.

# 09
# Communicating with the media

> *This is a tough time for public sector communicators. Austerity, a hostile central government, a hostile media environment – all of these things are making the job more challenging, yet from a professional development perspective, potentially more rewarding.*
>
> POLLY CZIOK, CHAIR CIPR LOCAL PUBLIC SERVICES GROUP 2011–14

> *Many of the old ways of doing things in the public sector simply don't work in a time of declining resources. The days of bolt-on comms teams that exist only to pump out positive news stories are over.*
>
> COUNCILLOR RUTH DOMBEY, DEPUTY LEADER SUTTON COUNCIL

*Can you get my name in the papers?* is the title of the only published autobiography of a council PR, Harry Diamond (1996). Diamond, head of public relations for Glasgow District Council from 1975–91, held what *PR Week* described at the time as the 'toughest council PR job in the UK'. His very personal story recalls his political battles and tribulations as he tried to boost Glasgow's – and its council's – poor media profile, locally, nationally and internationally. He remembers one councillor being scathingly dismissive of a positive feature about Glasgow in the *New York Times*: 'That's no use, Harry, I've got no punters (constituents) in New York!' Behind the book's title was the clamour from many elected councillors to get their name – and hopefully picture – in their local papers. Regardless of what was happening, the perceived job of PR was to put councillors in the media limelight with lots of good stories and pictures. A tall order then and less possible now, even with the best press officers. Councillors are not newsworthy unless they do or say something controversial, interesting or challenging; and councils or public services rarely hit the headlines for all the good things they do daily, but certainly do get their name in the papers when something goes badly wrong.

Council leaders, chief executives, directors and board chairs are most agitated when their organisation and its services are under media scrutiny. It is their PR moment – a reality check. 'One thing unites all senior people', says one senior communications adviser, 'the possibility that the things that could go wrong do and they end up unmanaged in public in a way that is fatally damaging' (Fletcher-Brown, 2009).

The job of today's press or media officer in a council or local public service is to manage professionally and timeously not just the media approach and response, but the misplaced expectations within their organisation. Expectations that PR can stop an uncomfortable story when there is a public interest to publish. Expectations that the PR should say little or nothing, and it will go away. Expectations that the PR should 'spin' an untruth, when the known facts will be rolled out sooner or later in the social media or forcibly disclosed under freedom of information. Expectations that PR can paint a rosy picture, when the organisation or its service is in deep trouble and knows it. Expectations that PR can do a cover up, when the services' reputation is already damaged and at further serious risk.

Robert Francis QC (2013a) in his final report on the serious care failings at Mid Staffordshire hospital has called for a 'duty of candour', enforceable by law, across the NHS. Senior managers, he stated, should be accountable, patients need to be protected and all staff should be empowered to be open and transparent when it comes to the well-being of the people in their care. The same should apply across councils and all public services. A deliberate judgement to 'cover up', as happened in Mid Staffordshire and has happened in other public services, is not in the public interest and is totally unacceptable. As Francis (2013b) says in his report:

> There is a difference between a judgement which is hindered by understandable ignorance of particular information and a judgement clouded or hindered by a failure to accord an appropriate weight to facts which were known.
>
> (Francis, 2013b)

The PR has a particular 'public interest' responsibility. Effective public relations requires judgement and an understanding of all the facts at the time, but much more. It demands an honesty, integrity and openness by the PR and those at the very top of the organisation into how they face up to the reality of a bad situation, the facts and the perceptions. Without that, there can be no credibility and ultimately no trust in the organisation's dealing with either the media or its publics.

Councils and public services still put a heavy emphasis on their portrayal in the traditional media – printed newspapers, television and radio, specialist and professional magazines – rather than other communications channels, including social media. On average, one in four staff of the communications function in local public services is specifically devoted to dealing with the traditional media. Daily or weekly press cuts or summaries of the organisation's media coverage will be circulated among the bosses, but there will be little or no report on what is being said that day about the council in the social media.

# Changing media landscape

Some 30 or so years ago, a council meeting report or council advert in a local newspaper could reach well over half, maybe three-quarters, of the households in the local area. Paid-for weeklies will never again achieve that level of reach. Similarly, a local news story, say about a council or health initiative, featured separately on both the tea-time regional news programmes of ITV and BBC would be watched by well over 80 per cent of the local viewing audience. That level of audience penetration for local news is never likely to be repeated. The segmentation of the media, and the multiplication of channels, including hyperlocal sites, presents a challenge.

But that total reliance on the media has changed over recent years with councils and public services communicating directly with their publics, for example through their own publications (newspapers and magazines, in particular) and now increasingly through the internet, their own website and social media channels (mainly through Twitter, Facebook, Flickr). So do public services still have to bother about the so-called traditional media?

Ofcom's annual tracker survey highlights that television has dramatically superseded newspapers as the UK public's 'main source of local news' in the first decade of the 21st century. In 2001, newspapers were top at 46 per cent, followed by television at 28 per cent, radio at 14 per cent and 'talking to people' at 7 per cent. In 2011, more than half the public, 53 per cent, said television was their main source of local news. Newspapers had dropped to 15 per cent and radio to 10 per cent. The internet share is growing at 6 per cent (from 2 per cent in 2005 survey) and 'talking to people' still around 7 per cent. Perhaps not surprisingly, given the regulatory framework at both BBC and Ofcom, three out of four people trust television most for fair and unbiased news (Ofcom, 2011).

The evening tea-time regional news programmes around 18.00 hours are consistently the most popular for local or regional news. BBC TV gets a 28 per cent share nationally, while the ITV stations get 18 per cent of viewing audience (Ofcom, 2012a) but only half the viewers watching TV at tea-time are tuned to news. But there are marked regional variation, with the highest local news viewing in south-west England, Border area and Northern Ireland (see Figure 9.1).

**FIGURE 9.1** Percentage of homes watching tea-time local and regional news programmes on BBC TV and ITV stations

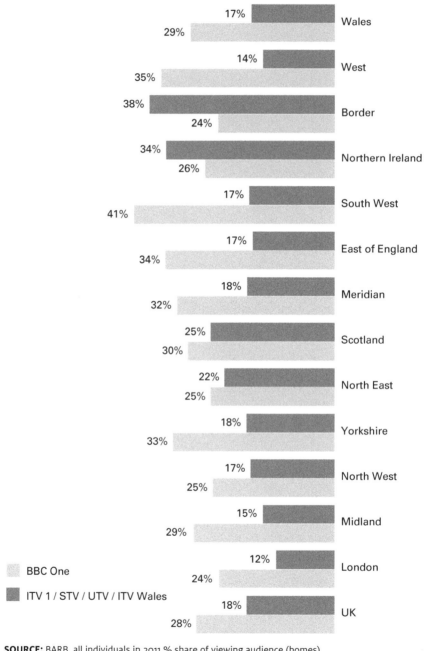

SOURCE: BARB, all individuals in 2011 % share of viewing audience (homes)
NOTE: Based on regional news programmes, start time 17:55–18:35, 10mins+duration, BBC One and ITV1, weekdays

When people were asked to score separately the importance of television, radio, paid-for local newspapers, and free papers for getting their local news, a more pluralistic picture emerges. 59 per cent say television is 'very important', 44 per cent radio, 43 per cent paid-for newspapers and 29 per cent free newspapers. So while television dominates, local radio, paid-for and free local newspapers still have a significant place as providers of local news (Ofcom, 2012b).

Communicators cannot do their job without an understanding of this evolving media landscape and how it impacts directly on the council or public services they work for. Printed newspapers are on a life-support machine as circulations fall drastically and they desperately develop apps, digital editions and a subscription base to fund their journalism. But whatever the print circulation, the fact remains that a bad press story or stories can dent reputation. Today that story is not thrown away or forgotten as quickly as yesterday's fish and chip wrapper; it can be e-mailed, blogged and tweeted across the internet and is digitally searchable by anyone months or years later.

*The Daily Mail*, often a critical voice when it comes to public services and social services, still has a strong print edition but its free access *Mail Online*, now profitable, is the biggest English digital newspaper, outstripping *New York Times*, with over 9 million browsers daily, a growing number on smartphones viewing 24 minutes a day on average (MacMillan, 2013).

Other news brands, such as the *Daily Telegraph*, *The Times*, *Independent*, *Guardian* and *Scotsman*, seek to underline online their distinctive journalism or regional and national strengths. On average, through their online versions the quality press have added almost 50 per cent to their current print readership, the popular red tops only 12 per cent (*Independent*, 2012). More people now read the *Guardian* online than buy the newspaper. The *Guardian* has online public services forums with its editors and readership and Twitter accounts for specialist areas, such as social care, education and housing. Trade journals such as *MJ* (*Municipal Journal*) and *LGC* (*Local Government Chronicle*) and a number of specialist magazines in the fields of health, planning, education and regeneration are still important. Many are slimmer now and some, like *Community Care* specialising in the social services, have moved totally from print to digital, as income particularly from public sector jobs advertising has collapsed.

The UK's evening newspapers, a ready outlet for local public services stories, are declining fast; some have turned weekly, others have their main print run during the night, rather than around midday. Almost 250 local papers have closed or merged in the six years to 2011. Media groups, such as Trinity Mirror, Johnston Press and Newsquest, have centralised their editorial and production teams to save costs, revamped their weeklies and developed local news websites. Trinity and Johnston alone run almost 500 local news websites, many funded on a shoestring, across the United Kingdom, compared to the 55 licence-funded BBC regional websites.

Ashley Highfield was appointed chief executive in 2011 to overhaul digital strategy for Johnston Press PLC, the UK's second largest publisher of newspapers. He believes local newspapers still have a print future, most weekly, a few in the bigger cities daily, but all embracing digital through an integrated or 'platform neutral' approach. Highfield (2012) is quoted in *The Drum*:

> We should look at the story first and foremost and then look at how we use all the different media to disseminate the story and make them all work together. I see the role of the editor changing because they are moving from a print deadline world to one of continual communication and engagement with their audience. That's probably the shift from light touch engagement with our audience to one where we curate quite a lot of user generated content in with, and always part of, and never superseding, our own journalists' content.

More fundamental changes are afoot as technology allows broadcast and broadband to integrate and news is delivered faster and richer through the internet in many formats and through many devices, especially mobiles. Robert Kynel (2012) head of content for YouTube, states smartphones will be the 'first screen', ranking above television as the place people will go to watch content. Some 20 million gigabytes of data was consumed over the country's mobile network in 2012, more than double the previous year (Ofcom, 2012b). The interactive smartphone makes it easy for anyone to receive news or proactively send pictures, words or video across the internet and direct into news desks. This user-generated content is being actively encouraged by most newspaper websites as well as BBC, Sky and ITV. Such ad hoc or committed 'citizen journalists' are an added source of news, together with a growing community of informed bloggers.

Public services should, too, be engaging differently with the media, particularly their local newspapers and their associated websites; pumping out press releases is not enough. First, there needs to be an understanding on the kind of content the media are now looking for, not just words but pictures, video and graphics. Second, councils and public services should embrace the locally trusted papers, their websites and social networks as they move to a more active engagement with their communities. Nesta (2013) highlights the growth of hyperlocal media and the value of trusted local news and information sites. The communicator's task must be linking into these more local e-networks.

# Real life TV documentaries

In recent years, television – not the news programmes, but real life documentaries and series – has given insights into the working of many of our public services.

Programmes like 'One born every minute' (Channel 4) about the maternity services at Princess Anne Hospital, Southampton or 'Protecting Our Children' (BBC 2) about the child care services in Bristol City Council bring to the viewer an intense, but captivating, picture of the day-to-day activity of midwives and social services and the varied and at times difficult interactions between professionals, public services and their patients or clients. 'Life of Grime' (BBC 1) focused on the unpleasant jobs of environmental health inspectors across the country. Such programmes raise the profile of the services.

But these documentaries demand total co-operation – and formal agreement – with the series producer and production team, the public services communications team and the specific front-line services. All have to be convinced on the purpose to get the necessary buy-in and commitment from all involved, including patients and the public. The producers and production teams for this genre of documentary-making are committed to telling the story with integrity, and are sensitive to the vulnerabilities of anyone taking part. But the filming commitment is immense; the Southampton maternity series of 12 programmes involved six weeks of filming 24/7 and up to 40 fixed and hand held cameras in the hospital.

Tower Hamlets London Borough's new chief executive, Kevan Collins, swapped his smart suit to go in disguise to work in different council jobs in the popular 'Undercover Boss' TV series (Channel 4, 22 July 2010). At the time the council, with a £1 billion budget and 10,000 employees, was facing up to £50 million in cuts or savings. The challenge was – as it is in every council – making savings without impacting too much on the front-line services. Viewers saw the dilemmas he faced as he worked with an enforcement officer, a pest control officer, and as a meals on wheels deliverer. There were too many meals to distribute and no time to spend with the vulnerable, lonely recipients of the service. Collins admitted doing the programme was a risk, but it offered an enlightening insight into the front-line. 'I want the council to get better and to get better needs taking risks,' acknowledged the undercover council boss.

Monmouthshire County Council also invited the cameras in for the BBC Wales current affairs programme 'Week in Week Out' (broadcast 30 January 2012). Communications Manager, Robert Webb (2012) says he 'choked' over the title 'Carrying on at the Council'. But the programme got a positive response from the public, on Twitter and from other professionals including the local newspaper editor.

Webb states:

> BBC wanted the human element and I have to say that came across massively. Staff from the council talked with clear passion and commitment about their jobs, we saw our gritters out and about keeping our roads safe, we saw our social services colleagues, the fantastic work we're doing on supporting business. Yes, we did get something on the massive savings we're managing to make in the way we work, in the way we collect waste and with our buildings. Most of all it portrayed an organization saying 'let's get on with it'.

# Local television

There will soon be more opportunities – and challenges – for public services locally. Up to 65 UK cities and towns – with the possibility of others in the future – have been earmarked for local digital terrestrial TV stations, partly seed-funded from the television licence. The first 14 local TV stations, many run by existing media groups, have got the go-ahead for a start in 2013/14. 'These new local TV services will be a fundamental change in how people get information about their own communities and how they hold their representatives to account', according to Jeremy Hunt, the then Secretary of State for Culture, Media and Sport (DCMS, 2011). Over the last 20 or so years, attempts at local TV services in Britain, for example in Birmingham, Edinburgh and with council support Lanarkshire, have failed dismally due to spectrum limitations, funding and insufficient viewers to support advertising. Unlike the United States, where local TV does well, the UK's media regulatory and competition regime, until recently, made it difficult for newspaper or broadcast companies to run local TV stations in the same area, so that early synergy was lost. Local TV will have to compete with an established network of local radio stations, both commercial and BBC, and a growing number of community-run radio stations, most only offering local programmes for part of the day. Plans to develop local TV over the internet are the next stage: more choice for local people or more unsustainable competition for local newspapers, their websites and local radio? The local TV stations offer potential, but could still fall flat on funding. Carnegie fellow and former senior broadcaster, Blair Jenkins (2012) argues communities need 'new sources of accurate information'. Local TV services should not be judged solely on commercial terms, as they have the potential to bring 'great social and democratic value'. Such services will have a licence commitment to produce a strong local news service; this claims Jenkins 'will present something fresh and valuable' and could 'empower communities to be producers and not just recipients of local content'. Jenkins advocates partnerships with civic society.

Councils and all local bodies delivering public services should be active partners, rather than bystanders, in the development of new local TV in their area. Alex Aitken (2012), then head of communications at Westminster City Council, hopes that local television creates 'a meaningful platform' for councils to speak to local people. 'Council communicators have the eternal task of explaining what their councils are doing and why. If local broadcasting can provide the medium, we'll provide the message'. But local TV will never be resourced as well, both in money and staff, as current broadcasters. It will be operating on very limited budgets. This opens up the new possibility of local public services produced or supported programmes or segments, but any such programming will have to meet the broadcasting rules.

## Social media and journalists

In this media transition from print to online, the convergence of broadcast and broadband, and the power of the social media to create and engage connected networks, public sector communicators cannot any longer media manage in terms of the old traditional silos of press and broadcast. Trusted news brands are across print, broadcast and online. And there are a growing number of e-newspapers, many local like *In Thurrock*. The internet and social media are transforming the way the public communicate and the way many journalists do their job.

The Social Journalism Study (2012) found that three out of four UK journalists use social media to promote their work and their engagement with their audience. One in four UK journalists said social media was essential to carry out their work and even more (39 per cent) claimed using social media improved their productivity. Twitter is the most popular among journalists; 80 per cent in the study tweeted and over 50 per cent were involved in publishing content on blogs and microblogs. 'Journalists are much more active general users and they play a key role in the world of social media through content creation, networking and other active uses.'

Media relations is now more online and unfortunately much less about face-to-face contact. Journalists sourcing and researching stories will be looking to the council's website and Facebook for current information about key people and services and to Twitter for the latest news alert. They can click into all the council reports and minutes, Google to check the organisation's past media coverage and current issues, and monitor voice on social media. Within a few minutes of online search a journalist can have a picture of the organisation – good and bad. For the public services, that means a crucial part of media relations is building trust and credibility in its own online presence and activity. Journalists should be able to rely on public services communicators (and their organisations) as trusted sources, online and offline. Mistakes or misjudgements by councils can go viral so easily and are much more difficult to manage. In June 2012, Argyll and Bute Council, already reeling from the suspension of their head of public relations and two press officers for alleged misuse of Facebook and e-mails respectively, will be remembered most for banning a nine-year-old primary school pupil, Martha Payne, from blogging her daily school meal photos (Neverseconds blog, 2012; Payne, 2012).

The issue came to a head when the *Daily Record*, a Scottish tabloid, ran a two-page feature with a picture of Martha and TV chef Nick Nairn beside a flaming frying pan with the tongue in cheek, but insensitive, headline 'It is time to fire the dinner ladies'. That headline inflamed passions at the council, calling the story an unwarranted attack on their catering staff. Their response – a ban on Martha from taking any more photos of her school meals. Martha blogged the decision to her few thousand online followers: 'I only write my blog, not newspapers and I am sad I am no longer allowed to take photos. I will miss sharing and rating my school dinners.' Overnight it became the most tweeted blog that day. (A full case study is included in the online resources for this book **http://www.koganpage.com/PRGov.**)

Viral outrage turned on the council, who struggled to justify their impetuous decision. Under pressure, the council did a U-turn. But not very graciously. Their full press statement from the council leader – the second within two hours – was a confused self-justification, refuting censorship and attacking an 'inaccurate and abusive' newspaper headline. Martha was not mentioned till the fourth sentence and the positive message about engaging was left to the very last paragraph. Why did the council leader not just tweet: 'Sorry, Martha. We got it wrong. Continue taking pictures of your school meals. We will listen to what you and other pupils are saying'? Or better still, think first about the implications before imposing the ban. Or even better, support Martha's blog and engage with her and other pupils in rural Argyllshire through the social media.

The Argyll council ban story is an example of council media mismanagement, coupled with no understanding of the impact of social media. There were three distinct media issues. First, Martha was a popular blogger with lots of followers, including well-known TV chefs and the media. The council clearly failed to consider their photo ban would go viral, then ricochet round the news desks and hit the headlines. Second, press statements need to be considered, get to the point and should be written with clarity. Adrian Short (2012) and Tom Chivers (2012) have critically dissected the council's first press statement confirming the ban. Third, the allegedly offensive headline that triggered the ban should have been separately managed and contained as an issue between the council and the newspaper. Other media had no interest in a tit-for-tat with another newspaper.

John Shewell (2011), head of public relations from Brighton & Hove, gave his professional assessment in *PR Week*: 'Argyll and Bute's U-turn is a classic example of spectacularly screwing it up. Instead of engaging with a young person legitimately expressing her views, the council gagged her. This is an anathema to social media and the notion of democratic participation.'

The forced eviction of travellers and their families from Dale Farm in Basildon in the autumn of 2011 put Basildon Borough Council in the eye of a media tsunami. For several weeks the UK and international media descended on the town to report the on-off eviction saga, as the travellers went to court to stop the action. Our Dale Farm case studies on the web look at both communications campaigns – the council and the travellers **http://www.koganpage.com/PRGov**.

Dale Farm had developed over 10 years without planning permission and most local residents nearby were frustrated that, despite earlier attempts, the council had not been able to take action. The issue was 'a significant reputational threat' to the council. The council's communications strategy was centred around three areas: the key messages, legality, equality and humanity; engaging the media and responding to volumes of media enquiries and interview requests; and media training for key council spokespersons, including the council leader.

Pitched against the council were the Dale Farm residents, who over several months had mobilised through the social media and their networks an impressive array of support from academics, personalities, church leaders, parliamentarians and even the United Nations. The Dale Farm Solidarity

Campaign focused on highlighting the travellers' plight and stopping the council's eviction. Volunteers came in to assist on public relations. The media, television, radio and press were invited in and several journalists were embedded within the site. Their communications strategy was to show the external support they had, involve and support the travellers as the spokespersons, encourage the media to interview them and to get across the injustice and prejudice they said underpinned the council's action.

The eviction, involving bailiffs and police, eventually took place on 19 October 2011. Who won? The council in securing their eviction objective, and gaining by the eviction date the wider public and media support for their actions. With the story ever-present on the media, support for the council's eviction action increased from 66 per cent in mid-September to around 90 per cent a month later. But the drawn out Dale Farm eviction gave a voice and a confidence to the travellers' case, and highlighted the need for official travellers' sites. In October 2012, the government announced changes in the law to stop unauthorised sites developing and £60 million to fund 'authorised pitches for travellers'.

# The media toolkit

## *Protocol*

Having an agreed media protocol is good practice for any council and organisation. The protocol will set out who should and should not deal with the media and who should act as official spokespersons and issue press statements. Clear published procedures minimise confusion and ensure transparency.

Most councils now have their own media, publicity or communications protocol and these are often formally approved by the council and published online (as part of their publication scheme) for anyone to see. Such protocols can at first sight appear very authoritarian and not consistent with a council pledged to openness. But the protocols reflect the statutory requirements and the Code of Practice on Local Authority Publicity all councils are bound by. There is a further bind: all officers of councils 'speaking' on behalf of the council to journalists and broadcasters are deemed politically restricted by statute.

So responsibility for dealing day-to-day with the media rests with head of communications, the media manager and the press office. Protocols usually underline that all media enquiries should be 'routed through the press office' (Walsall Council) or 'incoming press calls will be fielded by the press office or other communications staff' (Hackney Council). Or more explicitly 'employees and other staff should not communicate with press and other media unless authorized by the appropriate manager to do so' (Southwark Council) and 'no member of staff to speak to any publication, radio or television station on council matters without the knowledge and guidance of the press office' (Walsall Council).

The protocol often lists which councillors should be quoted in press statements or release. Usually that will be confined to the mayor (mainly on civic matters), elected mayor, council leader, deputy leader and councillors with portfolios, namely cabinet members and committee chairs or vice-chairs. 'Media statements on cabinet decisions will be made by the appropriate cabinet member (or their substitute), the mayor or issued by the entire cabinet and interviews on cabinet decisions will only be given by the appropriate member of the cabinet, their substitute or the mayor' (Hackney Council). 'Press releases containing quotes from councillors must be agreed and signed off by the appropriate councillor' (Southwark Council).

Behind these protocols is the ever-present issue of politics, and the statutory requirement not to be party political. For councils, statements and press releases are within the law if they are about services, functions and agreed council decisions, policies and priorities. Walsall Council has published online (see case study) a 'working protocols for the press' statement, which dismisses spin and says the council will 'never knowingly mislead the media' and will always acknowledge mistakes if something has gone wrong. The council says it will not respond to anonymous or unattributable allegations. But its reference to the press attending council meetings is wrong – the press are not there as 'a guest'. Since the 1960s, the press (and the public) have had a statutory right to attend all council and committee meetings and the council have a duty to provide appropriate facilities for journalists to do their job, including making available the relevant papers, agenda, minutes and reports, now usually online. The press can only be excluded on specific matters if councillors vote that 'publicity would be prejudicial to the public interest'; this can be, but rarely is, challenged. But an excluded item decision should be available to the press.

**CASE STUDY** Walsall Council: Working protocols for the press

The council does not wish to be involved in any notions of 'spin'. Instead we concentrate on promoting council services and how to access them, the democratic process and how to engage in it, and the council's decisions or plans and what they mean for our diverse communities.

The press office will never knowingly mislead the press, the public or staff on any issue. We will work with the media to aim to ensure that any publicity describing the council's policies, aims, decisions and services will be objective, concentrating on facts and explanation, and what the council aims to achieve for the people of Walsall. If the council discovers for itself that the council has made a mistake, in terms of the operation or delivery of its services, it will proactively tell the press and the public what has gone wrong and what it will do to put it right.

The value of integrity will be maintained. This sometimes means that there are matters where the council should properly respect confidentiality, particularly where it has a duty of care, for example to citizens, tax payers, staff or elected members. Where we are limited in what we can say to the media, we will explain the reasons why. The council will not comment on information provided to the press anonymously or comment on quotes that will not be attributed. Any anonymous quote is not a council quote.

The council will make committee meetings open to the press and encourage them to attend as a guest, offering good facilities for reporting the meeting. If previous media comment or reportage is discussed in committee it is done so as to establish facts.

In return the press are not permitted to enter council buildings unless invited to by the council, nor will it invade the privacy of individual staff members or harass them directly. Instead they will direct their questions to the press office only.

The council believes the press want to move Walsall forward too and will respect the role the press plays in holding the council to account and will make every effort to learn from press coverage to improve services. All this is both necessary and healthy. In all its communications, the council will not blame the media for performance of image problems.

These protocols and principles are designed to help the press do a demanding job and the council will seek to provide a professional and responsive service within the framework set out.

Walsall Council, 2013, accessed online 25 April 2013
**http://cms.walsall.gov.uk/communications_protocols.pdf**

## *Online newsroom*

Many local council and public services press offices still operate on traditional lines, but use the tools of e-communications and e-databases to distribute press releases and pictures and maintain media lists and monitor calls and responses. Some councils have a TV or radio station; a few also have developed a more integrated online newsroom, serving not just the media but bloggers, social network sites and others interested in local government news and information.

Shropshire Council no longer sends out press releases; the media are directed online to the Shropshire Newsroom (**http://shropshire.gov.uk/news/**). This gives residents and the press 'equal access to council news'. In addition, Shropshire has active online networks – over 30 on Facebook (recycling, family advice, food safety, museums etc) and 20 through Twitter. Monmouthshire Council effectively uses YouTube for video reports, liveblogs to keep journalists up to date on ongoing issues and, like many other councils, Twitter for alerts on road closures, gritting and school closures.

One of the best examples of an online newsroom is at Birmingham City Council (**www.birminghamnewsroom.com**). It was set up in 2009, following consultation with journalists and a growing band of local bloggers and citizen journalists. The council recognised that there is an 'online community out there that really takes an interest in local government news and their help has proved invaluable' (Birmingham, 2010).

With a budget of £150 and using the blogging platform Wordpress, its development involved many long hours of the committed press team at the council. It first proved its worth during the 2009/10 winter when the newsroom attracted 9,600 unique users in three days for gritting updates, school closures and other service information. The online newsroom operates 24/7 (see case study). The reaction in Birmingham from journalists and bloggers has been positive. 'Great resource for Birmingham journalists and residents alike' (editor), 'wonderful platform for a potentially whole new relationship between the council, the city and the media' (blogger), 'the audience is niche but those engaging with the online newsroom site has exceeded our expectations' (council deputy leader) and 'good to see that the public sector is making moves into social networking' (local government commentator).

## CASE STUDY  Birmingham Online Newsroom

www.birminghamnewsroom.com was launched by Birmingham City Council in late June 2009 to offer greater access to council news. The aim was and is to serve journalists, residents and a growing hyperlocal scene. In addition to news releases, the site features: videos, downloadable photographs (Flickr), maps, speeches and links to all council meetings, reports and agendas. The website also hosts blog posts from politicians and officers at all levels of the organisation.

### Setting up

Before launching our digital press office, the Birmingham City Council press office operated along traditional lines, issuing news releases to the mainstream media, organising briefings and press conferences etc. News releases did appear on the Birmingham City Council website but would first be sent to journalists. This meant that ordinary citizens were given secondary access to press releases and were entirely dependent on journalists for news about the local authority. The council was not engaging with the emerging social media platforms. The then Head of News Deborah Harries was keen to change this.

With no real budget, open source was clearly the way forward and after research, including useful chats with local social media specialists, Birmingham decided to build an online newsroom using Wordpress. Two members of the team learnt the basics and just got on with it. Much of the work was done outside office hours in evenings and weekends; a far cry from the highly paid 'Twitter tsars' often cited by local government detractors in certain sections of the media.

### Three years on

Three years on, 2012, the online newsroom now reaches traditional journalists, bloggers and residents. Keeping the newsroom up to date does take time but it also speeds up a number of processes for the press office because so much information is now stored online.

With releases, statements, videos and photographs stretching back to 2009, it is also a very useful searchable archive. But Birmingham's commitment is to 'as it happens' coverage and that does mean 24/7, with some postings, gritting alerts, school closures etc and tweeting undertaken through the night.

The Birmingham press office team is small, so the ability to point callers to information already available on the newsroom site certainly speeds up the information flow. That said, the newsroom continues to distribute content via traditional methods but increasingly reporters and bloggers go directly to the newsroom – primarily via RSS feeds and Twitter.

A new section featuring regular Freedom of Information requests and links to Open Data was added in 2011; in time this will also ease the pressure on the council's very busy FOI team. Since January 2012 council meetings have been streamed on the newsroom and footage from the first eight meetings was viewed over 45,000 times; all footage is archived.

## Impact

**www.birminghamnewsroom.com** is all about openness and transparency, says the council. Its intention has been to democratize council news and information, so there are easy links and access to reports, meeting agendas and minutes. A daily tweet points to scheduled meetings, giving readers links to more detailed information. The aim is to interest people in how the city is run.

In an average month, the online newsroom reaches around 35,000 unique visitors – this increases with events like elections, winter weather and riots. There are around 400,000 page views a month. This audience continues to grow and the site also has over 7,000 followers on Twitter. Journalists use the newsroom on a daily basis. It has also had a positive impact on the council's daily interaction with hyperlocal sites and Birmingham residents in general. The newsroom reaches a new emerging audience. It is still an ongoing and developing project.

(information provided by Geoff Coleman, Head of News, Birmingham City Council online newsroom)

## *Grid*

Most councils and public services organisations operate a media grid. Some have developed the grid into an online planning tool for media and communications; for others it is a simpler diary planner.

The purpose of the grid is to map out over the next few months or year all key communications activities across the organisation – for example, campaigns, launches, events, announcements, key cabinet, committee or board meetings, forthcoming elections. It must pinpoint potential known issues of concern or controversy, the publication of an inquiry report or controversial matter coming before the council, cabinet or board, so a specific communications plan can be ready in place.

Such a grid avoids clashes or overlaps and allows a much more co-ordinated approach to proactive media activity. The grid is useless if it is not kept constantly up to date and reviewed at least weekly, ideally with the full team. It is less effective if it does not include all the media and communications activities across the council or organisation, including section or departmental publications and internal communications.

Behind the grid should be detailed plans for the various communications activities and deadline dates for staff to ensure delivery within the timescale.

## *Press or media release*

For decades, the press or media release has had one intended purpose: to get media coverage about its contents through targeting specific journalists, news desks, feature desks, picture desks and forward-planning desks. Journalists and editors were – and still are – the filter. They decide which press releases would be followed up and, ultimately, whether or not the contents in press release – and in what form – should get to the public at large through the editorial pages of a newspaper or magazine or through news or other programmes on TV or radio.

Posting or e-mailing out press releases like confetti to everyone on the press list (which is the stated practice of some councils) makes no sense. Newsnight presenter Gavin Esler puts it bluntly: 'One thing that is really annoying is the rise in the PR equivalent of cold calling – people who send out press releases willy nilly. I get some extraordinary nonsense and it's very untargeted. When you send something out to a lot of people, you are just telling everybody to ignore it' (Esler, 2012).

Press releases have to be targeted. That involves taking time in earmarking the specific press release for the individual journalists, news desks and specialist publications that you know cover the subject matter. Talk to the local media on how best to get press releases into their news and content management systems or their forward planning desks. Check with named journalist contacts on how they would like any press release delivered to them, by Twitter or by e-mail. Many prefer the press release in the body of the e-mail, not as an attachment.

Most public services manage their media lists internally, and these should be updated very regularly, with full contact details and social media links.

The basic rules of the press release are:

- Tell the story, explain the decision or issue clearly and simply: use plain English.
- Put the main point in the first paragraph.
- Write and think as objectively as possible.
- Always use a named person quote: 'Council leader Jim Smith said...'
- Keep number of people quoted to a minimum (ideally one or two).
- If you use any statistics remember to footnote the source.
- Avoid clichés, jargon and council-speak.

- Consider the headline (for Twitter and link).
- Author the press release by name, contact details, social media links.
- Sign off with a sentence or two about the council/organisation.
- Say you have available supporting content – case studies, pictures, video, info graphics etc.
- Think SEO (search engine optimisation) for every release.

Many councils have an unnecessarily bureaucratic mechanism for press release approval, often leading to the chief executive or even council leader to sign off. Yes, there should be checks for facts, quotes should be agreed by the named person and a 'second sighter' should go over any press release, but ultimate responsibility for sign-off should rest with the media manager or the communications head. This is an issue of professional responsibility and trust.

With the internet and digital technology, the use of the press release has widened. It is now not just for journalists. The exact same press release is often being downloaded onto the council's or the organisation's website as a matter of course, and through social media, to followers on Twitter, Facebook and other channels. Interesting or relevant press releases will be re-tweeted and commented upon and that engagement itself may generate press interest. Web 'news' pages are refreshed by the latest press release; most sites have a helpful 'news' archive, but access is not helped by a poor search facility on many council websites.

This wider role for the press release needs rethinking, as we move from the linotype era of one-way communication into the digital era of engagement. Is the content, tone or style still right for both journalists and the website and social media? Should it be enhanced by pictures, video and graphics? Or with embedded links to more background? Has its content been optimised for search engines? Is it targeted or written best for local social e-networks? And, more significantly, is the council ready to engage on the issues posted in the press release.

## Press conference

Calling a press conference doesn't necessarily mean that journalists will turn up. Busy and understaffed news desks will not release journalists, interviewers or cameras for one or two valuable hours if there is no strong story or little media interest in what you have to say. The day chosen may be a very busy news day and there are always bigger stories to cover on the schedule.

The advice for councils and local public services is do not call a press conference unless you must. But even then, think carefully about what you want to get across and whether there are other – and better – ways to engage the media. An interview on radio or TV news? A feature? A photocall? Press briefing? Press release? Social media?

Getting your message across does not require a press conference. This is also true when councils and other public bodies arrange what they call a 'press launch' – an uneasy cross between a press conference and a project or service initiative launch event, with invites not just to the press, but a host of staff, councillors, directors and stakeholders. It is best to separate the media activity and the launch parts; that does not mean journalists or press photographers cannot attend the launch. It means that work with the media is done separately, maybe days before from an actual launch-speeches event.

Press conferences do have a place in major stories that are unfolding or continuing. For example, where there are several journalists and TV crews on location covering a child abduction, a murder enquiry, serious fire or flooding. Or when there is known press interest, a significant announcement or perhaps an investigation report is to be published. Greater Manchester Police (GMP) called two press conferences within hours of each other on 18 September 2012, the day of the tragic murder of two female police officers attending what they thought was a routine enquiry. The first was to confirm the deaths of the officers, PC Fiona Bone and PC Nicola Hughes. The second, later with the chief constable provided 'more detail than normal' around the incident and the arrest. 'We knew we had to put the details out there because of the intense media focus. If we hadn't been as transparent, the media would have started trying to find out what happened themselves' Amanda Coleman (2012) GMP's corporate communications director told *PR Week*.

Of all the public services, the police hold most press conferences, usually at police headquarters or a police office. Almost all are linked to ongoing police enquiries where the purpose of the press conference is to update the media, give an opportunity to answer media questions and, importantly, get press and public support for their investigation, help find witnesses, jog memories, trace vehicles etc. Several press conferences were held after the abduction, and subsequent murder enquiry, of five-year-old April Jones in Machynelleth in Wales in early October 2012.

Such police press conferences are usually filmed, and frequently televised live on Sky News or BBC News 24. The police limit the number of senior officers taking part to two, sometimes the chief, deputy, or assistant chief constable and the senior police officer in charge of the specific investigation. In serious cases of a missing child or adult, close relatives, often distressed and supported by a family liaison officer, have spoken at the press conference.

The police are adept at managing press conferences, perhaps through experience. The other public services less so. For councils and health services, there is a tendency for too many people to be at the top table, with councillors, officials or experts all given a chance to speak. It may add depth, but for the journalist covering the press conference there is a danger of information overload, blurred messages and mixed quotes. The child protection committees or children's safeguarding boards fall into that trap. Rightly, they wish all their board members, who are mainly drawn from the various children's services, to be seen united when they publish a report into a child abuse or child death investigation. A recent board press conference in England had nine people at the top table; it would have been better with only the chair and one other.

Sometimes in a fast-moving situation, an incident at a hospital, leisure centre, or disaster, a media huddle will converge around public officials looking for a statement. This is in effect an ad hoc press conference. The press officer on the scene should take a minute to manage the situation and organise the situation so that both the official spokesperson is not crowded out by the media scrum, and all cameras and microphones are in place. Control and credibility are critical. It is important in these situations for the most senior public official available to take responsibility and make a statement, show concern and indicate as far as possible what is being done by the authorities, without making any quick judgement on why it happened. In default of any official statement, there will be plenty of bystanders ready to fill the void.

When the media are invited to a planned press conference, make sure it is properly organised, the setting and backdrop are in place, and critically the messages and outcomes are clearly considered and discussed with those taking part. Key points for a successful press conference:

- test out possible questions and responses (Q & A);
- keep the top table to the very minimum – ideally one or two or at most three, with one taking the lead chair's role;
- ask media to sign in, with contact details;
- set the tone correctly in the opening statements;
- make sound and/or video recording for the record (also consider putting it on website or clips from it);
- allow an opportunity for questions and answers;
- do not let the conference drag out unnecessarily;
- allow time afterwards, if necessary, for separate interviews;
- issue at the start a press release with the key points and quotes.

If a weighty report (say an inquiry report or a major policy strategy) is being issued, have a prepared summary with extracts that reflect the tone and balance of the report and do not overlook the critical parts.

## Press briefing

Briefing journalists and broadcasters is a key part of media relations. Some will be specialists who will know the subject well and will not be fobbed off with standard lines and scant details; the majority will be generalists who will have a story to follow up or stand up.

Much of the briefing by public sector communicators is done on the phone or by e-mail, providing answers, background information to elucidate the issue or help put it in context. This will include making available or directing journalists to reports or documents, many of which will have been before cabinets or council committees or boards and in the public domain. Or perhaps arranging for the journalist to meet managers, visit a service or talk to front-line staff.

Individual face-to-face briefings are best. This would bring the journalist and the organisation's senior official or best expert together. A journalist may request such a briefing on a complex topic, like the council's budget or the impact of a policy proposal locally. Alternatively, the press office can take the initiative and offer briefings to a local, national or specialist journalist who from phone discussions or following them on social media have shown interest in an issue. These are best targeted, and on a one-to-one basis.

The press officer's job is to facilitate and host the briefing. Such briefings should mainly be 'on the record' – that is, everything said can be reported. Sometimes going 'off the record' (on a 'not attributable' basis) can put issues in context by providing sensitive or complex background information. But be very clear with the journalist the parts of the briefing that are on and off the record. Also be clear when the briefing can be used, for example after a council meeting or on publication of a report. The integrity and reputation of the organisation is at stake in these briefings. Organisations will be found out – sooner or later – if the briefing is misleading or deliberate spin.

Background briefings of the media can backfire spectacularly, even years later. The most serious example was over the Hillsborough tragedy when 96 Liverpool fans died in Britain's most fatal football crowd disaster on 15 April 1989. To shift any blame from themselves, high-ranking police officers in South Yorkshire and the local police federation actively briefed a local news agency and the local MP that it was the drunk, abusive and aggressive behaviour of the Liverpool fans that contributed to the tragedy and prevented the emergency services doing their job. These police briefings resulted in damning – and distressing – media coverage about the Liverpool fans' behaviour on the tragic day; the worst a front page in the *Sun* entitled 'The Truth' listing the awful allegations. It took 23 years to vindicate the fans conclusively. The 2012 Hillsborough Inquiry concluded there is 'no evidence to support these allegations'. The police briefings disseminating untrue stories could be viewed as a deliberate cover up or black propaganda (Hillsborough, 2012).

## Photocall, photographs and filming

That century-old phrase 'a picture is worth a thousand words' is still true today. Pictures and video can bring a story or issue alive and get more public attention. This is particularly so in the public services where there is a wealth of opportunities, and settings, for filming or photographing. But most good pictures will involve people – patients, vulnerable clients, residents, school pupils, children and staff – and that requires both sensitivity and consents.

Arranging a media photocall needs careful planning. There should always be a recce of the setting, for example the school, art gallery, residential home or public place and what, if any, additional props or arrangements need to be made. The individuals likely to be involved – a school class, clients in a centre and staff – must give consent; for children that requires parental consent which takes time.

Some councils use a general consent form for the school term; others the consent used is specific to the day's photocall's purpose. For all sensitive photos or filming, specific consent is best practice; that purpose should be clearly explained verbally or in writing to all giving consents. It has to be the responsibility of the media officer handling the photocall to ensure the media are aware that the pictures taken that day are specifically to illustrate and highlight the purpose or project and once in the media's library should not be used later for general visuals. The press officer should check any 'release forms' the media ask people to sign; these should be limited to the purpose of the filming and the programme.

Media photographers and film crews have a busy daily schedule. And there is no guarantee that the photocall will be covered. It is now always good practice to arrange for a freelance or in-house photographer to take both stills and video of the photocall event; these pictures and video (fully captioned, with names and summary story) can be downloaded onto the council's website and offered that day to the local news media. Digital cameras and smartphones make it easy to record the event, but check picture resolution is sufficient for all uses. Any contract with a freelance should cover all rights usage for promotional purposes by the council, including to other media and on the internet.

At many photocalls, there will be conflicting demands from television camerapersons and from press stills photographers to get the images they want to tell the story. It is very likely the stills photographer will be looking to create a picture with only one or two people in it. Television may also seek an interview or short vox pops with those present. The press officer managing the photocall has the task of facilitating and directing as may be required. The focus must be on the story. Not everyone attending the photocalls – including councillors – will be in the picture, and sometimes that can be a source of discontent.

Note that consent to be photographed and named for publication does not mean other information on the person can be revealed. Several complaints before the Press Complaints Commission (PCC) have been upheld where parents have objected to reference in local newspapers to their child's illness or specific disability in the picture caption or story.

*The Cambrian News*, for example, used a photo of a child using the council's school taxi service; the parents only gave permission for the child to be in the photograph. But the caption included the child's name, age and details of his medical condition provided by the taxi driver. 'The case demonstrates the paramount need for newspapers and magazines to establish in advance of publication, exactly what is the competent authority to grant consent' (PCC, 2011). Such cases have implications for councils and public services: if they are acting as the 'competent authority' they must stick to the terms of the parent's consent.

## The Q & A

The Q & A (question and answer) is a well-tested approach to bottom out the issues and is a valuable aid in the media officer's toolkit. A Q & A should be prepared for all issues or decisions that are likely to be controversial and hit the media. It must interrogate the difficult areas, for example where cuts or service changes are being proposed and the implications these will have on current service users.

Responsibility for preparing the Q & A has to be shared between communications and the service director(s) responsible; there should be joint sign-off and accountability for the Q & A. On most issues, this will almost certainly involve the political leadership or board chair.

## Specialists' list

All public services have specialists or practitioners who are expert on specific matters, for example, recycling, building control, fostering children, welfare benefits, school admissions, care of dementia patients etc. Local radio programmes, in particular, are always looking for such practitioners to take part, either in phone-ins, discussions or interviews. Too often councils do not grasp this opportunity and lose out to spokespeople from voluntary or campaigning organisations or academia.

It is a good idea for councils to draw up a media list of specialist areas and staff members (with their contact details) who are both subject knowledgeable and media friendly. That contact list could be circulated to local radio stations or alternatively just the subject areas and contact advised through the press office. Focused media training, particularly for radio and local TV, is strongly advised for all those on the list.

Sometimes the peg for the item on local radio, TV or the press will be a national story. This is an opportunity for the council to highlight their services and provide information locally. Be sensitive if the national story is controversial or critical and keep the focus on advice and what is happening locally.

## Bloggers and citizen journalists

Councils and public bodies cannot now ignore local bloggers and citizen journalists who occasionally or frequently focus, often critically, on the organisation. It is important to start engaging with them and include them in your e-mailings or press releases. Most will be known and they cannot be refused access to council meetings, or access to publically available reports. Councils and public bodies should allow blogging from any meeting open to the public and use the LGA 'social media' access logo.

Bloggers and citizen journalists will have a following on social media – assess that following and its importance to your organisation. Be aware if staff or opinion formers are following the blog. A decision has to be taken whether or not to respond to negative blogs or follow up postings. Ignoring wrong or misleading reporting and unjust criticism in the blog gives an impression that the blogger may be right. So engagement is often better in the long term. Focus on factual inaccuracies (and provide the correct information) rather than criticisms or opinions, but always encourage informed democratic debate. It is best policy to ignore offensive or overtly party political postings.

If engaging on the part of the council, say who you are. Do not hide behind a pseudonym. You will be found out, like the leader of Christchurch Council when he was unmasked as 'doomdodger' for his over-positive comments 'the council is doing a great job' (*Daily Telegraph*, 2012).

## Corrections and rebuttal

Correcting or rebutting inaccuracies or unfair criticisms in the media is a demanding task, especially when there is heavy pressure and anger to 'do something' from councillors, directors, board chair or the chief executive.

If there is a story running in the media or online that is blatantly wrong, and there are facts to show that, the priority is to be proactive and get these facts to the journalist, the editor on duty, or producer immediately by phone or e-mail. This will involve a professional – maybe heated – discussion that calls into question the journalist's story and sources. Always keep focused on what needs to be corrected. Hopefully agreement can be reached quickly and amendments made to the online story or corrections in the next edition of the newspaper or TV or radio bulletin. If there is no satisfactory outcome, bring together all the material and log all actions to prepare a formal complaint. Print off or download the offending story if online.

There will be other stories where there are complaints about the words in the headline, the quotes used (the councillor or director says he never said that), or some details are wrong or the story is misleading. Or that the council's statement has not been properly considered or incorporated in the story. The first task is to analyse the press story or the radio and TV transcript paragraph by paragraph or the recording frame by frame, underlining the areas of disagreement. Second, check if there are any breaches of the media's operating editorial guidelines.

For all BBC programmes, that is the BBC Editorial Code of Practice (or on issues of 'fairness' Ofcom); for newspapers currently the Press Complaints Commission (PCC) Editors' Code of Practice; and for all other television and radio broadcasting the Ofcom Broadcasting Code. The current codes should be available in every press office and studied by every council press officer. They cover a wide range of areas, accuracy, impartiality, privacy, harassment by journalists, intrusion, use of clandestine devices and secret filming and restrictions on journalists entering hospitals and care homes. The media can invoke a 'public interest' defence in their reporting and that covers, according to the PCC, detecting impropriety, protecting public health and safety, and 'preventing the public from being misled by an action or statement of an individual or organization' (PCC, 2012).

If there is believed to be a breach, it is best to take this up immediately with the media concerned. The media may agree to a correction in print, correct the online record, publish or broadcast an item on a future date giving the other side or publish a letter clarifying the matter. If this is not acceptable, a formal complaint is the next course to the appropriate authority, BBC, PCC or Ofcom. Complaints can take several weeks or months before a resolution or adjudication.

Most recent council or councillor complaints to the PCC, particularly on grounds of 'inaccuracy', have been resolved by a negotiated response, usually an agreed short statement in the newspaper. For example, a complaint in 2011 by Haringey Council in relation to a story in the *Evening Standard* about legal costs relating to the 'Baby P' case. It took six weeks for the correction to be published (see press complaints judgement). Such redress is unsatisfactory, given the time lapse and the prominence of the original story, compared to the correction.

Following Lord Justice Leveson's (2012) inquiry into the press, there will be a new tighter, regulatory framework and additional requirements for redress, but the key principles behind the Editors' Code will remain. The PCC will be replaced in late 2013 by a new regulatory body to adjudicate complaints, backed by a Royal Charter and separate powers to award damages.

Communications heads, and their staff, should be alert to these important changes when they happen.

## CASE STUDY

PRESS COMPLAINTS COMMISSION

COMPLAINANT NAME: **Haringey Council**

CLAUSES NOTED: 1 (Accuracy)

PUBLICATION: Evening Standard

### COMPLAINT:

Kevin Crompton, Chief Executive of Haringey Council, complained to the Press Complaints Commission that the newspaper had published the inaccurate claim that John Suddaby, the Council's former head of legal services, had spent 'thousands of pounds of taxpayers' money trying to "cover up"' failures by the Council that contributed to the death of Peter Connelly ('Baby P').

**RESOLUTION:**

The complaint was resolved when the PCC negotiated the publication of the following correction and apology, in the newspaper and online:

*Haringey Council*

*Our report on June 7 said that Haringey council's then-head of legal services John Suddaby led a bid costing thousands of pounds trying to 'cover up' failures that contributed to the death of Baby Peter Connelly.*

*In fact, Mr Suddaby and the council sought court orders restricting reporting of the case only to protect the welfare of children involved. We are happy to clarify this and are sorry for the misunderstanding.*

DATE PUBLISHED: 22/08/2011

# *Monitoring*

Keeping a log or record of all media enquiries and the response is not just best practice, but essential. This is usually maintained on a database accessible across the communications team to ensure consistency and continuity. The press officers and their manager are able to regularly review the workload and response times. The log should include additional notes on the contact from the service area in case of follow-up and any additional background. Care should be taken about data protection issues. Monitoring media coverage on the council and related issues is also a key duty of the press team and essential to evaluate PR effectiveness. This can be undertaken in-house or contracted to a press cuttings and media monitoring agency. Increasingly now, most of this is done online.

Evaluating both traditional media and online coverage can be undertaken on reach, mentions, key message penetration, and favourability of coverage or voice using a basic positive/neutral/negative scale or a more weighted ranking. The use of AVEs (advertising value equivalents) as a measure is now discredited and 'outlawed' by the PR professional bodies. AVEs measure the cost of media space and not the value of public relations (Barcelona Principles, 2010). Media measurement needs to be both quantitative and qualitative. The COI, the government's central office for information, before it was disbanded, set out a 'core standard evaluation metrics for PR evaluation' (COI, 2009).

Any organisation, including councils, photocopying or distributing press articles offline or online, need to have a licence from the Newspaper Licensing Authority. To keep NLA annual fees to the minimum many councils have severely restricted the distribution of their daily press cuttings offline and online; others now prepare a short summary statement of the main press stories with no links to the original articles. For example, Birmingham City

Council newsroom publishes a daily online 'media watch' summary (see **www.birminghamnewsroom.com**).

## Advertising

Taking paid adverts in the press or on radio or television is the only way to be certain the message exactly as presented is published in the commercial media. The Code of Recommended Practice states that any publicity – including advertising – must be cost-effective and non-political. Most public services will have negotiated rates directly with the local media or through an external media buyer.

Councils used to be big advertisers, particularly in local newspapers, with job vacancy and public notices adverts. But that has changed. With the financial pressures, there are now few job adverts being placed; those vacancies that are available are being advertised in job centres, the council's own website or government job websites. For example, Fife Council's spending on recruitment ads fell dramatically from £714,000 in 2007/08 to £23,000 in 2010/11 (BBC online, 2011). Public notice adverts for planning, licensing, roads etc are required by legislation dating back to the 1930s to be placed in a paid newspaper that serves the area. Councils, however, have been arguing that this is not only costly but unnecessary, when councils have at their disposal other cheaper and as effective channels, particularly their council publication, website, hyperlocal sites, e-mailing residents or through a central portal such as Tellme Scotland (**www.tellmescotland.gov.uk**). There is also a need to make further reforms and 'de-jargon the content of public notices'. In England and Wales it is estimated public notices cost councils a total of £67.85 million (Dale, 2012).

## Contact information

The authors, in researching this book, found it often difficult to find contact information on the communications or public relations team on many council websites. Council websites are now generally much more user friendly; their focus primarily on providing information to the residents of the area and promoting web transactions, from council tax payments to booking bulk uplifts. Many do not even have in their A–Z 'public relations' or 'communications' as a service! Or a mention in the 'contact your council' section. This is a gross omission.

Given that the website will be a starting point for many journalists and the public, councils should have a link from the home page to public relations or communications. Good practice is listing the communications team, with at least their specific portfolios, office contact numbers and e-mail.

# 10
# Communicating in a digital world

*As social media begins to mature, and the initial hype surrounding it subsides, it should be regarded as a credible channel that complements more traditional methods of speaking to the public. Used appropriately – to a targeted audience, with clear messages, and as part of a planned campaign – social media can be a powerful, cost-effective tool.*

DEAN SPURRELL, COMMUNICATIONS AND MARKETING MANAGER,
ASHFORD BOROUGH COUNCIL

**D**igital communication is an integral part of the contemporary landscape, impacting on the ways in which organisations communicate and operate. In May 2012, Twitter announced it had 10 million active users in the United Kingdom, superseding the combined total of those who buy national newspapers (Prescott, 2012). In 2009, Obama's successful election was in part attributed to the successful use of social media. Governments across the world have joined the digital bandwagon; however, now that the dust is settling, reflection on its use is beginning to happen.

Although 76 per cent of adults in the United Kingdom have access to broadband (Ofcom, 2011), Yaxley (2011) suggests that there is still a lack of equal access due to factors including location, age, educational attainment, gender, disability and ethnicity. In 2012, Westminster and Kensington and Chelsea Councils partnered with O2 to provide free Wi-Fi across the boroughs in an attempt to bridge the digital divide. While this provided broadband to residents and visitors, it could not reach those without the necessary equipment. Digital will therefore, as a channel, remain in a mix, selected on its ability to reach a desired audience. The challenge for councils is to reach both the digitally enabled and those without access – though these aren't always exclusive in an increasingly networked society. The impact of online communication is, however, much more far reaching than merely offering an expanded and more cost-effective range of channels. Reynolds (2012) notes that discussion in the PR industry has moved beyond the use of digital 'tools' towards a re-consideration of organisational approach. Yaxley (2011) identifies that the revolutionary aspect of the digital world is the ease in which communities can be networked and communicate independently.

'The expectations are growing on councils to engage, work openly, be more accountable and move quicker on issues' (Gibson, 2010). The digital environment has changed the working practice of local authorities. The broadcast model of communication has shifted towards fulfilling expectations of at least a two-way approach, in a world in which many to many communication is taking place regardless of organisational involvement.

It is far more risky for organisations not to engage than it is to engage: 'Citizens will still use these networks to talk about you whether you add your voice to the conversation or not. The choice for councils is stark: get on board, or get left behind' (Gibson, 2010). With reduced budgets, local authorities must re-engineer the way they work; digital communication provides opportunity to listen more, engage and involve communities in service delivery and design.

Challenges include changing the culture of staff and management to recognise that messaging and reputation can no longer be controlled and in embedding the technical knowledge of online participation in staff development.

Some local authorities have, however, been slow to adapt. Socitm research (2012) indicated that 54 per cent of councils still restrict access to Facebook and Twitter.

The approach that local authorities must take to operate in this digital environment will be embedded throughout the book. This chapter will explore the potential methods of digital communication that local authorities can utilise drawing on emerging good practice across the United Kingdom.

# Digital communication: moving beyond the tools towards the method

If councils do nothing else, they should at least understand who is online and what is being said about them. Grunig (2012) believes the greatest value of digital communication is in its use for environmental scanning.

For those actively engaging in digital communication, there is also the potential to deliver more convenient and personalised information in a more cost-effective way. New technologies drive down the cost of traditional communication such as printed materials, call centres and face to face (Socitm, 2012). Effective, proactive communication significantly reduces expensive one-on-one enquiries.

However, technology in itself is not the solution; there should be a sound business for going digital. Research should drive channel selection with on-going monitoring of content, delivery and reach as would be expected with more traditional choices. Signposting is key to driving the digital uptake. The challenge for communicators is in integrating and ensuring the consistency of messaging across multiple channels.

The Local Government Information Unit (LGiU) (2011) suggests that councils should prioritise e-mail in line with 'where the eyeballs currently are' but that social media should be developed in acknowledgement of its growth. The LGiU recommend that local authorities develop an opt-in subscription platform on the website, which allows visitors to select relevant information and preferred format. Councils can support the public in building their own bespoke communication portfolio by offering a range of categories, channels and signposting to partner organisations.

Most significantly, the potential digital audience is global, and propels a local authority into an international community. Online communication is not just about providing residents with what they want, when they want it and how they want it. Reynolds (2012) highlights that going digital enables a local authority to collaborate with the rest of the world. Camden Council engaged with a global audience in the redesign of their website; launching a blog and inviting readers to get involved, expressing their likes and sharing their thoughts on Twitter.

## Websites – interactional and transactional platforms

Local authority websites in the last 10 years have moved from being static providers of information to becoming interactive and transactional. In times of austerity it is the potential of websites to provide services that has been of greatest interest. Fox (2010) proposed that moving 30 per cent of government services online could generate savings of £1.3 billion a year, rising to £2.2 billion if 50 per cent went digital. Research undertaken by Socitm (2012) identified that local authority web transactions cost 15p on average, compared to phone costs of £2.83 and face-to-face transactions of £8.62. In 2011, the most visited communication channel in the United Kingdom was the government website (Azyan, 2011). Providing visitors to websites with easily accessible information can potentially divert them from seeking out more expensive ways to communicate. In driving down costs, it is crucial that local authorities identify the most popular transactions, clearly signposting these on the home page and ensuring that they are user friendly.

Ofcom (2011) identified that over a quarter of adults and almost half of teenagers now have a smartphone. If the trend continues, which saw 59 per cent of them acquire their phone that year, then local authority websites, like those of any other sector, must be geared up to meet the demand, providing content that can be easily accessed from a mobile device.

Providing website content that is free and easy to share can also extend the reach of your messaging. Monmouthshire County Council changed the licensing agreement of its website in 2012 to Open Government Licensing to enable developers and citizens to freely access and use data from the website to build applications that have a positive impact on people's lives. People are free to copy, adapt, distribute and transmit information published on the website. This is their first step in becoming an 'open data' authority, providing non-sensitive information free of charge to be recycled and amplified across the web.

## E-mail – a communication method to prioritise

LGiU (2011) found that councils identify e-mail notifications, Twitter and Facebook as the key priority for future digital communications. While many believe that e-mail will soon be superseded by social media, research suggests the opposite. E-mail use is predicted to rise to 1.9 billion by 2013 (Azyan, 2011). Research also suggests social media encourages more not less use of e-mail and that Generation Y who have grown up with this technology and who are now beginning to enter the workplace would be more reluctant to give up e-mail and text messaging than social media (Azyan, 2011).

E-mail, then, rightly remains a local authority priority, driving website usage and enabling measurement of click throughs and opened e-mails – more quantifiable than attempting to measure the more elusive, often intangible benefits of social media.

Norfolk County Council launched a personalised e-mail subscription service in 2005. By 2010, over 12,000 residents and businesses had opted in, and 1 million personalised messages had been sent, 68 per cent of which directed users to the council website (Govdelivery, nd). E-mail alerts sent to county councillors alone, when the latest committee reports were published, are estimated to have saved the council £20,000 per annum.

E-mail and text messaging alerts provide personalised immediate information, while social media has the potential to join up these subscribers, providing a platform for discussion and interaction on subjects that they have already expressed an interest in (LGiU, 2011).

## Social media

The CIPR Social Media Panel define social media as 'the term given to Internet and mobile based channels and tools that allow users to interact with each other and share opinions and content. As the term implies, social media involves the building of communities or networks, encouraging participation and engagement' (CIPR, 2011).

However, the term social media can be misleading. Socitm (2012) identified that one of the barriers to local authorities providing open access was the belief that staff would waste time. However, using social media as part of issues and crisis management is beyond that of the communication department. Kay (2012) suggests that social media enthusiasts across the council should be identified in advance and be used to provide support during a crisis.

Reynolds (2012) suggests the value of holding social media surgeries in embedding good practice and encouraging staff from across the organisation to monitor the environment. These sessions also identify those who could be drawn on in an emergency. Staff need to be trained and trusted to get on. After all, if people are recruited to do a job, they should be trusted not to spend all day on Facebook or be inappropriate. Reynolds (2012) also dismisses the idea of instilling a vibe or tone to those communicating online on behalf of the organisation. She believes that this isn't necessary if local authorities are recruiting the right people.

In addition to identifying and managing issues, and providing a cost-effective means of communication, social media can also bring savings through enabling a wider community to contribute to finding a solution. Collaborating and encouraging the co-design of services also builds relationships at a time when trust in organisations is at an all-time low.

## Blogs

Blogs, which are a type of website that allow the owner to publish web pages in chronological order, are commonly used by public figures within local authorities to share and exchange their views. Although some blogs attract huge readership, most have a small following. Live blogs, however, are increasingly being used by local authorities as a way of communicating with those who are unable to attend events such as consultations. Live blogs provide an online opportunity for those with a mobile device to participate in real time. Monmouthshire County Council held a series of 'big tent events' in 2011 that aimed to generate genuine conversation between staff and local people around the issues that mattered to them. The launch event 'Your places, your way' was an open session in which people, attending both in person and online decided what they wanted to talk about. At the end of the session they decided together what the most important points from the conversation to take forward were. The live blog also acts as an online record of the event, signposted by the website and social media channels, for those unable to participate or attend.

## Twitter

Although research undertaken by the Local Government Information Unit (LGiU), suggest that less than 1 per cent of the population follow their council on Twitter, Reynolds (2012) highlights the power of influence. Although acknowledging that the percentage may be small, she suggests that those engaged can be influential and spread the message through their own networks, which cannot be easily tracked. The reach and reputational impact of tools such as Twitter go beyond the local community; social media propels the organisation into a global forum. A Swedish follower of Monmouthshire Council on Twitter, transpired to be an ex pat, who communicated what was happening in the county back to his mother who was still resident. The word of mouth value generated by influential followers of social media is elusive: 'Would your managers ask you to prove the value of a telephone? How can we capture the true impact of social media?' (Reynolds, 2012).

LGiU research (2011) recommends local authorities use e-mail alerts and newsletters that are opted into by the resident, which then enable councils to signpost residents towards social media channels. Reynolds (2012) supports this as the key to developing followers on Twitter.

Many local authorities hold events such as a councillors' Q and A on Twitter, which enables those with mobile phones to follow and engage in the session in real time. This channel, in addition to a live blog, is an important part of the mix in engaging with those who are digitally connected and unable to make a visit to the Town Hall.

Walsall Council has used Twitter to raise awareness of the range of services they provide. Over a 24-hour period, as part of the Walsall 24 initiative, they sent tweets that aimed to capture the diversity of the work, the most powerful sent from staff on the ground in real time. They also ran a week-long initiative to highlight the role of social care workers, focusing on the calls made to social workers. The tweets sent from their health and social care Twitter account @whocareswalsall were retweeted by the Walsall Council account @walsallcouncil, raising both awareness of social care issues and the social care Twitter.

Twitter is an important part of monitoring what is being said about your organisation, spotting issues and identifying influential people. Hootsuite will identify any mentions of your organisation or related issues, and enable you to identify people to follow, providing a gateway into direct engagement. Hashtags also allow you to search for tweets related to a particular subject. #local gov will provide every tweet related to that subject from all over the world.

Social media and Twitter in particular has been recognised by many local authorities as an effective way to reach people quickly and to receive instant feedback. The 'Gritter Twitter' was adopted by many councils to update and work with the local community on keeping the highways accessible throughout the winter.

In 2011, the Information Commissioner's Office (ICO) validated the use of Twitter as a medium for sending Freedom of Information (FoI) requests. Monmouthshire County Council demands that FoI requests by Twitter include:

- '@monmouthshirecc': the Twitter @username so the council is aware of the request;
- name;

- contact details (eg e-mail address or home address);
- question.

eg '@monmouthshirecc FoI request: What did you spend on recycling collection 2009–10? Jo Blogs, joblogs@hotmail.com'

As tweets are restricted to 140 characters, the FoI request and contact details could be blogged and then sent as a link via twitter, eg '@monmouthshirecc FoI request: **www.joblogs.com/foirequestblogpost**'

Once the Monmouthshire team receive the tweet, they send it to the FoI team who will ensure the answer is blogged or e-mailed within 20 working days of getting the tweet. If the response is requested by Twitter, the team will reply with a link to a blog post with the answer.

In addition to monitoring how other local authorities are using social media, asking your own followers what information they would like should also guide content. There are a range of digital tools to measure engagement and influence, including Klout and Tweetlevel. Measuring the more intangible benefits of social media such as goodwill and reputation continue to remain elusive.

## Facebook

Coventry Council has more than 10,000 fans on Facebook, bucking the trend of unpopular local authority Facebook sites by repositioning its offer. Instead of presenting itself as the local council, it has instead designed a Facebook page around place. Wakeman (2009) suggests that creating pages around subjects that people have already developed an affinity with will be more successful than those focusing purely on the council as a distant corporate body. In Medway, they have used Facebook to promote theatre and events, tapping into a group of people who have already mobilised around an interest. This provides a good starting point for any Facebook page. Similarly, Birmingham City Council, which is one of the most prolific users of Facebook, has over 30 pages each dedicated to a different subject ranging from parks to dog adoption.

Opportunities presented by crisis situations such as the bad winter weather can attract fans who are keen to find out about school closures, and other weather related information. Blackburn with Darwen Council set up a BwDWinter Facebook page in 2010, which is estimated to have diverted 10,000 calls from being made to the customer services team, saving the council nearly £8,000. Positioning the local authority as an authority and providing timely, correct information builds trust within the online community.

In Monmouthshire, the Youth Service has set up a Facebook page, as a way of following up on face-to-face contact. They recognise that on the ground youth work can't be replaced but recognise the impact of Facebook. The page was developed following research that indicated 100 per cent of young people interviewed already used Facebook.

Dan Davies, Inclusion Worker, said: 'It's fantastic because it's being used not just as a way to push out messages to young people in the county (although it does do that), it has become the hub of all social activity, has saved the service money and is a genuine example of using tools to serve a purpose not just doing Facebook "because we should".'

The Youth Team manage the account, but there are plans to develop a team of young people who will eventually be the gateway for all the service's social media. The site is open and young people can post their own photos or tag themselves to images uploaded by the Youth Service. These will then appear on their profile.

The team recently used Facebook for organising end of year proms across the county. They set up a separate business page, from which all the ticketing was done through PayPal. Students bought their tickets through Facebook, which also enabled the organisers to ID them on the door using their profile picture. This approach has saved resources in the production and distribution of marketing materials.

Inappropriate or abusive posts have been a rarity with fans understanding the protocols of being part of the site. The page was set up first as an information hub, and once it became interactive a moderator was introduced to filter content, keeping posts hidden that include any of the terms agreed to be inappropriate.

The Youth Service Facebook page was set up before the council opened access and is an excellent example of why staff across the council should have access to use social media.

## *Flickr*

Flickr is a photo-sharing website that allows people to share their photos with friends, providing an online site to upload photos and tag keywords. Flickr groups usually mobilise around an interest or place. Many local authorities have initiated Flickr groups or engaged with those that already exist.

Like other social media groups it is a good way for local authorities to directly collaborate with the community. The first uploads by new members are checked before they are published and copyright remains with the photographer who may choose to sign up to a creative commons licence, which enables their images to be shared with others on the understanding they are acknowledged.

In Walsall, in 2012, the Flickr group, set up by residents, had 150 members and over 6,000 images. Walsall Council recognised that it would be a good idea to showcase these photos taken by their own community on their website. The web team designed a Flickr friendly header and a comment was posted on the Walsall Flickr page outlining what they were looking for. They asked people to tag 'walsallweb' if they wanted their picture to be considered. Over 400 images were tagged for consideration in three days. Images including people were avoided due to consent. The first image of a canal side was linked back to the original Flickr image and received over 150 hits in two weeks.

Dan Slee, Senior Press and Publicity Officer at Walsall Council, who initiated the scheme, suggests local government PR practitioners adopt the following Flickr approach:

1 Be a disseminator – use Flickr as a way of sharing council stock photography with the wider community, once permission has been granted.

2 Be a campaigner – create a Flickr group for a campaign. Walsall Council set up Willenhall, Aldridge and Darlaston in Bloom Flickr group to support their entry to Britain in Bloom, 2010.

3 Be a way to open-up museums – create a Flickr group for a museum exhibition.

4 Be an enabler – set-up a Flickr meet, providing access for photographers in a council building such as the Town Hall.

5 Be a Flickr Twitterer – link to pictures via Twitter. Pictures are more popular than straightforward links, brightening up your stream.

6 Be a marketeer – use Flickr images for marketing. Leaflets can be brightened up with Flickr shots, once permission has been granted.

7 Be a Flickr webbie – use Flickr on the council website.

8 Be a civic pride builder – create a Flickr group for an area.

9 Be a stock photography user – the Creative Commons is a licence that allows the use of shots with certain conditions. There is a category that allows for not for profit use, for example.

10 Be a digital divide bridger – featuring 'favourite walks' or a way to celebrate heritage is an excellent way to encourage people to log on.

(Slee, 2012)

# Social media evaluation

The Barcelona Principles (2010) state that social media can and should be measured, yet the CIPR (2011) acknowledge the difficulty in capturing the full impact of social media. The CIPR taskforce produced a series of recommendations focusing on directing social media outcomes; that these need to be defined in advance and are likely to span multiple business goals, to include a starter set of KPIs; which should consider quality over quantity, and that content sourcing should be part of the evaluation.

Social media is difficult to evaluate on its own as it usually works alongside a range of other approaches that aim to bring about an action within a target group. While followers and friends can be measured, these don't reflect the influence or the impact of engagement. The CIPR (2011) acknowledge that social media measurement is 'a work in progress' and echo the concerns and standpoints of many local government PR practitioners engaged in social media activity. Influence is key and identifying who you are engaging with on the web and why, and understanding the networks they are involved in, builds a rationale for you to allocate resources. As Reynolds (2012) highlighted, the benefits of social media PR are often intangible. If recognised to be part of the relationship-building process espoused by Grunig and Hunt (1984), the concept of capturing an exact return on investment will continue to remain elusive.

# The impact of social media on organisational approach

Providing open access to all staff across the local authority is important if staff are to understand the issues that relate to their work, if they are to network with peers and if they are to engage in conversations that will be taking place regardless of whether they join them or not.

Social media guidelines and training can be embedded in induction and social media surgeries held to share good practice, troubleshoot and to build a network of enthusiasts across the organisation. What is clear is that engaging in social media is beyond the remit of a single communications department. It should be part of the work of every member of staff – even if that is only to monitor the environment that relates to an area of work.

Barriers to providing access to all staff have commonly focused around fears that staff would waste time or be inappropriate (Socitm, 2012). Reynolds (2012) points out that this is a problem of recruitment and that when staff are trusted there are very few transgressions. Similarly, staff who have established Facebook pages for the community with open access have found that there is an implicit understanding of behaviour among its users.

A local authority's Code of Conduct and the Publicity Code apply on and offline. Data protection, legality issues, copyright and dealing with challenging members of the public in a professional way all apply when engaging in social media. Local authority staff must make their identity known online, and if wishing to set up a blog or social media account on behalf of the council it is good practice that they first present a business case to their managers outlining their rationale. Staff using social media on behalf of the council should be alert to political restrictions (see Chapter 2, page 37).

Walsall Council has established an online Social Media Directory to record public sector social media platforms such as Twitter, Facebook, Flickr and LinkedIn. The Directory was launched by the council who recognised that the public and local services needed to be able to access an up-to-date listing, particularly in times of emergency. This also provides an overview for residents and other stakeholders of the ways in which they can receive the information digitally.

Those local authorities that have open access are clear that social media can improve the way the organisation works both in empowering residents but also in opening up a world of contact and knowledge to staff and elected members.

Local authorities need to remain ahead of the expectations of consumers. LGiU research (2011) identified that just a quarter of council staff used social media to receive news and information personally. Local authorities need to get ahead of the curve.

Social media enables staff to make connections with people and build relationships. The potential of social media as an engagement mechanism is what PR practitioners should have been waiting for.

# The future

Social media is just one aspect of the digital landscape, and while providing opportunity to finally engage directly with our publics, it is in the mix, with e-mail remaining a local authority priority. LGiU (2011) best captured the relationship between social media and other digital channels in recognising that social media has the ability to join up groups who have already expressed an interest in a particular subject.

The surge in the use of mobile devices and smartphones (Ofcom, 2011) should be a consideration in any online developments. Local authorities are in a position to be the trailblazers in digital communication, with a large and diverse audience with whom they can pilot projects. The opportunity to collaborate and co-design services online has the potential to save money and build trust.

> The whole concept of digital engagement is to become one of the voices, to be part of the network. Once people understand that councils are made up of humans trying to solve problems, an organisation made up of people who care about their work, it recasts the concept of a local authority not as a controlling organisation but as one who people trust to possess the requisite knowledge to guide them.
>
> (Reynolds, 2012)

In order to be part of the network, local authority staff must be ahead of the curve, able to meet the expectations of the on and offline community. In understanding what these expectations are to begin with, digital engagement has a very important part to play.

---

**Checklist**

- Consider digital approach rather than digital tools.

- Work openly, be more accountable and move quickly on issues.

- Recognise many to many communication is already taking place, regardless of organisational involvement.

- Listen more, engage and involve communities in service delivery and design.

- Embed technical knowledge of online participation in staff development.

- Ensure open access is part of organisational practice.

- Develop interactive and transactional websites.

- Join up groups who have already expressed an interest in a particular subject through social media.

## KEY WORDS

Digital communication; networked society; engagement; accountable; global audience; interactive; transactional; conversation; transparency; monitoring; trust.

**CASE STUDY**   CIPR Local Public Services Awards – Digital Excellence

My County Council… Anywhere – Mobile Phone Project

Northamptonshire County Council

### 1. Objectives

In May 2011, Northamptonshire County Council launched the mobile phone project; two mobile apps and a mobile friendly website. The key objective was to transform how services were delivered to customers. The iPhone app, Android app and mobile web browser offered free, easy access to council information anytime, anywhere. The council wanted to exploit the latest technologies available to their customers and engage in the most cost-effective and convenient way.

The corporate aim was to achieve a 20 per cent channel shift over a year; moving customer contacts and transactions from more expensive channels like telephone and face to face, to less expensive self-serve web and digital channels.

Northamptonshire County Council would be the first local authority in the country to offer the complete mobile service – across Apple, Android and the mobile website. They aimed to achieve 3,000 app (Apple and Android combined) downloads within the first six months.

## 2. Strategy and Implementation

The strategy was to offer customers a self-serve application to meet their expectations which was easy and convenient to use.

The Council recognised it had a duty to ensure residents were able to access their services in a variety of ways and understood that mobile phones have quickly become a powerful tool and a huge area of growth and opportunity for any organisation. Smartphones with internet capability now account for 82 per cent of all phone contracts and by 2015, it is anticipated that 70 per cent of all internet access will be made using mobile phones. Therefore without this work, council customers who may have migrated from their PCs could be expected to ring the council if they couldn't use their preferred mobile channel.

The Council took the most popular pages from the website to develop the content of the app and browser. These included:

- the latest council news;

- contact details which could be saved in a phone directory;

- finding the nearest facility; library, recycling centre, country park, registration office with route mapping;

- bus times and nearest bus stops;

- council job vacancies;

- school term dates and closures;

- consultation information;

- schools directory – by distance or school name;

- free school meals form.

The Council worked in partnership with the University of Northampton to develop the apps and a local Northampton company Citric Technology, who support the website to develop the mobile web browser.

The marketing strategy, which aimed to raise awareness and encourage downloads, branded 'My County Council… anywhere!' involved:

- App Store, Android Market listings – achieving a ranking of 9th in the Top Free Reference category listings in the App Store.

- O2 Segmented text messaging to 27,000 Northamptonshire customers with iPhones or Androids.

- E-newsletters to over 30,000 contacts.

- Internal communications to council staff.

- Web pages on the council website – on the homepage and pages with services that featured within the apps.

- Twitter updates to over 1,400 followers.

- Radio Northampton interview with a Councillor.

- PR in local newspapers and the University of Northampton.

- A Quick Response (QR) Code – for scanning into your phone that automatically directs users to the website.

- Competition to win an iPhone 4 donated by O2.

The project was launched in three stages, starting with the iPhone app, followed by the mobile browser and the Android app. The staged implementation provided time to learn from customer feedback prior to the subsequent launch.

## 3. Creativity

The project was designed and developed around the customer using a technology that many of the council residents were already familiar with. Working with O2 to deliver a cost-effective and extremely targeted marketing campaign, and using e-newsletters allowed the council to maximise their return on investment.

The competition to win an iPhone ran for three months. Designed to appeal to a wider audience including those without a smartphone, the competition received over 2,500 entries.

Phase two is being planned to include service specific apps.

## 4. Budget

The total marketing spend was £5,788 in a campaign reaching over 73,000 residents.

## 5. Evaluation

The target of achieving 3,000 downloads in six months was reached ahead of schedule. For every person that uses the app instead of calling, the Council estimates it will save £2.22. 3,000 downloads used once will save the Council £6,600, exceeding £26,000 over the year if this trend continues.

# 11
# Communicating in a crisis

*The best laid plans are worthless if they cannot be communicated. Speed is of the essence. A crisis simply will not wait. Tell it all, tell it fast, tell it truthfully.*

**MICHAEL REGESTER AND JUDY LARKIN, 2008**

Over the last 30 years, academic literature and professional case studies have examined the relationship between issues management and crisis communications. An issue has been defined as an unsettled matter which is ready for a decision (Jones and Chase, 1979: 11) and by Hainsworth (1990: 3) as 'a point of conflict between an organisation and one or more of its publics'. In the digitally connected global environment there is more potential than ever for issues, which may once have been regarded as being of little significance, to develop into full blown crises. Yaxley (2011) suggests that this new environment has accelerated the speed in which crises develop, threatening the linear concept of issues management and its potential to avert a crisis.

In local government the range of stakeholders is extensive and monitoring these relationships on and offline is an activity that the whole organisation needs to be engaged in. Organisational behaviour is under more scrutiny than ever before. Regester and Larkin (2008) highlight the erosion of trust in those in authority following critical media reports spotlighting corporate failure and corruption in the financial and public service sectors. Behaving responsibly should be of paramount importance in this landscape amplified by the internet and the Freedom of Information.

Coombs (1995: 455) distinguishes crisis types based on the source of responsibility and degree of intentionality. He differentiates between internal sources such as poor operating procedures and external sources such as acts of god and terrorism. Both internal and external crisis types can be applied to local authorities who must consider not only their employees but their responsibilities to the community they serve.

The way that local authorities anticipate, plan for and act during an emergency can first and foremost save lives (LGA, nd). In recent years local authorities have dealt with flooding, swine flu, rail disasters, riots and terrorism. Public relations should be at the heart of issues, crisis and emergency management – communicating key messages has the potential to influence behaviour and keep people safe.

Preparing for an emergency is a legal obligation and 'Communicating with the Public' is one of the seven civil protection duties (Civil Contingencies Act, Part One, 2004). 'Warning and informing the public is no longer a nice to do but a must do' (Kay, 2012). The most difficult to plan for and anticipate are those situations for which no blueprint exists, and where the organisational response may act as a case study for scrutiny at a local, national and international level.

In the past it was generally held that if an organisation acted responsibly and engaged in effective issues management, they should be able to avoid development of most crises other than unforeseen physical disaster. However, digital communication has skewed this worldview. This chapter will explore the challenges of issues, crisis and emergency management in this emerging landscape.

# Issues management

Jones and Chase (1979) defined issues management as the process that companies could use to identify, analyse and manage emerging issues, so that they could respond to them *before* they became public knowledge. The impact of social media redefines issues management as public awareness has the potential to be immediate – the challenge and opportunity for organisations is to engage in discussion as soon as possible. The 'behind the scenes' stage that many issues management models include (Meng, 1992) has been eroded by social media, which plays out the potential and emerging stages on a public platform. Media coverage, which was recognised as being critical in advancement of the issue, is present at the outset and accelerates the speed with which issues develop.

'An issue represents a gap between corporate practice and stakeholder expectations' (Regester and Larkin, 2008: 44). When this gap fails to be closed and there is public outrage, an issue becomes a crisis and communication becomes much more reactive.

Potential local authority issues include changes made to the performance or delivery of services, budget cuts and the implementation of new legislation. For each service area there are a host of potential issues that should be identified through experience of what has happened to the authority before and others like it. Some issues such as critical inspection reports can be anticipated and included in forward planning, while new issues can be identified through monitoring traditional and online media. What is immediately clear is that this work is beyond that of a communications department and should be integral to the work of the whole organisation.

'A key maxim for avoiding a collision course with activists is for companies to switch on and monitor the radar' (Regester and Larkin, 2008: 15). This extends beyond identification to profiling personalities, networks and working practices. Social media monitoring tools such as Social Mention can be used to identify the top 10 people discussing an organisation online and the most commonly associated subjects. More often than not activists are seeking solutions, and establishing relationships ahead of an emerging issue is good practice. They will also have potential networks for you to engage with.

# Risk assessment

An important part of any issues and crisis management strategy should be a 'risk assessment' that identifies and analyses the level of perceived or real risk associated with issues.

Effective risk communication requires understanding of the dynamic of public emotion and the working practices of advocacy groups and the media. It is often unrealistic to change public opinion about the size of the risk. Emphasis should instead be placed on building trust and commitment to control, reduce or contain risk.

Regester and Larkin developed a series of questions for organisations to consider when identifying issues to prioritise:

- Are there linkages to other issues, and are there legacy problems?
- How strong are the key activists?
- How far have the dynamics of the issue lifecycle developed?
- What impact will dealing with this issue have on the organisation?
- What are the risks and opportunities if we ignore the issue?
- How are the company's key stakeholders likely to react and how strong is our support base on the issue?
- How confident are we that we can influence the issue in the way we want?
- What potential resources will be required?
- What are the potential benefits from actively seeking a solution?

(Adapted from Winter and Steger, 1998, in Regester and Larkin, 2008: 16)

# Emergency planning

Emergency planning is now a legal obligation for local authorities and communicating with the public one of the seven civil duties (Civil Contingencies Act, Part One, 2004).

The Emergency Planning College have developed an Integrated Emergency Management Model to capture how agencies should work together in an emergency. The Local Resilience Forum, which is required to meet twice a year, includes representatives from across local public and voluntary services, the military, Environment Agency, business and utilities to strategically co-ordinate emergency planning. This Forum usually has a number of sub groups, which commonly includes a 'Warning and Informing' group who are tasked with formulating the emergency communications plan.

## Crisis planning documents

The planning documents should be clear, well indexed and consistently formatted. The Emergency Planning College (2012) suggest the following index to guide content:

**FIGURE 11.1**   Integrated emergency management

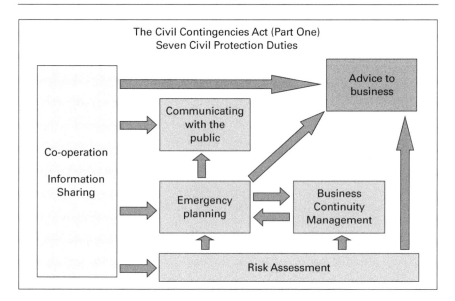

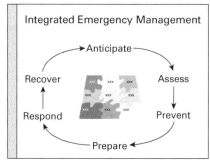

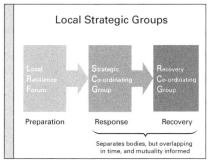

- version control;
- distribution list;
- aims: to warn, inform, and reassure;
- objectives (of this plan);
- alerting the public (when and by whom);
- alerting the public (radio, online, social media);
- roles and responsibilities (spokesperson, MLO etc);
- policies and protocols (eg naming of victims, interviews with survivors, pooling, VIP visits);
- checklists;
- emergency response kit (grabbing contents and maintenance);
- app 1 Media contacts;
- app 2 Internal contacts;
- app 3 Media inquiries logsheet.

This provides an outline guide and starting position that should be adapted to circumstance and be regularly updated with particular attention to the contact section. Social media should be an integral part of the plan.

Hillingdon Council have identified that having letter and briefing templates, prepared in advance to update information, can save valuable time in a crisis (LGID, 2009a). These are now a part of their emergency planning documents.

Partnership work is key and relations already in place with fire, police and health communication teams are crucial to effective practice. The plan should include an agreed protocol outlining who leads on communication in a range of potential emergency situations and how the information and messages will be disseminated across partner organisations.

The police provide greater reassurance than local or central government in a major emergency (Kay, 2012). In health-related matters, the NHS will lead, though this isn't always clear cut. In Hillingdon, until there was diagnosis of the cause of death of a pupil, the council communications team took the lead, speaking on behalf of the school.

The key to effective management of a crisis is to maintain effective control over the release of information and ensure that no unauthorised or incorrect information is distributed from formal channels. Monitoring social media is crucial in both rebutting inaccuracies and in gathering information.

In NHS Sussex, they have role cards that detail procedures and processes that need to be followed by the different members of the PR team during an emergency. The cards, which are A4, include bullet-pointed actions for roles such as the communication manager. These are presented in sequential order from assembling at the designated location for emergency planning through to protocols for working with partners and detailed information on organising press conferences. Laura Skelcey, Senior Communications

Manager at NHS Sussex, who utilised these cards through the swine flu pandemic, noted that they provided quick reference to the most important jobs, assuring the team of their roles and responsibilities so they could get on with the response.

Designated media spokespeople for key areas should be identified and receive media training in advance of the emergency. Annual refresher courses can be shared with other partner organisations to keep the costs down and managed in-house if there is the expertise. Contact details should also include key figures within the community such as religious leaders so they can be kept informed and keep their own networks abreast of the situation. The plan should also consider how staff from across the organisation could provide communication support. Kay (2012) suggests tapping into social media enthusiasts, who could be involved in monitoring conversations online. These staff should be identified in advance, receive training and be included in the plan.

Kay (2012) suggests that when you think you have a plan it is useful to ask what if? Possible scenarios might include considering the position of your organisation as a victim or when it is to blame and how an emergency would be managed across multiple sites or across boundaries.

## When it happens

It is crucial that the communication team work closely with the crisis management or emergency planning team. Access to restricted and accurate information is essential and that the facts are verified before dissemination. Public safety is of paramount importance and key messages should advise the public to 'Go in, Stay in, Tune in' (HM Government, 2004). If the crisis is expected to run into the night consideration should be given to sending half the staff home.

The press team should act as quickly as possible to deliver accurate information and keep channels of communication open where there are delays in obtaining this. An important part of the role of the communications team should be in predicting how the public will react and advising on what information they need at critical points. One of the most important lessons Newcastle City Council learnt in handling the chemical contamination of a stretch of land called Walker Riverside, was that it was essential to include non-technical staff in their meetings as they could ask the obvious questions sometimes missed by experts (LGID, 2009b). Communication should be in plain English, and terms should be tested to ensure that messages are clear and don't cause greater confusion. The 2009 Influenza Pandemic Report (Hine, 2010) highlighted the importance of the public clearly understanding the information, as certain terms used during the pandemic were unclear and caused confusion.

In Newcastle, people on the ground such as neighbourhood wardens, housing office managers and people involved in regeneration projects surrounding the contaminated land, could also have provided a valuable 'steer' as to what the community was feeling. Having established social networks already in place facilitates this process.

Transparency is key, and the organisation must continue to communicate, engage in online conversations and not hide information or refuse to comment. If the council is at fault, apologise swiftly and sincerely. The crisis surrounding Haringey Council and Baby P escalated as the *Sun* newspaper demanded an apology and resignation of the director of children's services, generating over 2 million online supporters and a protest march on Downing Street. It was at this point that the Secretary of State intervened.

It is important that communication is proactive and that regular updates are provided on a one-to-one basis where possible. Staff and service providers are an important group to keep informed and up to date as these are often the face of the organisation, the brand champions communicating directly with the public.

The communication messages must change through the lifecycle of the crisis, in tune with developments and in response to your audiences.

Ten principles of crisis management:

1 Be prepared.
2 Provide background information.
3 Manage information flow.
4 Agree ground rules.
5 Be authoritative.
6 Keep talking.
7 Say you are sorry.
8 Ensure accuracy.
9 Be sensitive.
10 Learn the lessons.

## Effective media handling in a crisis

The key spokesperson should be identified as soon as possible and briefed for the media response. A communication vacuum should be avoided as this will be filled by speculation and online conversation. Speed is of the essence; journalists driven by the nanosecond news agenda will find information from wherever they can if official sources do not supply it.

The summary statement should clarify:

- what happened (or what you know currently);
- what you are doing – focus on the consequences not the cause;
- when will you give your next release;
- where to get further information.

Admit what you don't know at this stage – be candid and honest. Manage expectations. Organisations should never accept liability, there will always be a formal enquiry.

Langford (2009) suggests that the spokesperson should follow a 5Cs model. First expressing *concern*; talking with *clarity* in conveying the key messages; taking *control* of the messages, the situation and the environment; speaking with *confidence* and finally demonstrating *competence* reflecting how the organisation will handle the situation. In a major crisis, a press office should be established to field media enquiries and release information. In hazardous situations this should be as close to the scene as possible. The crisis press team should focus on ensuring a constant flow of correct up-to-date information, monitoring media coverage and issuing corrections where there are errors in reporting.

The Pitt Review (2008) identified that Local Resilience Forums need to agree in advance a clear process that enables prompt sign-off from senior management. The Review also recommended concise but regular releases, with new information clearly highlighted. This practice also supports the generation of content for social media sites.

Developing a strong media culture throughout the organisation will provide an invaluable platform during a crisis; officers and members should already be aware of media guidelines and protocols.

Crisis situations provide the opportunity for organisations to demonstrate visible leadership. The Pitt Review, following the floods of 2007, urged local authorities to be proactive and to secure live broadcast of a prominent spokesperson as soon as possible to lead their community through the crisis. In a culture of digital communication, television is still regarded as the most trusted medium in the United Kingdom (see page 173). The value of a broadcast interview or statement cannot therefore be underestimated.

Kay (2012) suggests that providing journalists with what they need, 'loos, views and news', will usually keep them satisfied. He recommends 'letting them get on with it' and not interfering with what is aired. The BBC are bound by Editorial Guidelines, which requires coverage to 'balance the public interest in full and accurate reporting against the need to be compassionate and to avoid an unjustified infringement of privacy' (BBC, online, nd).

Contingency plans should outline where the media would be located, taking into account the potential number of vehicles and staff. In a major emergency the BBC could deploy over 100 people. In addition to the local, national and international media, Kay (2012) reminds emergency planners to be prepared for the trade press. Technical experts should be available at press briefings to answer more specialist enquiries.

It is good practice for a crisis bag to be prepared containing everything a communicator would need at the scene of an emergency. Contents could include technical equipment; tablet, dongle, mobile, charger, radio, refreshments, waterproofs/high-vis jacket, business cards, contacts, identification and a copy of the emergency communications plan.

The media should be invited to emergency planning exercises, as this will provide them with insight to the contingency measures in place and commitment of the organisation to continue to develop these.

# The role of digital communication

Crisis and emergency situations clearly present the business case for digital communication to be fully integrated into communication strategies. One of the key recommendations in the Influenza Pandemic Review (2010) was that the UK health departments should consider 'making more use of social networking and digital technology to reach specific sections of the public' (Hine, 2010). More than three-quarters of UK households have home internet access (Ofcom, 2011) and the resilience of the medium to reach the public has recently been demonstrated in a series of international natural disasters.

The use of social media in an emergency was one of the key recommendations of Exercise Watermark (2011). 'All emergency responders should assess social media capability, capacity and access and think about removing any barriers so they can start to lead the way in social media conversation' (Defra, 2011). The exercise revealed that many press officers still had to contend with firewalls and IT policies that prevented them from accessing social media in the workplace, and that many didn't have laptops or smartphones.

The Exercise highlighted the ability of social media to gather live information and to be used proactively as a tool to warn and inform. 'Mash up' sites, generated by the public in the Queensland Floods (2010) were identified as a successful way of communicating directly with people to ascertain their needs. Watermark also warned that the command and control communication structures of the past are not flexible or fast enough to respond to the public, who are now able to access live footage streamed from a mobile phone. Failure to respond quickly can severely damage trust and confidence in an organisation while successful engagement can build relationships beyond the life of the crisis or emergency situation.

Cornwall Council's award-winning response to the floods in 2010 demonstrated the role of social media in delivering key messages to a broad and diverse audience. Mobile communications and Twitter were key to the communications programme and were used to post regular updates about the incident and the recovery. Within 48 hours the website, which had a virtual information pack, received over 7,000 hits and the Cornwall Council Twitter page had attracted 2,000 visits.

During the London riots, many local authorities successfully used their Twitter feed to provide updated news. 'The feedback from residents was great. We've kept our followers and people now know they can trust us when it matters' (Stamper, 2012).

The *Guardian* project 'Reading the Riots' (2012) identified the significance of Twitter in dispelling inaccuracies and misconceptions, with the 'crowd' rebutting rumours often in the space of two or three hours. The study also found that Twitter was not used by rioters to directly organise themselves, although one rioter indicated that some had followed journalists' reports when deciding where to go.

The research, which examined 2.7 million tweets, found that the Twitter crowd quickly overturned statements supporting the riots and instead used this tool to mobilise community spirit and the clean-up operation. The tag #riotcleanup reached more than 7 million people, with 120 posted messages and 31,000 retweets. This crisis clearly demonstrated the power of Twitter, both in terms of the potential reach and discernment of the audience.

Digital communication has an important role to play in emergency and crisis communication. It is a robust medium with which to communicate key messages to large numbers of the public who may be otherwise hard to reach. It also provides the opportunity to gather and engage in conversation, connecting with those directly on the ground, the media and the wider public. Organisations need to be networked ahead of any crisis so that they are ready to engage when an emergency is triggered.

## CASE STUDY #riotcleanup case study

During the riots, Twitter demonstrated its potential to mobilise large numbers of people on the streets through the #riotcleanup. Dan Thompson, a Worthing-based artist who tweets as @artistsmakers encouraged Twitter users to lead a clean-up the following day. Overnight his followers grew from 4,000 to over 70,000 and the clean-up events snowballed from the first, which had 10 people, to the clean-up in Clapham, which was supported by over 2,000. Thompson (2012) cites Croydon Council as being exemplary in their involvement, responding quickly and sending down health and safety officers to support the clean-up operation. Generally councils were slow to respond, slowed down by bureaucracy and sign-off procedures within the organisation.

Although #riotcleanup was an example of Twitter harnessing positive activity, Thompson (2012) suggests that local authorities should consider how they would co-ordinate a response to such large numbers behaving negatively. He suggests that emergency planning documents should consider the organisational response to activists mobilising at this speed and in these numbers. The power of human contact should not be underestimated and Thompson (2012) recommends identifying the person at the heart of any demonstration and quickly establishing human contact. Issues management should include identifying the top 10 bloggers in the local community and engaging with them directly ahead of any crisis. Someone who has 10,000 followers on Twitter probably has a larger readership than the local newspaper. Although tools are available to evaluate social media, these should be treated with caution as numbers don't always equate with influence.

The challenges of digital communication during a crisis include the speed with which information travels, the global reach, potential for misinformation and the threat to reputation and operational security. However, this medium also provides one of the best opportunities to rebuild relationships and engage in genuine dialogue. The speed of communication provides the chance to publish updates immediately, and for the first time communicate directly with those on the ground in real time.

# Traditional channels of communication: direct communication matters

Depending on the type of crisis or emergency, traditional channels of communication continue to play an important role in the dissemination of key messages. In Cornwall, during the 2010 floods, detailed briefings to employees and councillors, daily media interviews and a dedicated flood line to talk to those affected directly were crucial. There was also a series of public meetings to provide residents and local councillors with the latest information regarding the situation in their areas and to offer support and guidance. Community bases and flood surgeries were also set up with staff from multiple agencies available to answer questions and give advice.

# Post-crisis communication

Crisis management is not only about handling the immediate reaction to a crisis but also involves communication in the aftermath. Kay (2012) suggests that community recovery is usually led by the local authority, but with continuing multi-agency engagement through a recovery co-ordinating group structure. This period is often long term and involves both a physical rebuild and restoration of confidence and cohesion in communities that have been destroyed.

An important part of the post-crisis period is to review procedures and identify the lessons to be learnt. Rebuilding the reputation of the organisation will demand an ongoing programme of communication with those stakeholders affected or by those who have questioned the organisation's ability to operate. Relationships nurtured pre-crisis will be crucial. A communications plan for this period should be agreed as soon as possible, in order to put in place the necessary resources. This may include a dedicated customer service phone line to provide information and support to local communities and specific partnerships to provide direct support to residents, businesses and organisations affected.

This period should also be used to spotlight the good practice of local organisations in managing the emergency. Cornwall Council's joined-up response to the 2010 floods was recognised by David Cameron and the Duke of Cornwall as a blueprint for how such incidents should be dealt with in the future. Pauline Causey, Managing Editor, BBC Cornwall, commented: 'We've appreciated enormously the speed with which interviewees, officials and experts have been arranged in response to our enquiries.'

While reflecting on what has happened is important, looking forward and adjusting practice is important. Communications plans should take into account trigger points that will cause the public and media to reflect on the crisis in the future. Many of the London boroughs acknowledged the first anniversary of the riots in their Olympic communication planning. An organisation may also become the first point of call for journalists wanting a comment on a similar emergency or crisis situation to one they have handled in the past. This continues to associate the organisation with the crisis, which though may have been handled well, may not be the story that the organisation wishes to define it.

Although there is no guaranteed outcome from an emergency or crisis situation, preparing and communicating clearly throughout each phase can support an organisation in achieving the best possible result.

### Checklist

- Nurture relationships with both on and offline media.
- Engage in social media networks.
- Agree the emergency communications plan and procedures with partner organisations.
- Invite the media to emergency planning exercises.
- Develop communication support across the whole organisation.
- In an emergency keep communication channels open.
- Provide a spokesperson as soon as possible.
- Ensure communication and messages are clear.
- Apologise if necessary.
- Plan for recovery.
- Learn the lessons and share practice.

## KEY WORDS

Issues management; stakeholder engagement; risk assessment; emergency planning; concern; clarity; control; confidence; competence; digital communication.

# 12
# Communicating the council brand

*The Hampshire County Council brand is one of our most powerful assets. It's who we are, it's how people recognise us and most importantly, it's about how people remember and relate to us.*

HANTSWEB, OUR BRAND

The brand of any organisation is much more than its visual identity; it represents the emotional connection that people have with it. The significant elements, which have been identified as contributing towards this relationship, include the symbolism, behaviour and communication of an organisation (Van Riel, 1995). Branding is an important part of reputation management, and should be just as important to the public sector as the private. Managing the brand is more challenging in the public sector because of the diversity of the ways in which services are delivered and the wide range of audiences.

In 2005, the Local Government Association (LGA) commissioned a series of focus groups across England and Wales. The findings were that most people perceived their council to be 'remote, low profile, bureaucratic and inefficient' (MORI, 2006). Further research revealed that only 1 per cent of people talked highly of their council unprompted and only 5 per cent knew what their council did. Quirke (2000) identifies the 'unknown incompetent' syndrome and uses research to draw a correlation between a lack of familiarity and low effectiveness ratings. The LGA concluded that the majority of councils were unable to project a coherent or consistent identity, confusing the public with a deluge of complex messages, too many sub-brands, inconsistent use of symbols and a credibility gap. The impact of this was likely to be the deep-rooted cause of low satisfaction ratings. Building the brand, therefore, became one of the core actions that the LGA (2005) identified to improve the reputation of local authorities. The Reputation Campaign catapulted the corporate identity into the consciousness of local authority leadership.

In 2009, the LGA found that a quarter of people thought councils provided hospitals and dentists. Informing residents of the services they provide clearly still needed to be a priority, and is particularly important when times are tough and residents need to understand what their council tax pays for. *The New Reputation Guide* (2010) identified the 'brand' as one of the three big issues for local government (LGA, 2010).

LGID (2009) identifies that building a strong brand has a range of benefits, including:

- improved staff morale;
- higher resident satisfaction and public profile;
- attracting new staff;
- acting as a powerful catalyst for a wider programme of culture change within the organisation;
- helping set new standards for communication, service, values and behaviour;
- leading to more cost-effective and speedier ways of communicating.

# The visual identity

The organisational identity should go beyond what Wathen (1986) calls the logo-motion and reflect the mix identified by Van Riel (1995) as behaviour, communication and symbolism. Visual identity should not be underestimated and is widely recognised as demonstrating the outward sign of inward commitment (Abratt, 1989).

Having a multiplicity of sub-brands within an organisation can be symptomatic of silos, as well as confusing to the public, preventing the council from taking the credit for the range of services they provide. Branding services consistently builds awareness and, in time, satisfaction. Getting your visual house in order, however, is increasingly challenging due to the diverse ways in which public services are delivered involving partnership organisations and arm's length reach companies.

The visual identity should aim to capture the overall look and feel of an organisation, which has emerged from engaging with those who have a relationship with it. Following an extensive consultation, the City of Edinburgh Council developed a brand wheel, which maps its values, tone of voice, personality and essence to a colour palette. They also replaced departmentally named straplines under the logo with those based on the nature of services – encouraging departments from across the organisation to select those applicable to audience and format. This approach provides a wide choice and reflects the diversity, which is often cited as a barrier to service areas getting on board.

The City of Edinburgh Council also developed stock images, which reflected the core values identified in the review process. Walsall Council worked with the local Flickr group, requesting the online community of photographers to tag the images they would like to be used by the council. This approach allows the visual identity to reflect the changing perceptions of the community.

Publications should look as though they belong to the same family. Although each material can have its own personality, the basic rules about written communication and design and visual imagery should apply. One of the simplest ways of achieving a stronger brand image is to ensure that all council publications sit together as a suite.

Developing a good, strong corporate identity can help promote a 'one council' approach that makes sense to your residents. It is important that your organisation takes credit for all its services, especially the most popular ones such as theatres, museums and sports centres. Although separate identities should be avoided, appropriacy is of paramount importance. In Rushcliffe, therefore, the council logo was deemed inappropriate on materials promoting civil ceremonies. Acknowledgement that this is a council service is included in the content.

# The behavioural and communicative identity

An important part of the brand is the behaviour of staff and how they communicate the identity of the organisation. Reynolds (2012) believes that staff induction and refresher courses to remind staff of the Code of Conduct that applies both on and offline is important, but going beyond this and trying to instil a tone of voice or vibe in both written and verbal communication is superficial and doomed to fail.

Organisations must instead ensure that employees understand their mission and recruit staff that share the values of the organisation and buy into the culture. Internal communication is important in keeping staff briefed on the services provided across the organisation and in engaging with them to identify any shift in perceptions. Every member of staff should be considered a potential brand champion as should elected members and staff working in partnership organisations.

Many local authorities have increasingly linked customer services to the communication department in recognition of the importance of these front-line staff in communicating the brand values of the organisation. Establishing a close relationship also enables the communication department to understand the perceptions of those interacting with the council.

Prioritising customer services has been high up on the agenda for many local authorities who recognise the importance of this team reflecting the values of the organisation and in raising awareness of the services through delivering accurate information.

## Where are you now?

The starting point for any rebranding exercise is to recognise that the brand for the local authority already exists in the perceptions of those who interact with the organisation. In order to benchmark, local authorities need to consider their relationships with a diverse range of stakeholders taking into account the full corporate identity mix of visual, behavioural and communication. These elements can be monitored through a range of methods that allow local authorities to consider the current perceptions of the organisation.

## What are the options – a council or place brand?

In the context of Total Place, a number of local authorities including Bolton, Salford and Oldham moved away from the traditional branding of organisation towards a branding of place. Semley and Powell (2010) suggest that one of the benefits of place branding is that it enables local authorities to reduce the political problems commonly associated with local authority rebrands. They argue that an identity of place secures a long-term life for the brand beyond changes in political administration and is more effective in securing the support of a wide range of stakeholders. In Bolton, the rebrand was managed by the Local Strategic Partnership (LSP), which was an effective way of bringing the town's partners together and ensuring shared ownership. Since LSPs have been disbanded, groups that have brought partners together, mobilising around a particular issue could present an effective mechanism in bringing stakeholders together to work through a rebrand of place.

Place branding is popular where there is shared recognition that there needs to be a collective effort to reposition the place, as part of regeneration work and to attract inward investment. In Bolton, there were more than 60 different logos when work began on the rebrand. The partners involved understood that there needed to be consistency of messaging if the town was to project its image. In Salford, repositioning the city, collectively as one, with a coherent set of values and messages is in part credited for attracting the BBC's relocation to the Quays.

Place branding necessitates external consultation with those groups who they are trying to attract, stakeholders from outside the city – the potential investors, relocators or visitors. For Bolton, this wider consultation resulted in a brand that went beyond being a 'traditional, Lancashire market town', which could have been the outcome if the consultation was confined to those who lived and worked in the town.

## Internal research

Staff are an important part of the brand, representing the organisation. Ind (2004) identifies that when there is inconsistency or when the promise of the performance is not delivered the organisation will be questioned. It is important therefore that employees across the organisation, not just those based in the town hall, are part of the consultation process. Quirke (2000) suggests that a greater level of discussion and involvement of organisational objectives is rewarded with a higher commitment from employees. He advocates a shift in attitude from seeing internal communication as a process of distribution to using it as a process of conversion where there is opportunity for dialogue and change.

Top down management is increasingly hard to sustain, due to the information now available to employees and a participative approach is recommended as the dividing line between senders and receivers is dissolving due to networking and customer integration. Internal and external relations to the corporate identity are inextricably linked and rather than delivering targeted internal communication as proposed by Quirke (2000) and Ind (2004), a strategy that works towards achieving buy-in from all the stakeholders must be adopted. Digital communication channels are ideal to use for engagement across internal and external groups as part of the decision-making process.

This process is crucial in developing a brand to which staff are committed, and in identifying any pockets of resistance and barriers to change. Buy-in needs to be achieved at all levels, with strong leadership at the top and involvement throughout. At the City of Edinburgh Council, sessions were also held with the cross-party political group to ensure that all parties were on board from the beginning and that the rebrand did not become a lightening rod for political differences. In these sessions the long-term cost savings made were highlighted, including reduced design time and reputational benefits. Rushcliffe Council also secured independent representatives from the LGA, to communicate the research-based benefits of a strong brand to employees and politicians.

If budgets are tight, a brand audit can be undertaken in-house with the communication team gathering feedback on the use of logo and design across the organisation. A visual audit can be undertaken examining buildings, signage, vehicles and uniforms. Mystery shopping exercises are a useful way to determine how the brand is communicated by staff. This will provide information on how the brand is being represented by staff; additional qualitative research such as focus groups will begin to identify the factors that underlie the visual and behavioural cues.

## External research

External research is an essential part of developing a brand that should be relevant beyond an internal audience. The LGID (2009) recommends the following cost-effective methods to identify what people think about the council and to keep in touch with the perceptions of a range of stakeholders:

- annual residents' surveys;
- citizens' panels;
- stakeholder surveys;
- feedback campaigns;
- mystery shopping exercises;
- feedback from public meetings and events.

Once a gap has been identified between an organisation's image and identity, and there are the necessary budgets in place, external agencies can be commissioned to analyse the views of both internal and external stakeholders. Hemisphere Design who have rebranded a number of local authorities suggest first drafting a target list of individuals and organisations to consult with, which can then be agreed with the lead officers from the project. The groups identified for consultation traditionally include local stakeholders and opinion formers and community research with local residents and businesses.

Hemisphere, working on place branding, went beyond the local area to get a qualitative view of how the area was perceived externally in the wider United Kingdom. They identified surrounding cities within a reasonable catchment area and the consultation included potential investors in these neighbouring cities, potential visitors and potential relocators. They highlight the importance of keeping people from the initial consultation involved throughout the journey and informed of the outcomes at the end. Documentary research including documents and strategies can be used to complement the results of the qualitative research.

The initial stages of consultation, both internally and externally, should provide the basis for brand positioning. Senior council officers and members should be involved in discussion and debate, as the themes associated with the council begin to emerge. This will then form the foundations on which to build the creative development.

## Consultation in more depth – investigating the brand

In establishing the branding position of an organisation, the research and consultation process should aim to elicit the current perceptions and the contributory factors. The research should also aim to establish the current values and characteristics of the council and perhaps most importantly the aspirations that those interviewed hold for the organisation, establishing their vision for the future.

Hemisphere (2012) suggest that perceptions are generated by factors including how people experience the brand and what they say. The brand analysis should identify the organisation's attributes and personality, and consider negative comments against the aims of the organisation. The brand values therefore should be aspirational rather than just capturing the current position of the organisation. From this initial stage, key themes from across different audiences will begin to emerge.

Local authorities should aim to capture what they stand for in a strapline, which communicates what they are committed to deliver. Rushcliffe Borough Council's 'Great place, great lifestyle, great sport' reflects their world-class sporting venues and the results of the Place Survey 2008, which recognised the borough as a great place, and the Comprehensive Area Assessment of 2009, which cited Rushcliffe as a top district council. Authenticity is key; the brand should communicate what the organisation stands for, which should be reinforced through delivery on a daily basis.

The brand of an organisation should capture both its tangible and intangible characteristics. The challenge is to ensure that the image in the minds of stakeholders is as close as possible to the identity projected by the organisation. Consultation throughout is essential in involving those who have relationships with the council in agreeing what its distinguishing features are.

The initial consultation exercise should identify the key words and statements that will be used to generate brand values, the visual representations and the relationships of the brand. The consultation should aim to establish a set of key values for the organisation that partners will sign up to support and that all stakeholders will recognise. Local authorities should recognise that brands are not static and that consultation should feature over the long term in the review and ongoing monitoring of the brand.

## Developing the brand

Many local authorities have introduced a visual rebrand over time, introducing the new visuals as materials need to be replaced. In Edinburgh, this was achieved over a four-year period. This is important in the context of potential criticisms of cost.

It is essential that the top team agree the corporate identity to avoid a cacophony of mixed messages and that the strategy has their full endorsement. Ind (2004), although arguing a 'bottom up' approach, acknowledges that employees will not live the identity if signals from management suggest it is unimportant. He suggests it is vital that there is at least one champion at senior management level.

The behaviour of senior management, presenting a strong consistent image, is particularly important in local government where the service silo culture may still exist. It is important that the local authority considers in advance the mechanisms that will be put in place in order to ensure that council services are consistently branded.

The findings of the research and consultation should be used to create a draft brand positioning that includes the values and personality traits, benefits and key attributes. A presentation should be made to senior management and a cross-party political group of the findings from the research and consultation followed by a discussion and debate of the suggested brand positioning. This session should aim to agree the personality and characteristics that will be needed for the creative brief for work on the visual identity.

The initial creative concepts that aim to capture the overall brand positioning should be presented to the lead project group, which includes the senior management team. At this stage the communications department at Tunbridge Wells Borough Council removed itself from the project team to ensure that the brand was owned by its stakeholders. This approach reduces the potential for the brand to become a future lightening rod between political parties, or subject to change if there is a shift in the overall political majority. The visual identity is the part of the rebrand that traditionally receives most criticism, generated by local councillors and the local news media. At Bolton Council, these two groups were targeted for a second wave of consultation to identify and address any concerns. This process identified that the main issues involved the expense of the rebrand and that there was a lack of understanding of how the rebrand would benefit local people. Understanding these issues led the project team to shape a document for councillors, the media and other stakeholders that identified the long-term efficiency savings and to compile a list of organisations committed to the brand. Semley and Powell (2010) note that achieving the buy-in of councillors and the media resulted in virtually no public or political backlash later. This additional stage of consultation is recommended for the long-term success of the brand.

Once the visual identity has been selected, the design agency should apply the creative concepts to a range of materials to evaluate its practical implementation.

## Launching the behavioural identity

The brand will manifest itself in a range of ways. The brand values that have been agreed will need to be embedded at the very heart of the organisation, in how the borough operates and in the initiatives and projects it is involved with. Initially the values could be applied to existing work, with future projects and initiatives considered in light of how they reflect the core values.

In Bolton, initiatives including steps to encourage a café society, improvement of the town's retail provision, securing developer interest and regeneration of Bolton's mills was underpinned by the aspirations of the town's brand.

## Launching the communication identity

The communication side of the brand can be delivered by embedding the values of the organisation into the key messages for each of its target audiences. It is essential that staff, who are the potential brand champions of the organisation, understand the values that they should have been involved in developing. Involving staff in the initial consultation and keeping them in the loop is essential for ownership of the brand. Staff need to understand the origins of the brand, what it represents and how their own behaviour should reflect the core values.

## Launching the visual identity

The style/brand guide should introduce the corporate logo, its applications across both on and offline materials illustrated with practical examples. A digital version will enable the communications team to keep the guide up to date, adding case studies and providing the opportunity for an online forum.

Many local authorities produce a suite of brand guides targeting different audiences. The City of Edinburgh Council launched a range of supplementary guidelines to provide more detailed information on a particular aspect of branding. This included guides for signage, uniforms, for schools and community centres, and for partnerships such as the Edinburgh Community Health Partnership.

In addition to outlining the technical requirements of logos, such as size, colour and positioning, there is opportunity to outline the expectations of the use of language. Plain English should be encouraged and reference made to the RNIB and RNID guidelines on producing accessible communication materials.

Developing templates that departments can use reduces design time significantly and contributes towards the long-term cost savings, important to highlight when building a business case to secure investment in a rebrand.

Within the communication department a designated member of staff should be identified to work with departments on the production of communication materials to ensure that they reflect the council identity. A list of approved designers and printers should have copies of the council logo in all its acceptable forms and be fully briefed on the corporate identity guidelines and corporate standards for producing publications. As part of their select list arrangement with the council, these suppliers could also be requested to provide electronic and hard copies of all publications to the communication team. Any instances where the brand has been used inconsistently can then be automatically picked up and fed back – both to the commissioning department and supplier. Rushcliffe Council credit the success of their rebrand in part with the vigour of the communications team in monitoring communication materials. Bolton Council's communication team were nicknamed 'the Talibrand' by staff; however, it was undoubtedly their commitment to ensuring consistency that has led to its success (Semley and Powell, 2010).

## Working with partnership bodies

Partnership work at local, regional and national level has increased over the last decade. Representation of all the agencies on communication materials can result in a confusing display of brands all jockeying for the bottom right hand position.

Local authorities need to consider their contribution and the appropriacy of representation. If a project has been funded entirely by the local authority then the style guide should be applied. In cases where the council is a major funder then negotiation should aim to achieve visual representation. Southwark Council have developed a useful guide to support decision making in partnership branding.

Talbot (2012) highlights the importance of explaining to partner organisations the pressure that local authorities are under, following the Reputation Project, to consistently brand their services. This can be interpreted as over zealous by partner organisations and build tensions.

Local authorities working in long-term equal partnerships should consider developing a brand that represents the partnership. In Edinburgh, the Department of Health and Social Care brought together the Council's adult social services and NHS Lothian's Edinburgh Community Health Partnership services under a joint senior management team. A brand was developed for Edinburgh Community Health Partnership to represent the work delivered by the Council and NHS. This brand brings together both organisations with a shared aim captured in a strapline that is used in conjunction with the council and NHS logos.

In Bolton, the place brand wasn't enforced but organisations were invited to join, and as highly regarded organisations signed up, others were keen to follow their lead. Giving organisations the option to sign up made their commitment more powerful. Similarly, in Edinburgh, the Council produced optional brand guidelines for schools, which enabled their identity to take priority, in recognition of their relationship with the local community. Supported by a presentation highlighting the benefits of using the brand, including cost savings through use of templates and the reputational impact of being associated with the Council, schools were encouraged to adopt the brand.

## National council branding

In 2008, the LGA launched the 'My Council' campaign to support local authorities in raising awareness of council services following research that indicated that the majority of people in England were not aware of the range of services councils provided. The campaign, built on research, aims to target the blind spots in people's awareness of council services. A series of posters visually reinforce what the council does by highlighting a service that is not highly recognised. The artwork provided by the LGA can be tailored to local needs, with the aim of building consistent messaging and visual imagery across the United Kingdom.

**FIGURE 12.1** A guide to partnership branding

With thanks to Southwark Council

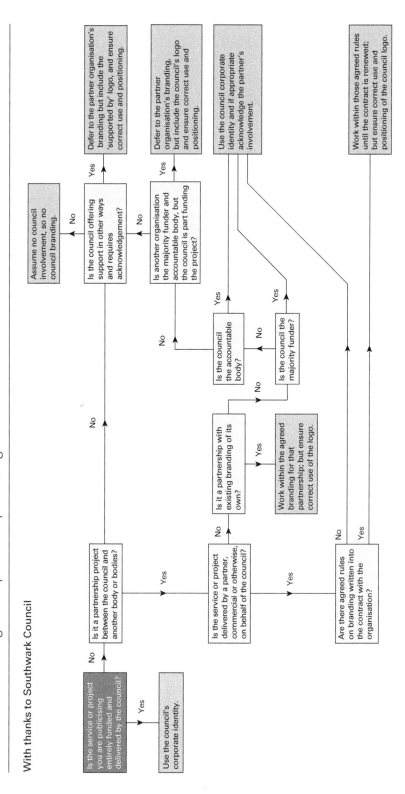

## *Maintaining the brand*

Individual services are rated higher than local authorities overall, therefore ensuring that there is consistency across uniforms, signage, vehicles and buildings is important in building recognition.

The corporate identity of any organisation is not static and is an ongoing process. Ind (2004) recognises that managing the identity is a long-term process, in which the values need to enter the systems of the organisation rather than being the crusade of a lone individual. Overseeing the identity of the council should therefore be more than just being a 'logo-cop', but should include ongoing dialogue and discussion around values and priorities with members, staff and stakeholders.

Meech (1996) suggests it should be routine management to review the corporate identity periodically. Gareth Morgan's (1987) use of the culture metaphor indicates a reason for this. He identifies the human side of organisations that communicate the key ideologies, values and beliefs that guide action to produce patterns of shared meanings. Thus organisational culture, he believes, is to a large extent self-generating – that is, not imposed from above.

Hatch (1997) similarly believes that culture should not be seen as a variable to be measured, accounted for and controlled, but as a context within which interpretations of organisational identity are formed.

Ind (2004) presents a bottom-up process involving employees from all parts of the organisation in discussing and defining a set of values that are authentic and usable. He argues that the time taken to define the values is offset by the resource implications to impose them from above. Hemisphere (2012) highlight the importance of external stakeholders, not just locally but regionally and nationally in the role that they can play in building an identity of place and shaping its long-term aspirations.

# Conclusion

To develop a strong identity, councils must first understand who they are, what they stand for and what they would like to achieve. This cannot be developed in isolation but must be developed with those who have relationships with the organisation. The brand lives among its publics and is not fixed. The on and offline community will shape the brand, whether the council engages with them or not. Involving internal and external communities in monitoring the position of the organisation and in identifying its aspirations should be part of ongoing brand management.

## KEY WORDS

Symbolism; behaviour; reputation management; consistent identity; symbols; place branding; dialogue; engagement; consultation; buy-in; brand value; behaviour.

# 13
# Communicating and promoting place

*Too few city leaders think about the number of jobs, businesses and other organisations that have a stake in their city's image and reputation. Unfortunately it is a value that goes unrecognised, unappreciated and unmanaged. It rarely gets measured and never appears on the balance sheet or the job evaluation of a mayor, city manager or city official.*

**BILL BAKER, 2011**

One of the real challenges for any council is how best to promote its area – a city, town, county or borough – in what is an increasingly competitive marketplace for jobs, business investment and government grants, or for tourists, day visitors and shoppers. Is there clarity on the purpose of the promotion? The target audiences? What are the area's strengths and weaknesses? What are people's perceptions of the area, from inside and outside? How do you differentiate an area, a city or a town from another? Can a slogan, logo or a catchphrase capture enough to sell an area? And can a city or place be branded like a product?

## Place promotion is not new

Promoting places is centuries old. Eastbourne, for example, published its first holiday guide in 1787, after King George III's children spent their summer in the seaside town. By 1937 the town's publicity department was promoting Eastbourne as both a tourist and conference destination, welcoming 2.5 million day visitors and almost half a million holidaymakers. Publicity and entertainments were merged in the 1960s, resulting in a 'far more effective machine, not only controlling the selling and marketing of the product, but having a large say in the product itself' (Bedford, 1973). Today, the borough council promotes Eastbourne as the 'sunniest place in the UK' with its own destination mobile app. It was a lead player in the 'Love Sussex' campaign to attract 2012 Olympics visitors from London, just over an hour away.

In the 1960s, selling a northern industrial city was much more difficult. Sheffield's main problem was image and 'eradicating a series of pre-conceived and ill-informed notions' (Wigley, 1973). Sheffield was one of the first UK cities to lead the way, addressing its image and promoting itself internationally. The council opened the city to nationally televised events and embarked on large-scale trade promotions for local businesses and inward investment: 'If you are promoting a major city of international standing, you simply have to do things on a grand scale or not at all.' Civic pride played a significant part. It was 'one of the main weapons in the publicity armoury' (Wigley, 1973).

New York's iconic red-hearted logo 'I love NY' reverberates civic pride and a real attachment to place. The logo, so easily transferable despite copyright challenges, has been adapted and imitated by many towns and cities around the world. No more so than after the worst riots to hit parts of London and several English cities in August 2011.

# After the riots: I love Hackney and Manchester campaigns

Hackney, one of the 2012 London Olympics host boroughs, with its new branding 'the real heart of London', picked up the red heart logo to underpin the immense council and community clean-up efforts after the rioting; 'We still love Hackney' was the supportive headline in the council's newspaper to its 180,000 residents. The logo 'I love Hackney', used by the council for several years for events around Valentine's day, was adopted by local shopkeepers, street traders, businesses and the council in the riots aftermath, as they successfully demonstrated that Hackney was still open for business. Badges, carrier bags and posters all proudly promoted the logo. The theme was developed further with the message 'Love Hackney, Shop Local' to encourage the borough's residents to make the most of what's on their doorstep, the local markets, local designers and stores.

Manchester's response to the riots was to launch within two days a 'I love MCR' campaign (see case study). Its primary aim was to get people back into the city centre for shopping, eating and leisure; footfall was down dramatically in days following the much publicised havoc caused by the riots and looting. So the campaign was quickly put together by Marketing Manchester, in partnership with the city council, the city centre's biggest shopping centre, the Arndale Centre, and the city centre management company, Cityco. Over 350 businesses signed up; the media came on side positively and tens of thousands of people backed it through Facebook and Twitter, using

#ILoveMCR. The campaign won the Purple Apple Marketing Award from the British Council of Shopping Centres. It was, said the judges, 'a shining example of professionals joining forces with the emotions and activities on the street with fantastic results... the short turnaround and quick thinking created great PR for the city in extremely negative circumstances'.

**CASE STUDY** After the 2011 Riots: I Love Manchester

On Tuesday 9 August 2011, following rioting starting in London, Manchester City Centre experienced some of the worst levels of disturbance and criminal activity. Footfall in the city centre was halved the next day.

### Objectives

- To galvanise the civic pride Manchester residents showed in response to the disturbances.
- To encourage people to return to the city centre to support the restaurants, bars and retailers affected by the downturn in business the disruption caused.
- To communicate a 'business as usual' message to restore order and confidence in Manchester city centre.
- To mitigate negative perceptions of Manchester locally, nationally and internationally.

### Implementation

A rapid response was essential to ensure immediate impact. A dedicated Facebook page (facebook.com/WeLoveMCR) and Twitter hashtag (#ILoveMCR) were set up for people to support the city within 48 hours of the rioting.

The 'I Love MCR' message spread quickly across the city, with outdoor sites, bus rears, lamp post banners and more for free. Major players in the city helped super-size the outdoor; CIS Tower and Bruntwood unveiled 'I Love MCR'. Manchester Airport posted the 'I Love MCR' logo above check-in desks and on terminal screens. Celebrity endorsement included Manchester City football team, Will Young during his European tour, and Jenson Button driving a Formula One car with 'I Love MCR' around the city. Week three switched to 'MCR Loves YOU'.

### Results

The three-week campaign increased footfall up 9.5 per cent (week 1), up 7.6 per cent (week 2) and up 12.3 per cent (week 3) compared to 2010. Facebook generated 21,000 likes, 1.8 million posts and 33,000 active users. Twitter, #ILoveMCR attracted 46,000 mentions. The ILoveMCR offers registered 14,481 page views. Overall, the campaign achieved a return on investment (ROI) of over 15:1.

See online resources for extended case study: **http://www.koganpage.com/PRGov**

The 'I love MCR' logo has become the lasting image of the city's resilience after the riots and symbolised Manchester's strength in trying times, according to one of the city's senior councillors, Pat Karney (Marketing Manchester, 2012). 'I love NY' logo, and its local interpretations, is resilient; it was created in 1977 out of adversity when New York was in decline, the city was bankrupt, companies were moving out and there was a big drop in visitors, especially business travellers.

The logo, probably the most successful of any city, lifted the city and boosted tourism by highlighting New York's strengths: Broadway shows, shopping, dining and museums. It still resonates as strong today. It is a 'citizen success' because it expresses a relationship rather than a difference or consumer benefit (Kapferer, 2011). Good slogans for a city have to come from inside, states Kapferer, as cities are first and foremost for their inhabitants. The slogan should express a sense of belonging, pride and symbolic proximity.

Wearing badges and T-shirts and tweeting with the logo, as they did in Hackney and even more so in Manchester, galvanised commitment and pride in their place; this spoke volumes to a watching media and outside world. Manchester's reputation as a safe place to shop and visit was successfully restored and Hackney was able to move forward positively with its plans for the borough and hosting the world's media at the 2012 London Olympics. Without these campaigns it may have been very different.

**FIGURE 13.1**   Mr Happy and Glasgow's Miles Better campaign logo 1983–89 and 1993–96

# Glasgow's Miles Better

Glasgow's Miles Better campaign, which ran from 1983–89, is considered to be one of the best city promotions ever mounted by any British city. It put a smile on a city that was both down on its heels and negatively perceived. The city's Lord Provost had initiated a public competition to find a slogan, like New York; but it was John Struthers and his Glasgow-based advertising agency who developed the idea and convinced the council to run with it. Struthers had earlier worked with Roger Hargreaves, the creator of the Mr Men series and got agreement to marry the Mr Happy figure with the cleverly duelled slogan 'Glasgow's miles better' or 'Glasgow smiles better'. Behind the phrase there was a little dig at Edinburgh. Glasgow, in fact, was always miles better than Edinburgh in terms of culture; its council-run galleries and museums were always free, and it was home to most of Scotland's cultural bodies and main broadcasters and media. Glasgow had a rich cultural, artistic and architectural heritage, but almost unknown to the outside world. Edinburgh, with its annual Festival and Fringe, was internationally known.

Mr Happy and the slogan was ever-present in the city and beyond. It did two things. First, it brought confidence back to the city, its people and the business community. Second, it was a catalyst in helping the city re-invent itself around culture and tourism, bringing additional spin-offs, and benefits to the city.

The launch year of Mr Happy coincided with the opening of the new Burrell Gallery in the city's Pollok Park; the shipowner Sir William Burrell had left his unique collection of art and artefacts to the city and the gallery opened to excellent media reviews and acclaim. The Burrell first put Glasgow, previously by-passed, on the coach tours of Scotland itinerary. Glasgow became a place to visit, rather than avoid. Glasgow opened its doors further with the successful Garden Festival 1988 with 3 million visitors, an ambitious and inclusive European City of Culture programme in 1990, and City of Architecture of Design 1999. These events added to the city's confidence and reinforced the city's inherent assets.

It is clear such promotions – but supported by other activities – can help turn around cities. The Miles Better campaign put Glasgow, once known as the 'second city of the empire', back on the map. Glasgow became for the first time a major tourist and conference destination, backed by a reinvigorated city offering of shopping, nightlife, dining, theatre, museums, galleries and sport.

Glasgow tried out other campaigns, 'Glasgow's Alive' and 'Glasgow – the friendly city', with limited success. A relaunch of Mr Happy in 1993 was short-lived when the cash-strapped new unitary city council had to pull the plug on cost grounds in 1996; one problem was that the council did not own the slogan or Mr Happy and the two rights fees accounted for a third of all promotion costs. Later, the Glasgow City Marketing Bureau, a public-private organisation with a board led by the council leader, was set up to 'communicate Glasgow's reputation as a world class city', attract conferences and events and promote the city as a tourist and leisure destination. It is custodian of the 'Glasgow Scotland with Style' brand launched in 2004 (see case study).

**FIGURE 13.2**    Glasgow: new branding since 2004

**CASE STUDY**    Glasgow: Scotland with style

### The creation and evolution of the brand

Greater Glasgow & Clyde Valley Tourist Board (GGCVTB) led the team tasked with rebranding the city of Glasgow in December 2003. Glasgow City Marketing Bureau (GCMB) took over in April 2005 as the official destination-marketing organisation for the city and custodian of the award-winning 'Glasgow: Scotland with style' brand.

### Aim

'Glasgow: Scotland with style' brand aimed to position Glasgow as a vibrant, dynamic and world-class city in which to live, work, study, invest and visit. It was to boost Glasgow's position in the European city league, as well as win the hearts and minds of Glaswegians. The creative rationale was inspired by Glasgow icon, architect, designer and artist, Charles Rennie Mackintosh (1868–1928) and the 'Glasgow style' movement.

### Launch and strategy

The brand was launched in 2004, with ads and banners dressing the city. And an intensive marketing communications campaign, targeted initially at the UK market then rolled out to Europe and the United States. First promotions were 'Discover Mackintosh's Art Nouveau masterpiece. It's called Glasgow' highlighting the global impact made by Mackintosh's global impact and 'Glasgow – the New Black' featuring the city's credentials as a major shopping and fashion centre. In June 2005, GCMB implemented the next phase of the brand's evolution – a £1.83 million campaign continuing to position Glasgow across key UK and international markets.

The 'Glasgow: Scotland with style' brand is woven into Glasgow's economic strategy and the city's tourism strategy for 2007–16. This demonstrates a clear vote of confidence in the brand to help deliver economic benefit for the city region. Glasgow now attracts 2.2 million visitors each year, generating £578 million for the local economy.

### Digital strategy

GCMB has developed a digital strategy putting the brand in the social space. The aim is to 'stimulate conversation about Glasgow' and create customers for the city.

GCMB's consumer Facebook page – under the banner 'we're the first to know what's going on in Glasgow and love to share it' – provide an interactive resource for residents and visitors. Other developments include '@seeglasgow' on Twitter; '@meetglasgow' and GCMB's LinkedIn page focused on business tourism and conference news. In December 2012, these four channels had in total 13,000 followers. Additionally there were over 30,000 downloads of the free Glasgow smartphone App, offering a real-time visitor guide.

### Partner and event alignment

Strategic alliances have been formed with city partners. Such is the brand's resonance, it has been adopted across various sectors from tourism and retail to transport and creative industries. GCMB target and secure events – in music, fashion, sports – that strengthen the brand's integrity and position Glasgow as a stylish, dynamic and cosmopolitan city.

See online resources for extended case study: **http://www.koganpage.com/PRGov**

# Event and place promotion

Specific visitor-focused projects, big events, special years or accolades can boost a city, town or area. There is no doubt the 2012 Olympics and Paralympics enhanced London's global reputation; the commitment of the London boroughs, the engagement of thousands of Games volunteers, and the participation of communities (and councils) across the United Kingdom in the Olympic torch relay added to that success, generating additional local media coverage and positive social media conversations.

Other accolades may not be so high profile, but bidding and securing them can make a difference. Glasgow and Liverpool certainly benefited from being garden festival cities in 1984 and 1988 and European cities of culture in 1990 and 2008 respectively. Commenting on Liverpool's 2008 success, city brands commentator Andrew Stevens said:

> There is often an element of scepticism as to the worth of such state-run festivals, especially during these more European Union bashing times, but research by Liverpool's two main universities in 2011 found that staging the event has led to an appreciable rise in positive coverage and perceptions of the city and its cultural offer, which had for the first time outweighed its unenviable tendency towards stereotypes.
>
> (Stevens, 2012a)

Similarly there were benefits for Sheffield and Preston as cities of sport in 2012, for Edinburgh and Norwich becoming UNESCO cities of literature in 2004 and 2011 and for Lanarkshire hosting the International Children's

Games, the world's biggest young sporting event, in 2011. Most of these bids are led by local councils. Preparing the bid documents can be time consuming and cathartic in putting together a deliverable proposal with vision. Successful bids involve working in partnership with other organisations, the community and the media. To maximise the impact of a winning bid (and for that matter dealing with the implications of a losing bid) there must be PR and communications input from the outset, with someone leading on the communication strategy and plan.

Since the turn of the century, there have been three opportunities for towns to seek city status, which is granted by HM the Queen: in 2000 at the millennium; in 2002 for the Queen's Golden Jubilee; and 2012 for the Diamond Jubilee. All the councils bidding – 38 in 2000, 42 in 2002 and 25 in 2012 – highlighted the prestige and advantages, as they saw it, of being called a city.

In the 2012 round, Chelmsford, Perth and St Asaph became cities and Armagh gained Lord Mayoralty status. Chelmsford's bid focused on 10 credentials and the city themes 'authenticity, intercity, capacity, tenacity, vivacity, and velocity... Chelmsford putting city into everything we do' (Chelmsford, 2011). Perth, on the other hand, was seeking to restore city status lost at the 1975 local government reorganisation; its bid received the most extensive media coverage locally, as well as an impressive list of third party endorsements (Perth and Kinross Council, 2011). Armagh's Lord Mayor Sharon Haughey said the new status 'can be a significant boost to Armagh's tourism and economy if we promote this in the right way' (Armagh City and District website, 2012).

One of the challenges councils – and places – face is promoting their efforts and activities to improve place to their own residents and voters. The Department of Communities and Local Government 2008 Place Survey in England found that 8 out of 10 residents were very or fairly satisfied with their area as a place to live. But, more significantly, less than 6 out of 10 people felt they belonged to their neighbourhood (Place Survey, 2008). Marketing internally to those residents is 'not as much a technical marketing problem of methods, messages and targets, as it is a political problem of defining place development in the public's own framework' (Kotler, Halder and Rein, 1993).

The Carnegie UK 'Pride in Place' initiative highlights other, but on a less grand scale, ways of recognising the importance of place, through tackling incivilities, such as litter or flytipping (Carnegie UK, 2011). These blight communities, trouble residents and deter visitors. Communicating such positive actions can impact on the image of place, internally and externally. Stockport Council's 'Stockport Boost' campaign in 2009 to support local residents and businesses in the recession put the council at the heart of its communities. And competitions, such as the Royal Horticultural Society's (RHS) annual Britain in Bloom awards, is yet another way councils can promote local areas, in partnership with local volunteers.

Broughshane, a village previously torn by sectarianism, won the top RHS award in 2012 as the 'cleanest, greenest and most beautiful location in

Britain'. The County Antrim village, which strived for community cohesion under their motto 'Plants, people and pride growing together', now welcomes 150,000 visitors a year. An earlier winner, the Welsh town of Holyhead, said the accolade boosted the town's regeneration. The RHS have reported that the Bloom awards raise esteem within an area, encourage voluntarism, generate visitors and business, and save councils money. Manchester spends £67,000 on bloom activities but the value to the council was at least 40-fold more (RHS, 2011).

Councils, too, have a responsibility to promote their area's assets, for example parks, museums, galleries, leisure centres – and most do, but sometimes not in a consistent or planned way. Events, council-run or council supported, are often well promoted and advertised, through the media, council publications, website and social media networks. Sponsorships and partnerships with local newspapers or radio stations can be cost-effective and mutually beneficial; but these need to be discussed and negotiated at an early stage and built into the communication plan, along with deadlines for events and tourist publications. Increasingly, social media and local microsites will play a bigger role in all communications; and for specific promotions and events, there has to be greater targeting of audiences. Post-event promotion in the media, on the website, or through social media, Twitter, Flickr or YouTube, through photographs, video and quotes, can help build engagement and interest for future events or activities.

Other initiatives can be maximised to promote place. In 2005, London Borough of Waltham Forest launched 'The Beckham Trail' – an annotated map and guide, now downloadable, for David Beckham fans tracing his early years in the borough, including his birthplace, school and the ground of Ridgeway Rovers, where he first played football for the under-10-year-olds team. Although the trail has not been formally endorsed by Beckham, the council's initiative brings visitors, including enthusiasts from Spain, the United States and France, to the borough and has received positive media coverage. *The Daily Mail* said the trail was 'fast becoming the holy land of the modern western world' (Waltham Forest London Borough Council, 2005).

Monmouthshire County Council and Wikipedia joined forces in 2012 to launch the Monmouthpedia, the world's first wiki project to embrace a whole town, Monmouth (population 9,000). The idea came from local resident, John Cummings, now appointed the Wikipedian in residence at the council's headquarters. The Welsh county town, with its culture, history, heritage and people, and offering free Wi-fi access for all, was an ideal pioneer.

Monmouthpedia covers all aspects of life in the town. It allows anyone to use their smartphones, tablets, iPhones and iPads to scan barcodes (over 1,000 QR codes on plaques across the town) to access a vast array of information instantly online in over 200 languages. Wikipedia's co-founder Jimmy Wales said: 'Bringing a whole town to life on Wikipedia is something new and is a testament to the forward-thinking people of Monmouth, all the volunteers and the Wikipedia UK team. I am looking forward to seeing other towns and cities doing the same thing' (Monmouthpedia, 2012).

# Essentials of place branding

The idea of branding places – particularly cities – is relatively new and several UK cities have developed what they call 'a city brand'. Birmingham, Edinburgh, Glasgow, Liverpool, Manchester and Newcastle with Gateshead, for example, have established, on the initiative of their city councils, strategic marketing public–private partnerships to develop and manage their city brand.

These organisations – Marketing Birmingham, Marketing Edinburgh, Glasgow City Marketing, Liverpool Marketing, and Marketing Manchester – are seen as 'city brand leaders' in the creativebrief blogs (Stevens, 2012a). Their focus is destination marketing, bringing tourists and conferences to the city, and high profiling the city for business and investment.

After extensive consultations, Edinburgh launched the 'Edinburgh Inspiring Capital' brand in 2005, as Scotland moved to a national, rather than local, framework to promote tourism, through VisitScotland. A brand pyramid (see Figure 13.4) summarised the brand, under the four themes: tone of voice, values, personality and essence.

**FIGURE 13.3**    Edinburgh: new branding since 2005

The 'Inspiring Capital' theme became 'an attack brand for Scotland, often with greater currency than the country itself', according to Kenneth Wardrop (2011), who headed up the new private–public Destination Edinburgh Marketing Alliance (DEMA). It was set up in 2009 charged with the destination promotion of Edinburgh and to address underperforming in the city's marketing, identified by the 2007 Anholt City Brand Index Survey. Although the city was ranked 22 out of 50, the view was it should rank stronger. It fell short on consumer perceptions and on recognition of the city's assets and achievements, especially when Edinburgh hosts 14 world-class festivals annually. Edinburgh has the credentials for a global brand and the ability to outperform the role of an attack brand for Scotland, a shop window and gateway for the country (Dinnie, 2012). But Frank

**FIGURE 13.4** Edinburgh Inspiring City: Brand Triangle

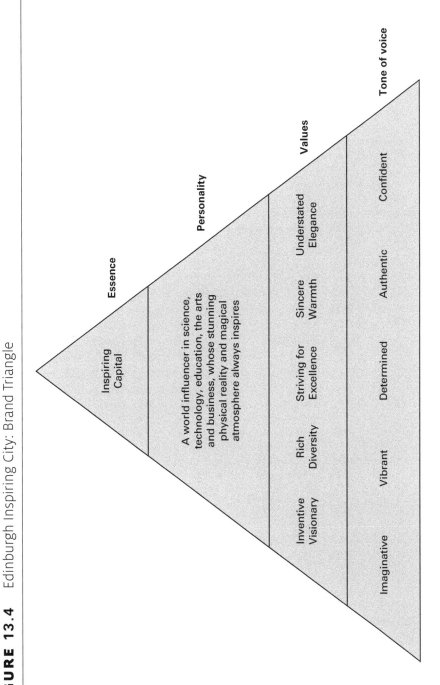

O'Donnell, editor of the *Edinburgh Evening News* is critical of the city's marketing approach:

> There's a fundamental mismatch between the external perception that the marketers buy into and the actual feeling on the ground, where the foot-soldiers who should embody the city's marketing message just give it a miss. It might just be the Scottish psyche but there's little local support for slogans like 'Edinburgh Inspiring Capital' – it might play well with marketers, but for the ordinary people who even know about it, it tends to just fuel the cynicism over what city marketing is about. Edinburgh certainly struggles compared to Glasgow, where its marketing efforts have been better geared to gain the support of the local population.
>
> (quoted in creativebrief blog, Stevens, 2012b)

In 2011, the city council decided to wind up DEMA and set up Marketing Edinburgh, bringing together under one umbrella the city's film office, conference bureau and destination marketing. Marketing Edinburgh, also a public–private partnership company, is now the custodian of the 'Inspiring Capital' brand, which still continues. In its first foray into place promotion, Marketing Edinburgh has been the butt of criticism from councillors and the media for a series of proposed slogans and hashtags for the city's campaigns in 2013. These included 'incredinburgh', 'aheadinedinburgh', 'romance is not deadinburgh' and 'paint the town redinburgh' (*Sunday Herald*, 2012).

Manchester's branding – the 'M' Original Modern brand – is uniquely different from other cities. Marketing Manchester says it is much more than a brand; the two simple words, original and modern, 'define what sets Manchester apart from our peers across the globe'. The 'M' is a 'brand signifier' for use in national and international communications by city partners across Greater Manchester. It contrasts markedly with the city's earlier promotions and the much-criticised marketing slogan of the late 1990s 'We're up and going'.

> The immediate choice of the city fathers would have been a conventional media or ad campaign for Original Modern Manchester. We knew that brand building was a broader, more grown up process that worked through experience, action and word of mouth.
>
> (Connor, 2012)

Manchester's approach is both creative and innovative; its new tourist centre is interactive and designed like an Apple store and Marketing Manchester's minimalist designed website includes a map (like a London tube map) of Manchester's online presence 2010/11, an 18 route guide to the city's digital connectivity, websites, portals, forums and social networks (Marketing Manchester, 2012). Manchester, according to Stevens (2012c), is 'not only punching above its weight, but is also generating an almost effortless template to which other city brands can inspire'.

In 2005, Bolton took a novel approach to place branding. The council and its private/public partners in Bolton Vision, the local strategic partnership, set out to develop one single brand for the council and the borough, banishing a myriad of some 60 or so different departmental brandings and identities. There were extensive consultations with residents, business and community leaders, council staff, visitors and opinion formers in the wider area to understand current perceptions, key attributes and future visions of Bolton. This engagement in the process won local support, and champions for the approach.

From this, the Bolton brand was developed and implemented – the use of the word 'Bolton' in a modified clarendon typeface was direct, solid and down to earth. The lettering was colour striped to reflect Bolton's DNA, the distinctive character of the town and its people. 'Place branding sits naturally with a local partnership approach, mirroring both current central government policy and likely future direction for local service provision' (Semley and Powell, 2010).

Belfast City Council, too, has opted for an inclusive branding to 'encourage other organisations in Belfast to use it and join us in promoting the city'. It is seen as a framework within which all those involved in marketing the city can operate and add value. In developing the new brand in 2008, the council, Belfast Visitor and Conference Bureau and their brand consultants involved businesses in various sectors, the tourist trade, community groups and councillors, mainly through focus groups. Once agreed, the city council got wide buy-in through a programme of 'brand adoption'.

**FIGURE 13.5**    Belfast: new branding since 2009

**CASE STUDY** Belfast brand guidelines

### What is a brand?

A brand is not just a logo. It is also about portraying a positive and consistent personality and image.

A logo does play a big part in this and it is important to have clear guidance on logo dimensions, placement and usage.

But a strong brand portrays an instantly recognisable visual image through other elements such as: typeface, writing style, colours, photography, and layout and design of publications.

A strong brand helps to build an image and supports what you do. By following a consistent and accurate identity, we are helping to create and maintain a positive and lasting impression of Belfast.

Our brands should not be used to promote anything that is detrimental to the city's reputation. For example, they should not be used to promote politically motivated causes or campaigns.

The Belfast brand is a city brand. We use it on our promotional material and would encourage other organisations in Belfast to use it and join us in promoting the city.

### Brand benefits

A city's brand is an extension of its reputation within every aspect of city life. The Belfast brand is therefore distinctive, creditable, sustainable and reinforces Belfast's position as:

- a confident and contemporary European city;

- a quality leisure and business tourism destination;

- a competitive place for companies to locate and grow their business;

- a great place to live;

- a place that attracts and retains talent; and

- a magnet for world-leading research and innovation.

By using the guidelines you are now helping to communicate these brand benefits by:

- ensuring the brand identity is highly visible across the city;

- providing a single and united message for all city marketing;

- creating a greater level of civic pride and encourage wider participation in city activities;

- uniting the public, private, and voluntary sectors in Belfast;

- enhancing the status and recognition of all those who associate with Belfast's unique qualities; and

- contributing to the long-term brand building exercise, changing perceptions and adding value.

### Brand essence

This is Belfast's moment.

### Brand proposition

A unique history and a future full of promise have come together to create a city bursting with energy and optimism.

### Brand attributes

- welcoming;
- sociable;
- witty;
- genuine;
- optimistic;
- determined;
- dynamic;
- vibrant;
- enterprising;
- inspiring;
- energetic;
- bold.

### Brand experience

For citizens: The time is right for us to use our resilience, enterprise, warmth and wit to build a thriving, vibrant, welcoming city. We're proud of heritage but we embrace the future with relish.

For visitors: Belfast is alive with possibilities and open to change – vibrant, energetic, genuine, warm welcoming and exciting.

For investors: A spirit of optimism and real sense of purpose fills the air, inspiring enterprise, creativity and change.

Extract from Brand Guidelines (Spring 2011) © Belfast City Council
**www.belfastcity.gov.uk/brand/docs/brandguidelines.pdf**

The Belfast Brand, as it says, is not just a logo but is about 'portraying a positive and consistent personality and image'. The detailed brand guidelines show how the solid B-heart brand with the word 'Belfast' sits with, rather than replaces, other logos, including those of the city council (armorial crest), Belfast Waterfront, Ulster Hall and Belfast Zoo. The Belfast Brand also worked beside the Northern Ireland Tourist Board's promotions, including the ribbons strapline 'Our Time, Our Place, Belfast 2012'.

Branding places is different from branding products. It is also significantly harder. Branding, too, is quite different from promotion. It requires a 'more open and critical debate about place and what it has to offer, both now and in the future' (Houghton and Stevens, 2012).

Using the term 'city brand' is generally accepted, but with some provisos. Places are not brands but have 'brand images'; they depend on the power and appeal of those images for their progress and prosperity. And the brand is best described as a 'competitive identity' (Anholt, 2010). The brand metaphor has its limits when one speaks of cities or places (Kapferer, 2011).

A place, unlike a product, has a richness and complexity; it is a human reality, anchored in a history, culture and an ecosystem that can change and adapt. A city brand is 'a vision with values', says Kapferer, and the brand should act as 'a lever of collective consciousness and commitment' to accelerate change. But encapsulating all that – the city's DNA and vision – defies the art of product branding; commercial branding practice 'does not apply in any straightforward way' to the management and promotion of places (Anholt, 2010). There are three clear defining issues for city branding: reputation, authenticity and stakeholder engagement.

First, public relations is essentially about reputation. Brand is a word that 'captures the idea of reputation observed, reputation valued and reputation managed' (Anholt, 2010). Safeguarding reputation is critical for any product or any organisation, but it is perhaps more so for places, particularly towns and cities. There is much more at stake. A damaged or poor city reputation can impact adversely on the whole city's economic and social ecosystem, as investment decisions are diverted to other cities, skilled workers look elsewhere for employment, and tourists, visitors and shoppers go elsewhere. A city's name – and reputation – is tied up in 'huge financial, political and social value'. Baker (2011) puts it more bluntly:

> Too few city leaders think about the number of jobs, businesses and other organisations that have a stake in their city's image and reputation. Unfortunately it is a value that goes unrecognized, unappreciated and unmanaged. It rarely gets measured and never appears on the balance sheet or the job evaluation of a mayor, city manager or city official. The level of esteem that a city's name evokes has a direct impact on the health of its tourism, economic development, prestige and respect. With so much riding on its image, it makes sense to have a plan to cultivate, manage and protect the most valuable of city assets.

The annual international index, the Anholt-GfK Roper Brands Index, measures the image and reputation of many of the world's cities, including those in the United Kingdom. It is a key benchmarking index for anyone involved in city branding. Cities are ranked in terms of six 'P's: presence (international status and standing), place (physical environment), pulse (how exciting the city is perceived), pre-requisites (schools, hospitals, transport, sports), people (friendliness and safety) and potential (economic and educational opportunities).

Secondly, any place branding has to be authentic – both internally and externally. Place brand messages have to resonate with both residents and others outside. A city's branding exercise is a continuous process and the city's brand has to be built up from the bottom (Ooi, 2011). Cities often look to reposition themselves, especially when they are in the doldrums. New York in the 1970s and Glasgow in the 1980s are classic examples. Both sought to turn around the negative perceptions by authentic campaigns that built relationships and through those relationships people were able to see the city, and what it had to offer, in a different light.

Branding can help shape a person's – investor, employer, tourist or resident – perceptions of a city or place, but if that branding is not an accurate representation or in tune with the place as experienced, it can quickly rebound. There will be chatter and conversations on the social media channels for all to see, add to, retweet and act on. Social media is increasingly impacting on places: the experiences and perceptions can shape a concerted view, positive or negative. Failure to be authentic in either place branding or promotions is an open invitation to criticism or worse ridicule. Dinnie (2011) succinctly makes the point: 'A city brand needs to be rooted in reality, rather than a delusion peddled by mendacious marketers. Making exaggerated claims for a city will backfire as soon as target audiences realise that they have been misled.' This is true for all places.

Thirdly, most commentators agree that stakeholder engagement is critical in city or place branding. According to Houghton and Stevens (2012), such engagement introduces a level of 'invaluable real world testing'. Ideas too abstract, superficial or distant from the reality and the assumptions and preconceptions of partners will be challenged. Engagement also helps to counter scepticism and hostility towards branding.

> Stakeholders are a diverse group, individuals, businesses, communities and agencies and need to be engaged proactively from the start. They need to be engaged on the basis of evidence. City branding does not start with a blank sheet. Cities are already branded whether or not they realise or recognise the fact. Starting point is to take a critical look at what the city has to offer to current and potential residents, visitors and investors, what unique assets and strengths can be developed and what flaws and weaknesses addressed.
>
> (Houghton and Stevens, 2011)

Gelder (2011) argues that for city branding to be successful it is necessary for key stakeholder organisations to come together in partnership 'to jointly develop, create and lead on the implementation of the brand of the place under shared responsibility'. More recently, Kavaratzis (2012) has advocated the 'centrality of stakeholders in the creation, development and ownership of place brands'. He says that current place branding practice focuses too much on the communication, for example logos, catchy slogans and advertising, rather than on the engagement of stakeholders in a 'collective exercise' in defining the meaning of place. The contribution of residents is underestimated.

There needs to be a re-examination and re-appreciation of the role of stakeholders, including residents, in place branding, states Kavaratzis (2012). More focus and budget has to go into engagement for three reasons. Place branding is a 'public management activity' and must have public support for legitimacy. The approach should be more transparent and participative, so that the brand is co-created and stakeholders empowered. And thirdly the online world changes things; it makes direct engagement and a multilogue with residents and stakeholders easier.

## Checklist

- Be clear on purpose for promoting place.
- Always first identify a place's strengths and weaknesses.
- Research and understand both internal and external perceptions.
- Bidding for events and projects, that underpin strengths, can promote place.
- Place promotions can make a difference, set targets and evaluate.
- Logos, slogans and hashtags can work for places, but not always: so test first.
- Branding places, towns and cities is different from product branding.
- Place branding is about reputation, must be authentic and involve residents.

## KEY WORDS

Civic pride; attachment; riots; resilience; belonging; negatively perceived; turn-round; city brand; accolades; events; city status; place survey; marketing; defining place; Beckham trail; Monmouthpedia; place branding; public–private partnerships; global brand; logo; brand images; competitive identity; vision; values; reputation; image; authentic; engagement; stakeholders; public management activity; transparent; multilogue.

# 14
# Communicating with confidence

*"Public relations practitioners must be confident professionals acting in the public interest. Having confidence takes you into the heart of all decision making, to advise about the impact for reputation on all strategies and to influence the way forward. It gives you the ability to stand up for what is good about your service against detractors and for the publics who depend upon it.*

SUE WOLSTENHOLME, CIPR PRESIDENT 2013

*First and foremost we are about professional development. Our sector is changing rapidly and so is what's expected of us. We must continue to acquire the skills to succeed in what's probably the most challenging PR job there is.*

CARL WELHAM, CHAIR CIPR LOCAL GOVERNMENT GROUP 2000–03

Major changes are underway in the way our local public services are run and delivered. Significant reductions in council funding over the coming years and an increased demand on services from an ageing population are driving the changes. By 2030, Barnet Council's 'graph of doom' predicts that there will only be money to provide adult care and children's services (Brindle, 2012). Birmingham's 'jaws of doom' highlight the ever-widening gap between money needed to run services and money likely to be available (Butler, 2012).

For Birmingham, the UK's largest council, the gap is £600 million by 2016/17. A doomsday scenario that means the axing of entire services and the 'end of local government as we know it', according to city council's leader Sir Albert Bore. Bore (2013) argues there is 'no more capacity for salami-slicing', making savings across the various council services. Birmingham – like many councils – is reviewing every one of its hundreds of service lines 'to decide what is statutory and/or fit for purpose and if it is neither, then it is likely to be stopped altogether'. Westminster's leader Councillor Philippa Roe (2013) says the funding challenge is an opportunity to break free of orthodoxy and review all the services provided and how they can be delivered more efficiently.

The current local government map frustrates change. In England, for example, there is a patchwork quilt of too many councils – unitaries, counties, districts and boroughs – of widely differing sizes and responsibilities. Lord Heseltine (2012) called for a new localism, single tier councils outside London, beefed up Local Enterprise Partnerships (LEPs) and a transfer of all central government budgets supporting growth to local areas. Scotland's eight regional police and fire and rescue services were merged into single national bodies in April 2013, but its set-up of 32 unitary councils and 14 health boards remains. Legislation is required to reorganise councils and their boundaries; but that can be a fraught process for any government. In Northern Ireland, where there are separate boards for education and joint boards for social services and health, plans are afoot to reduce the current 26 councils to 11 and return powers, like planning, to the new councils in 2015.

In default of legislative change and for financial expediency, more and more councils are working together to find synergies and efficiencies in both front-line and back-office services; the LGA (2012) reports that millions can be saved by sharing services and LGA have mapped 337 councils across England now sharing, saving over £263 million. The tri-county alliance of Staffordshire, Shropshire and Worcestershire councils is the biggest.

> Shared services could be more attractive to some councils than outsourcing. One of the reasons for this is that the council can retain more control over the shared service than an outsourced service. If an outsourced service fails the council has to find a different way of providing the service – either by taking the service back in house – if this is possible – or finding a different provider. Either option is likely to be expensive. Through the level of control and influence a council has over a shared service it can be argued this option provides a level of resilience an outsourced service does not.
>
> (LGA, 2012)

More integration of local NHS and council social services is likely, following examples of Wye Valley NHS Trust and Herefordshire Council creating a joint company, Hooper Ltd, to provide social care and acute community services, or of Highland Council and NHS Highland where the council now leads on children's services and the NHS on adult services. This will accelerate as English councils incorporate public health and through their health and wellbeing boards strategically link health with social services and other local services. Thraves (2013) calls on councils to integrate public health across all service areas.

Councils, too, may come together or merge, like Worthing and Adur or Barking and Dagenham and Thurrock or Stirling and Clackmannshire, with their elected councillors at the core of each council but a unified team managing and delivering services. Three London councils (Westminster, Hammersmith & Fulham, Kensington & Chelsea) have cross-border partnerships including school IT and support services, which are now being delivered by 3BM, a joint venture with the staff owning 75 per cent of the business.

What is certain is that more services will be managed on a shared or joint basis across councils or with other services, particularly the local NHS, and police and fire for public safety. Some will be provided in-house or through arm's length companies and new mutuals, but others will be contracted out to commercial companies or to charitable or voluntary organisations. The Public Services (Social Value) Act 2012 puts a new onus on public authorities in England (and Wales, if Welsh ministers decide) to 'have regard to the economic, social and environmental wellbeing' of the local area when procuring services. This could open up opportunities for local communities and businesses to get a share of public contracts. The public themselves may favour not-for-profit providers, but research shows they are 'increasingly agnostic' about who provides council services (PwC, 2012).

It is difficult to predict how councils or public services will operate in the future. Tomorrow's council could look and feel very different, as new models are being explored – the 'easyCouncil' offering a no-frills service, with all extras being charged separately; a self-build 'Ikea-council' of differently-run services; the outsourced council where many, if not all services, are contracted out externally; and the 'John Lewis-type council' of a co-operative or mutual business providing the services.

What does this all mean for public relations? It means doing more for less – and being more agile and strategic. Council PR and communications budgets have been cut by around 20 per cent on average and staffing reduced by 14 per cent on average (Cartmell, 2012). Linking up with other local public services PR teams is the way ahead to avoid duplication (the focus is often on similar messages or the same publics) and to maximise resources and skills. This is happening but slowly: East Sussex and Medway councils are developing a partnership for a shared communications agency for local public services, Westminster working jointly with Southwark on communications, policy and public affairs or Brighton & Hove providing a PR service to Lewes District Council.

Public relations should be an asset to decision making, offering a 360-degree view and intelligence on how the council, its services, plans and policies are perceived. Public relations staff should be in the eye of the storm, communicating and engaging. It requires confidence to tell it as it is. And confidence to stay the course. The five essentials – the five 'e's – that should underpin the way ahead for public relations are:

# 1. Embrace change

Council communications and public relations teams must embrace change – but not without question. If they have the task of promoting that change internally and externally they must work to ensure that the change proposals or service reconfigurations have been rigorously considered and that citizens, service users and staff have been fully engaged in the process. But change will not go away. The agenda has to be positively grasped by communicators.

> ... councils are moving into a period of sustained public expenditure constraint where choices will be ever more challenging and the public attitude less forgiving. The most important message for the sector is that there should be no letting up in the pace of change that it has demonstrated over the last year, that it needs to continue to focus relentlessly upon driving out inefficiencies from within and that simultaneously it should be looking to manage demand for services in more innovative and effective ways.
>
> (PwC, 2012)

Communicating change is difficult, especially when it is synonymous with cuts. The reality is that there is less money, but the rationale for change must be much deeper – reshaping local services in tune with the public's expectations and the public's willingness to pay up in tax. This means dialogue, or more likely multilogue, with our different publics.

A key aspect of public relations is building relationships. Local public services are about people – citizens, service users and staff – and it is important not to forget the feelings, anxiety and fears around change, and the need for understanding and reassurance.

L'Etang (2008) has indicated that emotion has been little considered in public relations practice and theory. During winter 2012/13, many local councils, thanks to an LGA initiative, stepped up their preparedness for bad weather conditions. Cave (2012) has shown that behind all plans and the Twitter, text and news road alerts, there was an understanding about how people feel about cold and icy conditions. It is not just about keeping the pavements and roads clear, but addressing fear of having an accident or paying the extra heating bills.

With the transfer of public health promotion to councils in England, there will be new skills and experience available to public relations teams. Public health communicators have led in social marketing and behavioural change campaigns from tackling smoking, drug taking and binge drinking to advising on healthy eating. Council public relations will also have to draw on this skill set – understanding emotions and human behaviour, social marketing and 'nudge' techniques – to manage demand and public expectations.

Public relations teams, too, have to change and skill-up for the tasks expected of them. These must include digital and social media, engagement and consultation, demand-management promotion, and effective evaluation.

# 2. Engage locally

There has never been a more important time to engage with residents and the business community – as citizens, customers and clients – on the future of local public services.

Many councils have initiated public consultations on changes to their services. Some of these consultations have been judged flawed by the courts because councils failed to follow the basic rules on consultation. Annual budget 'consultations', now undertaken by many councils, also fell short. As noted earlier, this is a new and complex area of engaging citizens, and most felt they had 'very little influence' on the actual decisions (see Chapter 4, page 90). Many budget consultations were seen cynically as rubber-stamping the cuts and priorities proposed by council officials.

The survey report 'The (local) state we're in' (PwC, 2012) starkly highlights an awareness chasm between what council leaders and chief executives think the public actually know about current spending cuts and what they actually know. Three out of four council leaders and half of the chief executives surveyed thought the public were informed or fairly well informed about the reasons and scale of the council cuts. But only 26 per cent of the public felt informed when asked the same question.

> ... there is a significant and continuing need for councils to engage more effectively with their local communities about the challenges they face, the options they need to consider and the decisions they need to take. If councils do not do so effectively, they are unlikely to be able to drive through the changes that are implicit in a continued period of severe financial pressure.
>
> (PwC, 2012)

There is a warning in the PwC survey that there could be a number of serious council failures sooner or later. So PR has a big task to address the issues both internally and externally. Surrey County's Head of Communications Louise Footner (2012) puts it succinctly:

> I believe that now more than ever communication and engagement is vital. The changes in local government mean that it is more important than ever to help people understand and play a role in these changes.

The conversation also needs to move on positively to what the council can or should be doing now and in the future with the year-on-year funding available. Councils should be leading that conversation locally through their public relations teams, but it requires listening to citizens, service users and the wider community, as well as an openness to follow up and act on their ideas. A bottom-up approach to service transformation may unleash untapped potential and new solutions, or engage the previously unengaged.

The digital world allows local public services to connect better, listen better and respond better, but only if public services really embrace online engagement. Followers can become influencers. PwC's report recommends, as part of a 10 point agenda for action, that councils embark on an ambitious social media programme which it claims could help reduce the digital divide.

Councils are good at using social media as a means of exchanging information with residents, but we believe it can do more than that. We believe social media can transform services, change behaviours and improve councils' relationships with their citizens, even as it saves them money.

Councils should not always have the last word. 'Mr Reasonable' (2012), the Barnet blogger, has questioned the council's 'graph of doom'. With the help of freedom of information requests, he has produced a 'graph of choices' which he hopes will start a 'constructive and meaningful dialogue between [Barnet Council] and residents into what choices we need to be taking to secure the best possible future for all our residents'.

# 3. Elevate leadership

Local government is something to be valued, not just tolerated. Democratically-elected councils and elected mayors have a duty to represent and be a strong voice for their area and their citizens. They should be leaders in their area.

Elected councillors are the local voice in their ward and community. The elected police and crime commissioners in England and Wales also have a specific role and are making an effort to engage with their communities and their local councils. In Scotland, the new national chief constable has said that he aims to engage at ward level. Councillors should be leaders in their wards.

It is the task of the public relations professional to actively promote and support the elected council, as well as the councillors separately, in their local leadership role. At times of change and uncertainty, leadership with engagement is critical both for the citizens and communities served by the council and the staff who provide the services. Councils are pretty good at managing budgets, staff, and services but are less effective when it comes to leadership. All councils should adopt a culture of leadership, operating more corporately and with strong political and officer engagement.

This has implications for public relations. Simon Hope (2012), Communications Head at Wakefield Council, argues rightly that the role of the communications team will have to change, if it is not already changing:

> ... this means moving from talking about what is important to the council to talking about what is important to residents. Communications teams are going to have to get used to marrying the needs of the traditional and social media, both of which are needed. They are also going to have to learn to let go. By that I mean the all-controlling communications team will need to relax the reins in some areas and just allow staff to do their own thing, especially in social media. This is a big challenge for communications teams, but an even bigger challenge for the culture of councils as a whole.

Public relations has a crucial leadership role to play. We have seen in Chapter 2 (see page 31) that public relations influence at the decision-making table is too low and many directors or heads of communications are short on the strategic business and leadership competencies required by chief executives to contribute at the highest level. LGCommunications (2009) has set out the competencies needed and runs a leadership academy for council public relations. Public relations is, according to Moss and DeSanto (2012), a 'natural component of leadership'. But public relations practitioners need to up their game, look beyond the status quo, innovate and be creative and proactive. And, more than anything else, be strategic in order to lead on the change agenda.

# 4. Emphasise brand and reputation

The council brand and reputation have a resonance locally. In a national poll for LGA (2013), 73 per cent of the public are very or fairly satisfied with the way their local council runs things and 61 per cent trust their local council to make decisions.

So, as services are re-configured with the different options of delivery – shared services, arms-length companies or mutuals, charitable or voluntary organisations or commercial companies – it is important not to carelessly discard the council brand or reputation, especially for something new which will have little public traction. The local public services are littered with new or joint services logos that have been devised in enthusiasm, but in haste. There is a strong case for retention of the known (and trusted) council logo as a signifier, perhaps alongside the logo of the provider. Councils should be allying themselves with trusted partners, whether not-for-profit or commercial. Detailed consideration needs to be given to such branding and messaging, whether it be for refuse collection or children's services (see Chapter 12, particularly Southwark Council's guide to partnership branding on page 234).

Too often, because of contractual oversights or default, the council is sidelined altogether and the contracted-out services are branded by the contracted provider, not the paymaster, the council. This confuses residents, distances the service from council taxpayers and fails to acknowledge that the council is ultimately responsible for the quality or failure of that service.

Councils have to be seen to be doing what they say they are doing in the annual bills for council tax and business rates or in the charges they make for services. The branded visible and tangible link between the council and its services is important for reputation, and should be a factor in reputation management. Reputation isn't yours to control, argue Earl and Waddington (2012). It always rests with your publics and the way you engage.

> The future of organisational communication and therefore the future of reputation management lies in the participation of the brand with its

audience. That is achieved by understanding the audience and building editorial influence across all forms of applicable media.

# 5. Embed public interest

Over 65 years ago, the 'municipal group' who were instrumental in founding the Institute of Public Relations (now CIPR) brought to the embryonic public relations profession the values of serving the public interest and the need for truthfulness in information to the public (see Chapter 1, page 3).

There are numerous examples of these values being ditched: councils, hospitals, the police and fire services deliberately covering up and suppressing serious complaints or information. But few officers or professionals are seen to be accountable. The Chartered Institute of Public Finance and Accountancy (2010) expelled John Lindsay, formerly East Lothian Council's chief executive for a 'breach of trust with the residents' by not declaring a conflict of interest and suppressing crucial information in a council report. Lindsay was later stripped of his OBE, awarded for public service.

The principle of public interest – truth, openness and transparency – needs to be embedded now more than ever if councils, health services and public services organisations are to retain the trust of the public they were set up to serve. This is particularly so during a period of transformation and change.

All local public services' PR teams must be equipped for the challenge and prepared to communicate with confidence in the public interest.

# APPENDIX 1
# The code of recommended practice on local authority publicity in England (2011)

This revised code came into force on 31 March 2011. It applies to all unitary, county and district councils in England, London borough councils, the City of London Council, Metropolitan Police Authority, police authorities in England and Wales, passenger transport authorities, fire and civil defence authorities, the National Parks authorities, the Broads Authority, the Manchester Combined Authority, the Council of the Isles of Scilly and parish councils in England.

In April 2013, the coalition government issued a consultation to make the 2011 Code mandatory and to give the Secretary of State new powers to direct a council to comply (see pages 13–15).

## Introduction

**1** This code applies to all local authorities in England specified in section 6 of the Local Government Act 1986 and to other authorities in England which have that provision applied to them by other legislation. Where the term "local authorities" is used in this code it should be taken as referring to both those categories of authority. References to "the Act" are to the Local Government Act 1986.

**2** Local authorities are required by section 4(1) of the Act to have regard to the contents of this code in coming to any decision on publicity. Section 6 of the Act defines publicity as "any communication in whatever form, addressed to the public at large or a section of the public". The code therefore applies in relation to all decisions by local authorities relating to paid advertising and leaflet campaigns, publication of free newspapers and newssheets and maintenance of websites – including the hosting of material which is created by third parties.

**3** Nothing in this code overrides the prohibition by section 2 of the Act on the publication by local authorities of material which in whole or in part appears to be designed to affect public support for a political party. Paragraphs 21 to 24 offer some guidance for local authorities on the management of publicity which may contain or have links to party political material.

# Principles

**4** Publicity by local authorities should:

- be lawful;
- be cost effective;
- be objective;
- be even-handed;
- be appropriate;
- have regard to equality and diversity;
- be issued with care during periods of heightened sensitivity.

# Lawfulness

**5** Local authorities should ensure that publicity complies with all applicable statutory provisions. Paid-for advertising must comply with the Advertising Standards Authority's Advertising Codes.

**6** Part 3 of the Communications Act 2003 prohibits political advertising on television or radio. Local authorities must ensure that their publicity does not breach these restrictions.

**7** Section 125 of the Political Parties, Elections and Referendums Act 2000 places a specific restriction on the publication by a local authority of material relating to a referendum under Part 7 of that Act, during the period of 28 days immediately before the referendum is held.

**8** Regulation 5 of the Local Authorities (Conduct of Referendums) (England) Regulations 2007 (SI 2007/2089) prohibits local authorities from publishing material in the 28 days immediately before a referendum which expresses support for, or opposition to a particular answer to a referendum question relating to the constitutional arrangements of the authority.

**9** Regulation 15 of the Local Authorities (Referendums, Petitions and Directions) (England) Regulations 2000 (SI 2000/2852) prohibits local authorities from incurring expenditure to publish material which appears designed to influence people in deciding whether or not to sign a petition relating to the constitutional arrangements of the authority, or to assist others to publish such material.

# Cost effectiveness

**10** In relation to all publicity, local authorities should be able to confirm that consideration has been given to the value for money that is being achieved, including taking into account any loss of potential revenue arising from the use of local authority-owned facilities to host authority publicity.

11 In some circumstances it will be difficult to quantify value for money, for example where the publicity promotes a local amenity which is free to use. In such a case authorities should be able to show that they have given thought to alternative means of promoting the amenity and satisfied themselves that the means of publicity chosen is the most appropriate.

12 If another public authority, such as central government, has issued publicity on a particular topic, local authorities should incur expenditure on issuing publicity on the same matter only if they consider that additional value is achieved by the duplication of that publicity. Additional value might be achieved if locally produced publicity gives a local context to national issues.

13 The purchase of advertising space should not be used as a method of subsidising voluntary, public or commercial organisations.

14 Local authorities should consider whether it is appropriate to seek advice from economic analysts, public relations experts or other sources of expert advice before embarking on a publicity campaign involving very large expenditure.

## Objectivity

15 Local authorities should ensure that publicity relating to policies and proposals from central government is balanced and factually accurate. Such publicity may set out the local authority's views and reasons for holding those views, but should avoid anything likely to be perceived by readers as constituting a political statement, or being a commentary on contentious areas of public policy.

16 Any publicity describing the council's policies and aims should be as objective as possible, concentrating on the facts or explanation or both. Local authorities should not use public funds to mount publicity campaigns whose primary purpose is to persuade the public to hold a particular view on a question of policy. It is acceptable for local authority publicity to correct erroneous material which has been published by other parties, despite the fact that the material being corrected may have been published with the intention of influencing the public's opinions about the policies of the authority. Such publicity should seek to explain the facts in an objective manner.

17 Where paid-for advertising is used by local authorities, it should be clearly identified as being advertising. Paid-for advertising, including advertisements for the recruitment of staff, should not be used in any publication owned or controlled by a political party.

**18** Advertisements for the recruitment of staff should reflect the tradition of political impartiality of local authority employees and should not (except in the case of advertisements relating to the appointment of staff pursuant to section 9 of the Local Government and Housing Act 1989 (assistants for political groups)) refer to any political activities or affiliations of candidates.

# Even-handedness

**19** Where local authority publicity addresses matters of political controversy it should seek to present the different positions in relation to the issue in question in a fair manner.

**20** Other than in the circumstances described in paragraph 34 of this code, it is acceptable for local authorities to publicise the work done by individual members of the authority, and to present the views of those individuals on local issues. This might be appropriate, for example, when one councillor has been the "face" of a particular campaign. If views expressed by or attributed to individual councillors do not reflect the views of the local authority itself, such publicity should make this fact clear.

**21** It is acceptable for local authorities to host publicity prepared by third parties – for example an authority may host a blog authored by members of the authority or a public forum on which members of the public may leave comments. Maintenance by a local authority of a website permitting the posting of material by third parties constitutes a continuing act of publication by that local authority which must accordingly have a system for moderating and removing any unacceptable material.

**22** It is generally acceptable for local authorities to host publicity, such as a blog, which itself contains links to external sites over which the local authority has no control where the content of those sites would not itself comply with this code. This does not amount to giving assistance to any person for the publication of material which local authorities are not permitted to publish. However, particular care must be taken by local authorities during the period before elections and referendums to ensure that no breach of any legal restriction takes place. It may be necessary to suspend the hosting of material produced by third parties or public forums which contain links to impermissible material during such periods.

**23** It is acceptable for publicity containing material prepared by third parties and hosted by local authorities to include logos of political parties or other organisations with which the third parties are associated.

24  It is acceptable for publicity produced or hosted by local authorities to include a logo associated with a particular member of the authority, such as a directly elected mayor, or leader of the authority. Publicity material produced by local authorities relating to a particular member must not seek to affect public support for that individual.

25  Where local authorities provide assistance to third parties to issue publicity they should ensure that the principles in this code are adhered to by the recipients of that assistance.

# Appropriate use of publicity

26  Local authorities should not incur any expenditure in retaining the services of lobbyists for the purpose of the publication of any material designed to influence public officials, Members of Parliament, political parties or the Government to take a particular view on any issue.

27  Local authorities should not incur expenditure on providing stands or displays at conferences of political parties for the purpose of publicity designed to influence members of political parties to take a particular view on any issue.

28  Local authorities should not publish or incur expenditure in commissioning in hard copy or on any website, newsletters, newssheets or similar communications which seek to emulate commercial newspapers in style or content. Where local authorities do commission or publish newsletters, newssheets or similar communications, they should not issue them more frequently than quarterly, apart from parish councils which should not issue them more frequently than monthly. Such communications should not include material other than information for the public about the business, services and amenities of the council or other local service providers.

29  Publicity about local authorities and the services they provide should be freely available to anyone who wishes to receive such information in a format readily accessible and understandable by the person making the request or by any particular group for which services are provided.

30  All local authority publicity should clearly and unambiguously identify itself as a product of the local authority. Printed material, including any newsletters, newssheets or similar publications published by the local authority, should do this on the front page of the publication.

# Equality and diversity etc

**31** Publicity by local authorities may seek to influence (in accordance with the relevant law and in a way which they consider positive) the attitudes of local people or public behaviour in relation to matters of health, safety, crime prevention, race relations, equality, diversity and community issues.

**32** Local authorities should consider how any publicity they issue can contribute to the promotion of any duties applicable to them in relation to the elimination of discrimination, the advancement of equality and the fostering of good relations.

# Care during periods of heightened sensitivity

**33** Local authorities should pay particular regard to the legislation governing publicity during the period of heightened sensitivity before elections and referendums – see paragraphs 7 to 9 of this code. It may be necessary to suspend the hosting of material produced by third parties, or to close public forums during this period to avoid breaching any legal restrictions.

**34** During the period between the notice of an election and the election itself, local authorities should not publish any publicity on controversial issues or report views or proposals in such a way that identifies them with any individual members or groups of members. Publicity relating to individuals involved directly in the election should not be published by local authorities during this period unless expressly authorised by or under statute. It is permissible for local authorities to publish factual information which identifies the names, wards and parties of candidates at elections.

**35** In general, local authorities should not issue any publicity which seeks to influence voters. However, this general principle is subject to any statutory provision which authorises expenditure being incurred on the publication of material designed to influence the public as to whether to support or oppose a question put at a referendum. It is acceptable to publish material relating to the subject matter of a referendum, for example to correct any factual inaccuracies which have appeared in publicity produced by third parties, so long as this is even-handed and objective and does not support or oppose any of the options which are the subject of the vote.

Department for Communities and Local Government, Circular 01/2011. Published here under the Open Government Licence.

# APPENDIX 1a
# The code of recommended practice on local government publicity (1988)

The 1988 Code only applies to councils in Scotland.

This Code applied to England and Wales until 2001. It was amended in 2001 for England and Wales only and was replaced by the 2011 Code for England (see Appendix 1). In 2013 a new Code for Wales was published. There is no similar Code for councils in Northern Ireland.

## Introduction

### Status of the Code

1 This Code is issued by the Secretaries of State for the Environment, Scotland and Wales in pursuance of their powers under section 4(1) of the Local Government Act 1986. The Code was drawn up following the consultations with interested parties in local government required by section 4(4) of the Act. It has been approved by a resolution of each House of Parliament. Local authorities are required by section 4(1) of the Act as amended by section 27 of the Local Government Act 1988 to have regard to the Code in coming to any decision on publicity.

### Why have a Code?

2 Local authorities are accountable to their electorate. Local accountability requires local understanding. This will be promoted by local authorities explaining their objectives and policies to their electors and ratepayers. In recent years authorities have increasingly used publicity to keep the public informed, and to encourage greater participation. Local authorities also need to tell the public about the services which they provide. Increasingly, local authorities see the task of making the public aware of the services available as an essential part of providing all kinds of services. Good, effective publicity, aimed at improved public awareness of a council's activities, is to be welcomed. This Code is not intended to discourage such publicity.

3 Publicity is, however, a sensitive matter in any political environment, because of the impact which it can have. Expenditure on publicity by some local authorities has been significant. It is essential, therefore, to ensure that local authority decisions on publicity are properly made, in accordance with clear principles of good practice. The purpose of the Code is to set out such principles. It reflects the conventions which should apply to all publicity at public expense, and which traditionally have applied in both central and local government.

4 The principles set out below recognise the political nature of local government. They take account of the fact that some local authority publicity will deal with issues that are controversial because of particular local circumstances, or because of a difference of view between political parties locally or nationally. The principles do not prohibit the publication of information on politically sensitive or controversial issues, nor stifle public debate. They set out the matters a local authority should consider, to safeguard both the proper use of public funds and those members of the public at whom publicity is directed. They apply to all publicity, but some aspects will be especially relevant to publicity which deals with controversial or sensitive issues. The underlying objective of the Code is to ensure the proper use of public funds for publicity.

## Scope of the Code

5 The Code is not concerned with the interpretation of section 2 of the Local Government Act 1986. (That section provides that a local authority shall not publish (or assist others to publish) material which, in whole or in part, appears to be designed to affect public support for a political party.) The Code is concerned with all the other publicity which a local authority may publish. In particular, it highlights factors which should be borne in mind in decisions on publicity which deals with matters or issues which are, politically or otherwise, controversial, but which are not prohibited by section 2.

6 Section 6 of the 1986 Act defines publicity as 'any communication, in whatever form, addressed to the public at large or to a section of the public'. The Code will therefore be relevant across the whole range of local authorities' work. It covers all decisions by a local authority on publicity and most public relations activities, such as paid advertising and leaflet campaigns, and local authority sponsorship of exhibitions and conferences, as well as assistance to others to issue publicity.

7 The Code has no relevance to the methods which a local authority may use to make its views known where these do not involve publicity in the sense of the 1986 Act.

8 The Code does not affect the ability of local authorities to assist charities and voluntary organisations which need to issue publicity as part of their work, but it requires local authorities, in giving such assistance, to consider the principles on which the Code is based, and to apply them accordingly.

9 By virtue of section 6(6) of the 1986 Act, nothing in the Code is to be construed as applying to any decision by a local authority in the discharge of their duties under the Local Government (Access to Information) Act 1985.

# Code of recommended practice

## Subject matter

1 Local authorities have a variety of statutory powers which enable them to produce publicity and circulate it widely, or to assist others to do so. Those commonly used include the powers in sections 111, 142, 144 and 145 of the Local Government Act 1972, sections 69, 88 and 90 of the Local Government (Scotland) Act 1973 and sections 15 and 16 of the Local Government and Planning (Scotland) Act 1982; but there are several others.

2 Some of these powers relate directly to the publishing authority's functions. Others give a more general discretion to publicise matters which go beyond an authority's primary responsibilities. For example, sections 142(1A) of the 1972 Act and 88(1) of the 1973 Act authorise local authorities to arrange for the publication within their area of information as to the services available in the area provided by them or by other local authorities; and Section 54 of the Public Health (Control of Disease) Act 1984 empowers local authorities to arrange for the publication within their area of information on questions relating to health or disease.

3 This discretion provides an important degree of flexibility, but also heightens the need for a responsible approach to expenditure decisions.

4 In considering the subject areas in which publicity is to be issued, the following matters will be important:

(i) the publicity should be relevant to the functions of the authority.
(ii) it should not duplicate unnecessarily publicity produced by central government, another local authority or another public authority.
(iii) in areas where central government, another tier of local government, or another public authority have the primary service or policy responsibility, local authorities should issue publicity only on matters that are directly relevant to their own functions.

## Costs

**5** Local authorities are accountable to the public for the efficiency and effectiveness of their expenditure, in the first instance through the audit arrangements.

**6** For publicity, as for all other expenditure, the aim should therefore be to achieve the greatest possible cost-effectiveness.

**7** To achieve this, there may well be cases where the benefit of higher expenditure to gain better presentation or improve other aspects of publicity will justify the extra cost.

**8** Local authorities should therefore always have in mind the extent to which expert advice is needed for publicity.

**9** In some cases publicity may justify its cost by virtue of savings which it achieves. More commonly it will be necessary to take a view of the importance of the unquantifiable benefits as compared with other uses to which the resources could be put.

**10** In deciding whether the nature and scale of proposed publicity, and consequently its cost, are justified, the following matters will be relevant:

(i) whether the publicity is statutorily required or is discretionary. (ii) where it is statutorily required, the purpose to be served by the publicity. (iii) whether the expenditure envisaged is in keeping with the purpose and expected effect of the publicity.

## Content and style

**11** Local authorities produce a variety of publicity material. It ranges from factual information about the services provided by the authority, designed to inform clients or attract new ones, to material necessary to the administration of the authority, such as staff recruitment advertising. There will also be publicity to explain or justify the council's policies either in general, as in the annual report, or on specific topics, for example as background to consultation on the line chosen for a new road.

**12** Any publicity describing the council's policies and aims should be as objective as possible, concentrating on facts or explanation or both.

**13** Where publicity is used to comment on, or respond to, the policies and proposals of central government, other local authorities or other public authorities, the comment or response should be objective, balanced, informative, and accurate. It should aim to set out the reasons for the council's views, and should not be a prejudiced, unreasoning or political attack on the policies or proposals in question or on those putting them forward. Slogans alone will not be an adequate means of justifying or explaining the authority's views or their policy decisions.

**14** Publicity relating to the provision of a service should concentrate on providing factual information about the service.

**15** In some cases promotional publicity may be appropriate – for example about the local authority's sports and leisure facilities or about tourist attractions.

**16** Publicity touching on issues that are controversial, or on which there are arguments for and against the views or policies of the council, should be handled with particular care. It should not over-simplify facts, issues or arguments. Again, it is unlikely that slogans alone will achieve the necessary degree of balance, or capture the complexities of opposing political arguments.

**17** Publicity should not attack, nor appear to undermine, generally accepted moral standards.

**18** Publicity campaigns by local authorities are appropriate in some circumstances: for example, to promote the effective and efficient use of local services and facilities, or to attract tourists or investment. Publicity campaigns may also be an appropriate means of influencing public behaviour or attitudes on such matters as health, safety, crime prevention or race relations.

**19** Legitimate concern is, however, caused by the use of public resources for some forms of campaigns which are designed to have a persuasive effect. Publicity campaigns can provide an appropriate means of ensuring that the local community is properly informed about a matter relating to a function of the local authority and about the authority's policies in relation to that function and the reasons for them. But local authorities, like other public authorities, should not use public funds to mount publicity campaigns whose primary purpose is to persuade the public to hold a particular view on a question of policy.

## Dissemination

**20** The main purposes of local authority publicity are to increase public awareness of the services provided by the authority and the functions it performs; to explain to electors and ratepayers the reasons for particular policies and priorities; and in general to improve local accountability.

**21** Information and publicity produced by the council should be made available to all those who want or need it. Local authorities should not discriminate in favour of, or against, persons or groups in the compilation and distribution of material for reasons not connected with the efficiency and effectiveness of issuing the publicity.

**22** Where material is distributed on matters closely affecting vulnerable sections of the community – for example, the elderly – particular care should be taken to ensure that it is unambiguous, readily intelligible, and unlikely to cause needless concern to those reading, seeing or listening to it.

23 Local authority newspapers, leaflets, and other publicity distributed unsolicited from house to house are inevitably more intrusive than publicity available on application to the council.

24 Publicity that reaches the public unsolicited should be targeted as far as practicable on those whose interests are clearly and directly affected by its content.

25 Material touching on politically controversial issues should be distributed unsolicited only where there is a strong case for letting a particular group of people have information of direct concern to them and no other equally efficient and effective means can be found.

26 Local authority newspapers or information bulletins are a special case. They are often a cost-effective means of disseminating information, but they may touch on controversial issues. If they do, they should treat such issues in an objective and informative way, bearing in mind the principles set out in paragraphs 11–19 of the Code.

27 Where it is important for information to reach a particular target audience, consideration should be given to using the communications networks of other bodies, for example those of voluntary organisations.

## *Advertising*

28 Advertising, especially on billboards or on television and radio, is a highly intrusive medium. It can also be expensive. It may however provide a cost effective, efficient means of conveying public information to the widest possible audience. Advertising on local radio networks has, for example, been used as a relatively inexpensive means of telling potential clients about local authority services. Advertising can also be the most cost-effective means of publicising a local authority's activities on tourism, and in the area of economic development generally.

29 The primary criterion for decisions on whether to use advertising should be cost-effectiveness.

30 Advertisements are not normally likely to be appropriate as a means of explaining policy or commenting on proposals, since an advertisement by its nature summarises information, compresses issues and arguments, and markets views and opinions.

31 Advertising in media which cover an area significantly wider than that of the authority is not likely to be an appropriate means of conveying information about a local authority's policies as opposed to attracting people to the authority's area or to use its facilities.

**32** The attribution of advertising material leaflets and other forms of publicity that reach the public unsolicited should be clearly set out.

**33** It is not acceptable, in terms of public accountability, to use the purchase of advertising space as a disguised means of subsidy to a voluntary, industrial or commercial organisation. Such support should be given openly through the normal grant arrangements. However, the conditions attached to a grant may require the provision of publicity, including publicity for the work of the authority.

**34** Any decision to take advertising space in a publication produced by a voluntary, industrial or commercial organisation should be made only on the grounds that it provides an effective and efficient means of securing the desired publicity.

**35** Local authorities should never use advertising as a means of giving financial support to any publication associated with a political party.

## Recruitment advertising

**36** Local authorities have respected in their staff employment policies the tradition of a politically impartial public service. Their recruitment publicity should reflect this tradition, and the fact that local authority staff are expected to serve the authority as a whole, whatever its composition from time to time.

**37** The content of recruitment publicity and the media chosen for advertising job vacancies should be in keeping with the objective of maintaining the politically independent status of local authority staff.

**38** Advertisements for staff should not be placed in party political publications.

## Publicity about individual members of an authority

**39** The functions of a local authority are discharged by the council corporately. It is therefore inappropriate for public resources to be used to publicise individual councillors.

**40** In the interests of public accountability, however, it may be appropriate to give publicity to the views or activities of individual members when they are representing the council as a whole: for example, when the chairman of a council speaks or acts as the first citizen of the whole community, or when a chairman of a committee opens a new scheme or launches a policy approved by the council or by his committee on the council's behalf.

**41** For the same reason a local authority may justifiably in certain circumstances issue press releases reporting statements made by individual members. Examples of cases where such press releases may he appropriate are as reports of the discussion at the meetings of the council or committees, or quotations of comments made by leading members of the council in response to particular events which call for a particularly speedy reaction from the council.

**42** This does not prevent a member of staff of a local authority from responding to questions about individual members, since that is not publicity as defined in the 1986 Act.

## Timing of publicity

**43** Particular care should be taken when publicity is issued immediately prior to an election or by-election affecting the authority's area to ensure that this could not be perceived as seeking to influence public opinion, or to promote the public image of a particular candidate, or group of candidates. Between the time of publication of a notice of an election and polling day, publicity should not be issued which deals with controversial issues, or which reports views or policies in a way that identifies them with individual members or groups of members.

## Assistance to others for publicity

**44** The principles set out above apply to decisions on publicity issued by local authorities. They should also be taken into account by local authorities in decisions on assistance to others to issue publicity. In all such decisions local authorities should, to the extent appropriate:
   **(a)** incorporate the relevant principles of the Code in published guidance for applicants for grants;
   **(b)** make the observance of that guidance a condition of the grant or other assistance;
   **(c)** undertake monitoring to ensure that the guidance is observed.

**45** It can be appropriate for local authorities to help charities and voluntary organisations by arranging for pamphlets or other material produced and paid for by the organisation to be available for collection by the public in public libraries and other suitable locations. Such material should not offend against any legal provision, but (subject to this) any such facility should be made available on a fair and equal basis.

# APPENDIX 2
## Performance Framework

**A**useful example of a Performance Framework demonstrated at Delivering Excellent Communications, a two-day development and learning event for communicators in local public services hosted by the CIPR local public services group and Thurrock Council, November 2012. Developed by Phil McCusker, Head of Communications for Thurrock Council.

## Communications Team – Performance Framework

### Planned Approach

| Competency | Good/Excellent |
|---|---|
| Proactive, planned and consistent | • Consistently seeks out information from a range of sources and manages issues to promote and/or defend the council's reputation.<br>• Organises and plans communications to achieve impact and value for money.<br>• Ensures consistency of message across all channels and activities.<br>• Adopts project management approach to all activities. |
| Evidence-based | • Seeks out and analyses data to identify issues.<br>• Produces plans based on research data with clear objectives and metrics.<br>• Seeks out best practice and benchmark data to improve performance.<br>• Understands and interprets complex issues and information.<br>• Seeks regular feedback from customers about services provided and uses this to undertake and/or recommend continuous improvement to services. |

## *Political Awareness*

| Competency | Good/Excellent |
|---|---|
| Political awareness | • Understands the role of politics in a council and works effectively with all politicians, within the LG code of publicity.<br>• Advises and consults with senior politicians on a range of reputation management issues.<br>• Ensures elected members are well informed about issues affecting their wards.<br>• Have good antennae and are stimulated by a degree of curiosity. |
| Organisational awareness | • Understands the overall functions, aims and direction of the council, including the vision and priorities and associated strategic objectives and action plans.<br>• Ensures all communications are linked to the vision and priorities of the council.<br>• Understands the council's business and the range of services and promotes in a co-ordinated way.<br>• Demonstrates an emotional connection to what the business is trying to achieve and links communications objectives appropriately.<br>• Adapts to changing environment and context. |

# Technical Proficiency

| Competency | Good/Excellent |
|---|---|
| Writing | • Writes in clear, concise and plain language, with excellent grammar and spelling.<br>• Writes creatively and with impact. Effectively conveys a message to a variety of audiences.<br>• Is sensitive to how different audiences may react to different issues and displays good judgement in dealing with different people.<br>• Develops and maintains a consistent and compelling story about the council, its services and its performance.<br>• Translates complex information and produces clear, easy to understand copy/editorial for a variety of channels. |
| Innovation and creativity | • Seeks out new ways of doing things, thinks laterally, joins up activity to create greater impact.<br>• Adopts a flexible and creative approach, redefining problems based on information gathered or changes in context.<br>• Creates original campaign concepts, writes creatively, and always linked to communication objectives.<br>• Inspires others to think and do things differently in order to change perceptions, attitudes and behaviours. |
| PR planning, delivery and evaluation | • Understands and applies the core principles of developing and delivering successful media, internal and marketing campaigns – applying research, setting clear objectives, audience and message management, clear and relevant strategy, implement using appropriate channels and evaluate performance.<br>• Examples of organising and executing successful campaigns applying the above concepts.<br>• Commissions and manages printers, designers, agencies, external professionals, to achieve excellent results and value for money. |

# *Ambition*

| Competency | Good/Excellent |
| --- | --- |
| For self | • Minimum qualifications and experience for role achieved. |
| | • Clear understanding of communications excellence and self-awareness about own performance. |
| | • Ambitious to improve own performance and career in communications – links training and development needs to current and future roles. |
| | • Strong track record of continuous professional development with a relevant professional body over several years. |
| | • Has a strong network of professional contacts. |
| | • Uses a range of techniques to enhance performance, in addition to training courses and qualifications. |
| | • Shares and applies learning with others. |
| For the Council | • Complete focus on promoting and defending the reputation of the council in everything you do. |
| | • Operates a 'one council' approach to communications thinking and activity. Protects the council's brand at all times. |
| | • Driven by a desire to ensure communications adds value to the whole council and clear about how to achieve that. |

# Personal Impact

| | Good/Excellent |
|---|---|
| Presentation | • Communicates orally in a manner which is clear, fluent, concise and appropriate, and which holds people's attention both in groups and in one-to-one situations, encouraging feedback as appropriate. |
| | • Able to present compelling copy and visual communications to get message across. |
| | • Behaves consistently with clear personal values which complement those of the organisation. |
| | • As a representative of the council and the team, takes pride in working environment, personal appearance and presentation of own work. |
| Teamwork | • Shares responsibility, experience and ideas in pursuit of team goals. |
| | • Has a desire to work as part of a top performing team and put maximum effort and commitment into achieving team goals. |
| | • Is supportive and cooperative with team and department. |
| | • Makes things happen. |
| Relationship building | • Builds strong, positive working relationships with contacts and primary stakeholders, that inspire trust and respect. |
| | • Influences the attitudes and opinions of others, gaining their agreement through persuasion to ideas, proposals and courses of action, including selling in news stories. |
| | • Seizes opportunities and takes the initiative in moving things along in a positive way. |
| | • Delivers advice and consultancy on a range of communications issues, with confidence and style. |
| | • Works effectively with partners and stakeholders on planned and crisis communications. |

# APPENDIX 3
# Chartered Institute of Public Relations Code of Conduct

**F**or full regulations see online resources and **www.cipr.co.uk/content/about-us/about-cipr/code-conduct**

## 1 Principles

Members of the Chartered Institute of Public Relations agree to:

I   maintain the highest standards of professional endeavour, integrity, confidentiality, financial propriety and personal conduct;

II   deal honestly and fairly in business with employers, employees, clients, fellow professionals, other professions and the public;

III   respect, in their dealings with other people, the legal and regulatory frameworks and codes of all countries where they practise;

IV   uphold the reputation of, and do nothing that would bring into disrepute, the public relations profession or the Chartered Institute of Public Relations;

V   respect and abide by this Code and related Notes of Guidance issued by the Chartered Institute of Public Relations and ensure that others who are accountable to them (eg subordinates and sub-contractors) do the same;

VI   encourage professional training and development among members of the profession in order to raise and maintain professional standards generally.

## 2 Putting the principles into practice

Examples of good public relations practice include:

### Integrity and honesty

- Ensuring that clients, employers, employees, colleagues and fellow professionals are fully informed about the nature of representation, what can be delivered and achieved, and what other parties must do in order to enable the desired result.

- Never deliberately concealing the practitioner's role as representative of a client or employer, even if the client or employer remains anonymous: eg by promoting a cause in the guise of a disinterested party or member of the public.
- Checking the reliability and accuracy of information before dissemination.
- Supporting the CIPR Principles by bringing to the attention of the CIPR examples of malpractice and unprofessional conduct.

## Capacity, capability and competence

- Delivering work competently: that is, in a timely, cost-effective, appropriate and thoughtful manner, according to the actual or implied contract; applying due professional judgement and experience; taking necessary steps to resolve problems; and ensuring that clients and other interested parties are informed, advised and consulted as necessary.
- Being aware of the limitations of professional capacity and capability: without limiting realistic scope for development, being willing to accept or delegate only that work for which practitioners are suitably skilled and experienced and which they have the resources to undertake.
- Where appropriate, collaborating on projects to ensure the necessary skill base.

## Transparency and avoiding conflicts of interest

- Disclosing to employers, clients or potential clients any financial interest in a supplier being recommended or engaged.
- Declaring conflicts of interest (or circumstances which may give rise to them) in writing to clients, potential clients and employers as soon as they arise.
- Ensuring that services provided are costed, delivered and accounted for in a manner that conforms to accepted business practice and ethics.

## Confidentiality

- Safeguarding confidences, eg of present and former clients and employers.
- Never using confidential and 'insider' information to the disadvantage or prejudice of others, eg clients and employers, or to self-advantage of any kind.
- Not disclosing confidential information unless specific permission has been granted or if required or covered by law.

## 3 Maintaining professional standards

CIPR Members are encouraged to spread awareness and pride in the public relations profession where practicable by, for example:

- identifying and closing professional skills gaps through the Institute's Continuous Professional Development programme;
- offering work experience to students interested in pursuing a career in public relations;
- participating in the work of the Institute through the committee structure, special interest and vocational groups, training and networking events;
- encouraging employees and colleagues to join and support the CIPR;
- displaying the CIPR designatory letters on business stationery;
- specifying a preference for CIPR applicants for staff positions advertised;
- evaluating the practice of public relations through use of the CIPR Research & Evaluation Toolkit and other quality management and quality assurance systems (eg ISO standards); and constantly striving to improve the quality of business performance;
- sharing information on good practice with Members and, equally, referring perceived examples of poor practice to the Institute.

# APPENDIX 4
# PR 2020: The future of public relations

Between July and October 2011, Dr Jon White FCIPR conducted a series of scenario-planning meetings with members of the Chartered Institute of Public Relations across the UK.

Recommendations for action emerging from examination of the scenarios include:

1 Encouragement to the Institute to provide leadership and meet expectations for its leadership

2 Education and training for public relations practice need to be taken to higher levels, which will involve greater collaboration with education for public relations

3 Practitioners need greater confidence in what they do, and should lead practice development by example

4 There is a need for clearer thinking and guidance on measurement and evaluation

5 Codes of conduct should be strengthened

6 Practitioners need to move faster to develop their knowledge of digital communication

7 There is a need for better definitions of public relations and what it is to achieve

8 Change should be embraced

9 Industry bodies should commit to research and development

10 There is a need to synchronize experience and fresh talent, and to celebrate young people in practice

For the full report, see **www.cipr.co.uk**.

# REFERENCES AND FURTHER READING

## Chapter 1

Aiming for the Best (2011) *Aiming for the Best – Using Lessons from complaints to improve public services*, Centre for Public Scrutiny/Local Government Ombudsman, www.lgo.org.uk

Anthony, S (2012) *Public Relations and Making of Modern Britain: Stephen Tallents and the Birth of a Progressive Media Profession*, Manchester University Press, Manchester

Audit Commission (1995) *Talk Back: Local Government Communication with Citizens*, HMSO, London

Bains, M (1972) *The New Local Authorities: Management and Structure*, London, HMSO, para 7.35 and 7.36

Bates, D (2006) *'Mini-Me' History: Public Relations from the Dawn of Civilization*, London, Institute for Public Relations

Birmingham City Council [accessed 30 August 2012] *Report on an Investigation into a complaint No 11009273*, Local Government Ombudsman [Online] www.lgo.org.uk

Calderwood, R (2008) 'NHS Greater Glasgow', *Health News* newspaper.

Communities and Local Government (2011) *Code of Recommended Practice on Local Authority Publicity*

Connecting with Communities (2002) *Five Years of Communications: A Review of Local Authority Communications*, London, Office of the Deputy Prime Minister

Cooper, D (2012) quoted in *Plain English*, Spring 2012

Corkey, J (2013) 'Communicating council tax budgets', *PR Week* [Online] 8 February

DCLG, (2013) 'Protecting the independent press from unfair competition', *Consultation on Publicity Code*, Department of Communities and Local Government, April

Dutch, H [accessed 20 August 2011] *Public Relations Annual Report 1 April 1992 to 31 March 1993*, Report to the General Purposes Committee, Strathclyde Regional Council Global Alliance for Public Relations and Communication Management *PR Landscapes* [Online] www.globalalliancepr.org/download.php%3Ffilename%3DPR%2BLandscape

Gordon, A (2011) *Public Relations*, Oxford, Oxford University Press

Gregory, A (2003) *Public Relations and the Age of Spin*, Inaugural lecture as professor of politics, Leeds Metropolitan University, 28 February 2003

Harrison, S (2000) *Public Relations: An introduction* (2nd edition), Routledge, London

Harvey, B (1995) Public relations in local government, in *The Practice of Public Relations*, ed Black, S, Butterworth-Heinemann, Oxford

HAT [accessed 20 August 2012] *History of Advertising Trust Archive* [Online] www.hatads.org.uk/collections/professional-bodies/61/Chartered-Institute-of-Public-Relations-CIPR/

Haywood, R (1991) President IPR in Foreword to *Public Relations for Local Government*, ed Fedorcio, D *et al*, Longman, Harlow

House of Commons (2010) Culture, Media and Sport Select Committee, *Future for local and regional media*, The Stationery Office, London

L'Etang, J (1999) Public Relations Education in Britain: An Historical Review in the Context of Professionalization, *Public Relations Review*, 25 (3), pp 261–89

L'Etang, J (2004) *Public Relations in Britain: A History of Professional Practice in the Twentieth Century*, Lawrence Erlbaum, Mahwah, NJ

L'Etang, J (2008) Writing PR History: Issues, Methods and Politics, *Journal of Communication Management*, 12 (4)

Lewis, G (1973) *Public Relations for Local Government*, Business Books for the Institute of Public Relations, London

LGcommunications [accessed 20 September 2012] *New Reputation Guide* [Online] www.westminster.gov.uk/workspace/assets/publications/WCC_LGcomms_ReputationGuide-1276523500.pdf

LGcommunications (2011) *Cracking the Code*, Bevan Brittan LLP and LGcommunications, London

Local Government and Health Services Ombudsmen (2011/12) *Annual Report 11/12 Delivering Public Value*, Commission for Local Administration in England, www.lgo.org.uk

Miller, D and Dinan, W (2000) The rise of the PR industry in Britain 1979–98, *European Journal of Communication*, **15** (I), pp 5–35, Sage, London

Milton, Sir S, LGA [accessed 28 September 2012] *What does your council do for you?* [Online] www.lgcareers.com/news/what-does-your-council-do-for-you/

Minogue, M (1977) *Documents on Contemporary British Government: Volume 2*, Local Government in Britain University Press, Cambridge

Ofcom (2013) 'In breach: Advertisement by Major of Tower Hamlets', *Ofcom Broadcast Bulletin*, Issue 222, 21 January 2013

Office of National Statistics (ONS) [accessed 2 December 2012] *ONS Home* [Online] www.ons.gov.uk/ons/index.html

Scottish Public Standards Commissioner (2011) Complaint Number LA/G/1127, reported 12 October 2011, www.publicstandardscommissioner.org.uk

Seymour, W (1948) An invitation to the critics, *Public Relations*, **1** (1)

South Bank University [accessed 10 December 2012] *Research led by LSBU academic professor Gill Rowlands highlights the need to simplify health information* [Online] www.lsbu.ac.uk

Thatcher, M (1960) *Maiden speech to parliament* introducing second reading of the private members bill, Public Bodies (Admission of the press to meetings) Bill on 5 February 1960, Hansard HC 616/1350-58

Wakeman (2012) *The Public Relations Handbook* (4th edition), ed Alison Theaker, Routledge, Abingdon

Walker, D (1997) *Public Relations in Local Government: Strategic Approaches to Better Communication*, Pearson Education, London

Watson, T (2011) [accessed 25 November 2012] *The evolution of evaluation – the accelerating march towards the measurement of public relations effectiveness* [Online] http://eprints.bournemouth.ac.uk/19076/1/Watson_(2011)_The_evolution_of_evaluation_(IHPRC).pdf

Widdicombe, D (1985) *Local Authority publicity: interim report of the Committee of Inquiry into the conduct of local authority business*, HMSO, London

Wonnacott, G (1994) Achieving Effective Advertising, in *Marketing, Competition and the Public Sector*, ed H Tam, Longman, London

Yeomans, L (2009) *Exploring Public Relations* (2nd edition), eds Tench, R and Yeomans, L, FT Prentice Hall, Harlow

*Yorkshire Post* (2013) 'Commissioner's first police plan in line for golden bull award', 5 February 2013

# Chapter 2

Audit Scotland (2012) *Managing performance: are you getting it right?* Audit Scotland, October 2012

Bhurji, D (2012) 'Skilling Up for the future', in *Share This, The Social Media Handbook for PR Professionals*, ed Waddington, Wiley, London

Bolton (2006) *Communications and Marketing Agency: Background*, Bolton Council

CIPFA (2010) *Communications Function*, Chartered Institute of Public Finance and Accountancy, www.vfmindicators.co.uk

CIPR (2012) *Essex Communications entry for best in-house team*, Chartered Institute of Public Relations South East PRide Awards 2012

CIPR [accessed 28 September 2012] *CIPR Code of Conduct* [Online] www.cipr.co.uk/content/about-us/about-cipr/code-conduct

Corkey, J, Wholey, N and Compton, J (2009a) *How Leicestershire County Council currently communicates Part 1 As is*, Report by Westco Trading to the council, November 2009

Corkey, J, Wholey, N and Compton, J (2009b) *Improving Communications at Leicestershire County Council Part 2 – recommendations*, Report by Westco Trading to the Council, December 2009

Cornelissen, J (2008) *Corporate Communication: A guide to theory and practice* (2nd edition), Sage, London

Day, Dong and Robins (2001) *Public Relations Ethics in Handbook of Public Relations*, ed Heath, Sage Publications, London

Department of Communities and Local Government [accessed 1 May 2013] *Place Survey Results 2008* [Online] data.gov.uk/dataset/england-place-survey

Essex County Council (2012) *Essex Works Communications and Marketing Strategy 2012–2017*, Essex County Council

Fletcher-Brown, M [accessed 24 September 2012] *Do you have walk in rights with your CX?* [Online] reputationstuff.wordpress.com/2012/09/24/do-you-have-walk-in-rights-with-your-cx/

Glasgow City Council (2012) Communication and Service Development, *Insider* magazine, February 2012

Greaves, L (2012) *Fourteenth Benchmarking Report*, Liza Greaves Public PR Confidential study for contributing authorities, 69 across the UK, www.publicpr.co.uk

Gregory, A (2008) Competencies of senior communication practitioners in the UK: An initial study, *Public Relations Review*, **34**, pp 215–23

Gregory, A (2009a) *Ethics and professionalism in public relations in The Public Relations Digest*, ed Wolstenholme, Pearson Education, Harlow

Gregory, A (2009b) in *Exploring Public Relations* (2nd edition), ed Tench and Yeomans, Prentice Hall, Harlow

Ipsos MORI/Local Government Association (2008) *The Reputation of Local Government*, LGA, London

LGcommunications (2008) *The Chief Executives' Challenge, Commission on Communications*, LGcommunications, London

LGcommunications (2009a) *Proving Communications Works – the impact of Council Publications, Phase 1*, LGcommunications, London

LGcommunications (2009b) *The Commission on Competencies for Senior Communication Roles*, LGcommunications, London

LGcommunications and Bevan Brittan LLP (2011) *Cracking the Code*, LGcommunications, London

LGcomms (2010) *New Reputation Project: Summary Report for Consultation*, Local Government Association and LGcommunications *New Reputation Guide*, www.lga.gov.uk/reputation

LGA & London Councils (2012) *Are you being served: benchmarking resident satisfaction data, question set and guidance*, Also *Annex A: sample questions*, Local Government Association, London

Marjoribanks, J, Local Government Political Restrictions Exemptions Adjudicator for Scotland in an email to author, 11 September 2012

Moss, D and DeSanto, B (2012) *Public Relations A Managerial Perspective*, Sage Publications, London

Parsons, P J (2004) *Ethics in Public Relations: A Guide to Best Practice*, Kogan Page, London

Tench (2009) *Community and Society: Corporate Social Responsibility (CSR) in The Public Relations Digest*, ed Wolstenholme, Pearson Education, Harlow

Tozer, J (2012) e-mail to author, 8 November 2012

UK Audit Agencies (2010) *Communications performance indicators*, UK Audit Agencies, licensed under the Open Government Licence

White, J [accessed 11 December 2011] *Scenario Planning with members of the Chartered Institute of Public Relations*, July–Oct 2011 [Online] www.cipr.co.uk/content/pr-resources/research-reports/cipr-research-and-reports

The following websites may be useful:
Chartered Institute of Marketing: www.cim.co.uk/Training/TrainingHome.aspx
Chartered Institute of Public Relations: www.cipr.co.uk/content/training-qualifications
CIPR Local Public Services Group: www.cipr.co.uk/content/membership-networking/member-groups/local-public-services
Consultation Institute: www.consultationinstitute.org/
Local Government Association: www.local.gov.uk/
LGcommunications: www.lgcomms.org.uk/
Local Government Information Unit: www.lgiu.org.uk/
Public Relations Consultants Association: www.prca.org.uk/

# Chapter 3

Allerdale Borough [accessed 11 November 2012] *Council Plan 2011 to 2015* [Online] www.allerdale.gov.uk/council-and-democracy/council-news/spotlight-on.aspx
Cornelissen, J (2005) *Corporate Communications: Theory and Practice*, Sage, London
Cutlip, Centre, Broom and Glen (2000) *Effective Public Relations*, Harlow, Prentice Hall
Department for Communities and Local Government (2011) *Code of Recommended Practice on Local Authority Publicity*, TSO (The Stationery Office), London
Essex County Council (2012) *Essex Works Communications & Marketing Strategy 2012–2017*
Gregory, A [accessed 4 January 2012] *CIPR Skills Guide, Strategy: Strategic Strategy and other Confusions* [Online] www.cipr.co.uk/sites/default/files/Strategy_members.pdf
Gregory, A (2010) *Planning and Managing Public Relations Campaigns* (3rd edition), Kogan Page, London
Gregory, A (2009) Management and Organisation of Public Relations, in *Exploring Public Relations* (2nd edition), eds Tench and Yeomans, Prentice Hall, Harlow
Grunig, J E (2006) Furnishing the Edifice: Ongoing Research on Public Relations as a Strategic Management Function, *Journal of Public Relations Research*, **18** (2) pp 151–76
I&DeA Improvement and Development Agency for local government (2009) [accessed 27 December 2011] *Strategic communications* [Online] www.idea.gov.uk/idk/core/page.do?pageId=9656591
Ipsos MORI (2008) [accessed 28 December 2011] *The reputation of local government*, research study conducted for LGA [Online] www.ipsos-mori.com/DownloadPublication/1248_sri_localgovt_the_reputation_of_local_government_092008.pdf
Ipsos MORI [accessed 27 December 2011] *Adding Value and Insight* [Online] www.ipsospublicaffairs.co.uk/
Kelly, K S (2001) Chapter 21 in *Handbook of Public Relations*, ed Robert L Heath, Sage Publications, London
LGcommunications (2008) [accessed 3 January 2012] *The Chief Executives' Challenge Report* [Online] www.lgcomms.org.uk/documents/LGcomms_research.pdf
Local Government Association (2006) [accessed 03 January 2012] *Original reputation campaign* [Online] http://reputation.lga.gov.uk/lga/core/page.do?pageId=922700
Local Government Association [accessed 27 December 2011] *Local government reputation* [Online] www.lga.gov.uk/reputation
Local Government Association [accessed 03 January 2012] *Local government reputation campaign* [Online] http://reputation.lga.gov.uk/lga/core/page.do?pageId=1
Local Government Association (2008) [accessed 27 December 2011] *The reputation of local government, literature review to support the my council campaign*, conducted by the Ipsos MORI Social Research Institute [Online] www.ipsos-mori.com/DownloadPublication/1248_sri_localgovt_the_reputation_of_local_government_092008.pdf

LGA (2012) [accessed 28 October 2012] *Media and communications Councillor Workbook* [Online] www.boston.gov.uk/CHttpHandler.ashx?id=7669&p=0

LGA/LGcommunications (2010) [accessed 14 May 2012] *New Reputation Guide* [Online] www.lga.gov.uk/reputation

Local Government Improvement and Development (2009) [accessed 03 January 2012] *Strategic Communications* [Online] www.idea.gov.uk/idk/core/page.do?pageId=9656591

North Ayrshire Council (2012) [accessed 9 May 2012] *Communications Strategy 2012–15* [Online] www.north-ayrshire.gov.uk/CouncilAndGovernment/CouncilInformationPerformanceAndStatistics/NorthAyrshirePerforms/CommunicationsStrategy.aspx

Oliver, S (2007) *Public Relations Strategy* (2nd edition), Kogan Page, London, pp 61–72

Stevenage Borough Council (2007) [accessed 18 October 2010] *Communications Strategy 2007–2010 Investing in Effective Communications* archived as PDF [Online] 19dec07–item7-appendix1 (1).pdf

Stevenage Borough Council (2011) [accessed 30 December 2011] *Let's Talk – Corporate Communications Strategy 2011–2014* [Online] www.stevenage.gov.uk/content/comms/chronicle-dwnlds/24227

Taylor, S and Williams, B (2006) *The Communities and Local Government Report: Perceptions of Local Government in England: Key findings from qualitative research*, BMG Research Ltd, Department for Communities and Local Government, London

the3towns-archive (2011) [accessed 21 July 2012] *Council's new Communications Strategy* [Online] http://the3towns-archive.blogspot.co.uk/2011/12/councils-new-communications-strategy.html

Wellingborough Borough Council (2012) [accessed 29 October 2012] *Corporate Communications Strategy 2012–2015* [Online] www.wellingborough.gov.uk/.../communications_strategy_2012–15

# Chapter 4

Barnet (2012) *Corporate Plan Consultation Findings*, London Borough of Barnet Council

BIS (2008) *Code of Practice on Consultation*, HM Government Department for Business, Innovation and Skills, London

Bristol (2012a) [accessed 8 November 2012] *Bristol Citizen's Panel: Bristol's Biggest Think Tank* and *Feedback Newsletter*, Issue No. 30 September 2012 [Online] www.bristol.gov.uk

Bristol (2012b) [accessed 9 November 2012] *Code of Good Practice on Consultation* and *Consultation Toolkit*, Bristol City Council 2012 [Online] www.bristol.gov.uk/node/8291

Cabinet Office (2012) *Consultation Principles – guidance*, www.cabinetoffice.gov.uk/resource-library/consultation-principles-guidance

Commons Committee (2010) 'Future of local and regional media', *Fourth Report of the House of Commons Culture, Media and Sport Committee*, Session 2009/2010, vol 1, March

Consultation Institute (2012) *Code of Practice for Using Social Media for Public and Stakeholder Consultation*

Consultation Institute (2010) The Consultation Charter, http://consultationinstitute.org

Dale, R (2012) *Why social media will solve the problem of local voter apathy*, The Guardian Local Government Network Blog, 20 August 2012

Davie, E (2012) Comment on the The Guardian Local Government Network blog, 20 August 2012

*Guardian, The* (2011) *Local referendums are nothing new*, by Martin Wainwright 5 May 2011

Headland, P (2012) *Involving Citizens in the Budget Challenge: A study of the experiences of consultation practitioners*, Consultation Institute, Biggleswade

Independent (2012) *Cuts put hundreds of libraries at risk of closure and thousands of jobs on the line*, 31 July 2012

International Association for Public Participation (2007) *IAP2 Spectrum of Public Participation*, www.iap2.org

Involve & National Consumer Council (2009) *Deliberative Public Engagement: Nine Principles*, www.ncc.org.uk and www.involve.org.uk

Jones, R (2012) *Putting Principles into Practice: Understanding the new Cabinet Office Statement of Consultation Principles*, Briefing Paper 32 Consultation Institute, Biggleswade August 2012

Jones, R (2010) *Public Engagement Aspects of the Localism*, Bill Briefing Paper 26 Consultation Institute, Biggleswade

Jones, R and Ashton, J (2006) *Consultation and the Media A Joint White Paper*, Consultation Institute, Biggleswade

Jones, R and Gammell, E (2009) *The Art of Consultation*, Biteback Publishing Ltd, London

LGIU (2009) *Local Government 3.0 How Councils can respond to the new web agenda*, Local Government Information Unit

Lopata, R, Jones, D and Headland, P (2011) *Local Authority Budget Consultations* Briefing Paper 29 Consultation Institute, Biggleswade September 2011

Mundy, D and Umer, Q (2012) *An Analysis of UK Council use of the social network*, Twitter Paper to the European Conference of E-Government, Barcelona

Ofcom (2012) *Standards Cases: In Breach Advertisements for Union Terrace Garden Referendum Aberdeen*, Ofcom Broadcast Bulletin Issue 213

Pasquier, M and Villeneuve, J-P (2012) *Marketing, Management and Communications in the Public Sector*, Routledge, London

Payne, M (2012) At the heart of the matter, *Cllr Magazine*, June 2012, Local Government Information Unit, London

Pickles, E (2013) Why councils should heed our quiet revolution, *Daily Telegraph*, 28 January 2013

Regulations (2012) [accessed 1 May 2013] *The Local Authorities (Conduct of referendums) (Council Tax Increases) (England) Regulations 2012* and *The Neighbourhood Planning (Referendums) Regulations 2012* [Online] www.legislation.gov.uk

Sawyer, A (2009) Introduction in *Local Government 3.0 How Councils can respond to the new web agenda*, Local Government Information Unit (LGIU), London

Tee, M (2009) Foreword in *Effective Public Engagement: A guide for policy makers and communications professions*, Cabinet Office/COI, London

Watson, T (2010) reported in *Future of Local and Regional Media* Fourth Report of the House of Commons Culture, Media and Sport Committee – Session 2009/10 Volume 1, March 2010

# Chapter 5

Belfast City Council [accessed 23 September 2012] *Belfast City Council Awards* [Online] www.belfastcity.gov.uk/citymatters/awards.asp

Blackburn with Darwen [accessed 26 September 2012] *Learning disability partnership board* [Online] www.bwdld.org.uk/

Brennan, C (2013) *Grumbles, Gripes and Grievances: the role of complaints in transforming public services*, Nesta, April

Brighton and Hove City Council [accessed 12 August 2012] *Residents Guide to Brighton and Hove Services* [Online] www.brighton-hove.gov.uk/downloads/bhcc/counciltax/2012-13_Residents_Guide_to_Brighton___Hove_Services.pdf

CIPR (2011) [accessed 23 September 2012] *Northern Ireland PRide Awards* [Online] www.cipr.co.uk/sites/default/files/NI-12175859.pdf

CIPR PRide Awards (2010a) [accessed 21 September 2012] *Dacorum Digest* [Online] www.cipr.co.uk/sites/default/files/Cat%2015_%20Dacorum%20Borough%20Council.pdf

CIPR PRide Awards (2010b) [accessed 21 September 2012] *Hertsmere News* [Online] www.cipr.co.uk/sites/default/files/Cat%2017_Hertsmere%20Borough%20Council.pdf

CIPR PRide Awards (2010c) [accessed 22 September 2012] *Community Pride*, City of Bradford Metropolitan District Council [Online] www.cipr.co.uk/sites/default/files/ City%20of%20Bradford%20Metropolitan%20District%20Council_Cat%2015.pdf

CIPR PRide Awards (2011) [accessed 21 September 2012] *In-House Public Relations Team*; Essex Communications; Essex County Council [Online] www.cipr.co.uk/sites/default/files/ EA-12118371%20(1).pdf

City of Bradford Metropolitan Council website [accessed 22 September 2012] *Community Pride Newsletters* [Online] www.bradford.gov.uk/bmdc/community_and_living/community_pride

Corrigan (2008) [accessed 21 September 2012] *The Telegraph*, 'Disgusting' council poster campaign criticised [Online] www.telegraph.co.uk/news/2217329/Disgusting-council-poster-campaign-criticised.html

Cumbria County Council [accessed 30 August 2012] *Customer Services Strategy 2011–14* [Online] www.cumbria.gov.uk/elibrary/Content/Internet/536/647/4080594226.pdf

Dacorum Borough Council (2010) [accessed 21 September 2012] *Dacorum Digest wins gold* [Online] www.dacorum.gov.uk/default.aspx?page=6477

Derbyshire County Council [accessed 17 September 2012] *Your Council Tax 2012–13* [Online] www.derbyshire.gov.uk/images/DCC%20Council%20Tax%20Leaflet%20 2012-2013_v11_tcm44-200647.pdf

Derbyshire County Council website [accessed 16 September 2012] www.derbyshire.gov.uk/education/default.asp

Dunning, A (2005) *Information, Advice and Advocacy for Older People: Defining and Developing Services*, Joseph Rowntree Foundation, York

Grunig, J E (2009) [accessed 19 September 2012] Paradigms of global public relations in an age of digitalisation, *PRism* 6(2) [Online] http://praxis.massey.ac.nz/prism_on-line_journ.html

Grunig, J and Hunt, T (1984) *Managing Public Relations*, Holt, New York

Hartlepool Borough Council [accessed 17 September 2012] *Communicating with Your Council* [Online] www.hartlepool.gov.uk/info/200024/consultations/740/communicating_with_ your_council/1

HM Treasury/Communities and Local Government (2010) [accessed 16 September 2012] *Total Place: a whole area approach to public services* © Crown copyright [Online] www.hm-treasury.gov.uk/d/total_place_report.pdf

ICE Inclusive Communication Essex [accessed 24 November 2012] [Online] www.essexice.co.uk/

IDeA (2010) [accessed 16 September 2012] *Customer insight: through a Total Place lens* [Online] www.local.gov.uk/c/document_library/get_file?uuid=a32db84c-1224-4f0b-80e9-af0527e5c0b6&groupId=10171

Inclusive Communication in Scotland [accessed 24 November 2012] [Online] www.inclusivecommunicationscotland.org.uk/project-summary/

Ipsos MORI (2010) [accessed 26 August 2012] *One world, many places; Citizen's views of municipal government and local areas across the world* [Online] www.ipsos-mori.com/ researchpublications/publications/publication.aspx?oItemId=1361

Ipsos MORI (2009) [accessed 26 August 2012] *Timely Information to Citizens; Identifying and evaluating best practice* [Online] www.ipsos-mori.com/researchpublications/ publications/publication.aspx?oItemId=1308

Leicestershire County Council (2009) [accessed 26 September 2012] *Equalities Impact Assessment; Corporate Communication Strategy and Action Plan* [Online] www.leics.gov.uk/corporate_communications_strategy_and_action_plan_eia.doc

L'Etang, J (2004) *Public Relations in Britain: A History of Professional Practice in the Twentieth Century*, Lawrence Erlbaum Associates, Mahwah, NJ

Lewis, G (1973) *Public Relations for Local Government*, Business Books for the Institute of Public Relations, London

LGA (2010) [accessed 16 September 2012] *Developing Customer Insight* [Online] www.local.gov.uk/web/guest/home/-/journal_content/56/10171/3511511/ ARTICLE-TEMPLATE

Local Government Association (2006) [accessed 03 January 2012] *original reputation campaign* [Online] http://reputation.lga.gov.uk/lga/core/page.do?pageId=922700

LGID careers (2008) [accessed 25 August 2012] *What does your council do for you?* [Online] www.lgcareers.com/news/what-does-your-council-do-for-you/

LGID (2011) [accessed 26 August 2012] *Customer led transformation programme; Case study – East Riding of Yorkshire: A local strategic partnership approach to understanding our customers* [Online] https://knowledgehub.local.gov.uk/c/document_library/ get_file?p_l_id=904624&folderId=6728865&name=DLFE-31140.pdf

LGID (nd a) [accessed 21 September 2012] *Number of councils* [Online] www.lgcareers.com/ what-is-local-government/facts-and-figures/number-of-council/

LGID (nd b) [accessed 26 August 2012] *Local government hot topics* [Online] www.lgcareers.com/what-is-local-government/local-government-hot-topics/

Norfolk County Council 2011–12 [accessed 18 September 2012] *Norfolk County Council's customer service and communications unit* [Online] www.norfolk.gov.uk/Council_and_ democracy/Council_departments/Communications_and_customer_services_unit/index.htm

Norfolk County Council (November 2011) [accessed 24 November 2012] *Customer Service Strategy 2011–14* [Online] www.norfolk.gov.uk/view/NCC105429

Norfolk County Council (May 2012) [accessed 24 November 2012] *Customer Service Strategy, six month progress* update [Online] www.norfolk.gov.uk/view/ carp220512item16pdf

Office for Disability Issues (2007) [accessed 17 September 2012] *Improving Information for Disabled People Crown copyright* [Online] http://odi.dwp.gov.uk/docs/wor/imp/ODI_ FivePrinciples_2007_main.pdf

Office for Disability Issues (2008) *Producing better information for disabled people: A toolkit for local authorities*

Pembrokeshire County Council (2012) [accessed 17 September 2012] *Our Customer Charter* [Online] www.pembrokeshire.gov.uk/content.asp?nav=2%2C101%2C1581%2C114

2020 Public Services Trust (2010) (in partnership with RSA Projects) *What do people want, need and expect from public services?* Ipsos MORI Literature Review Paperback

Rinehart and Winston (2012) [accessed 21 September 2012] *Hands off Old Trafford Library* [Online] http://hootlibrary.wordpress.com/

SOCITM Consulting (2012) [accessed 17 September 2012] *Understanding customer needs* [Online] www.socitmconsulting.co.uk/page/understanding-customer-needs

Staffordshire County Council website [accessed 23 September 2012] www.staffordshire.gov.uk/Homepage.aspx

Stockport Council (nd a) [accessed 30 August 2012] *Customer Focus – Overview* [Online] http://democracy.stockportItem%205a%20-%20Customer%20Focus%20Annual%20 PPRR%202011-12.pdf

Stockport Council (nd b) [accessed 30 August 2012] *Customer Charter* [Online] www.stockport.gov.uk/services/councildemocracy/your_council/performance/customercharter

Suffolk Free Press [accessed 21 September 2012] *Hundreds sign up to save parks* [Online] www.suffolkfreepress.co.uk/news/campaigns-and-fundraising/hundreds-sign-up-to-save- parks-1-2375824

Wakeman (2012) *The Public Relations Handbook* (4th edition), ed Alison Theaker, Routledge, Abingdon

Wigan Council website [accessed 23 September 2012] [Online] www.wigan.gov.uk/

# Chapter 6

Allerdale Borough Council [accessed 12 July 2012] *Internal communications strategy and action plan* [Online] http://webapps.allerdale.gov.uk/moderngov/mgConvert2PDF.aspx?ID=11759

Audit Commission (2012) [accessed 8 August 2012] *Comprehensive Performance Assessment What we did* [Online] www.audit-commission.gov.uk/inspection-assessment/cpa/pages/default.aspx

Bernstein, D (1989) *Company Image and Reality; A critique of corporate communications*, Cassell, London

Braiden, G in *The Herald* (August 2012) [accessed 24 November 2012] Council staff morale 'hits rock bottom' [Online] www.heraldscotland.com/news/home-news/council-staff-morale-hits-rock-bottom.18336169

Briggs, D (2011) [accessed 1 August 2012] *Radical transparency in local government – what can you do?* [blog Online] http://kindofdigital.com/tag/wikileaks/

Caveney, D (2011) (head of communications and marketing at Walsall council) in Groves N, *Guardian Professional* [accessed 24 July 2011] Making internal communications count [Online] www.guardian.co.uk/local-government-network/2011/feb/14/local-government-internal-communications-q-a

Cornelissen, J (2004) *Corporate Communication: A Guide to Theory and Practice* (3rd edition), Sage Publications, London

East Midlands Improvement and Efficiency Partnership (2010) [accessed 8 August 2012] *Good Practice Case Study* EM IEPCS25 [Online] www.eastmidlandsiep.gov.uk/uploads/case-studies/EMIEP%20-

Fitzpatrick, L (2012) chapter in *The Public Relations Handbook* (4th edition), ed Alison Theaker, Routledge, Abingdon

Groves, N (2011) [accessed 24 July 2011] *Guardian Professional Making internal communications count* [Online] www.guardian.co.uk/local-government-network/2011/feb/14/local-government-internal-communications-q-a

Grunig, J E (1992) *Excellence in Public Relations and Communication Management; Symmetrical Systems of Internal Communication*, Lawrence Erlbaum Associates, Mahwah, NJ

Grunig, J E (2008) [accessed 6 August 2012] *Excellence Theory in Public Relations* [Online] http://kdpaine.blogs.com/files/encylopedia-of-communication-9781405131995_chapter_399.pdf]

Investors in People [accessed 8 August 2012] *Engaging Employees* [Online] www.investorsinpeople.co.uk/About/PolicyDevelopment/Pages/Engagingemployees.aspx

Ipsos MORI [accessed 24 November 2012] [Online] www.ipsos- Glasgow City Council Staff Survey 2011-12 mori.com/researchpublications/researcharchive/3068/Glasgow-City-Council-Staff-Survey-201112.aspx

Ipsos MORI [accessed 9 September 2011] *Survey 2003, Communicators in Business/MORI, Trust and Mistrust at Work* [Online] www.ipsos-mori.com/researchpublications/researcharchive/941/Trust-And-Mistrust-At-Work.aspx

LGA [accessed 6 August 2012] 'How to Guide 3', *Engage your staff and improve your performance*' [Online] http://reputation.lga.gov.uk/lga/aio/11478167

LGA [accessed 6 August 2012] *Reputation Campaign* [Online]

Local Government Improvement and Development [accessed 8 August 2012] *Internal Communications* [Online] www.idea.gov.uk/idk/core/page.do?pageId=7816302

News & Star (January 2012) [accessed 24 November 2012] *Morale among Cumbria council staff at rock bottom – survey* [Online] www.newsandstar.co.uk/morale-among-cumbria-council-staff-at-rock-bottom-survey-1.914491?referrerPath=2.1853

O'Dea (2011) [accessed 14 July 2011] Guardian Local Government Network, *Faced with cuts internal communication is even more important* [Online] www.guardian.co.uk/local-government-network/2011/jan/14/faced-cuts-internal-communication-more-important

Oliver, S (2007) *Public Relations Strategy* (2nd edition), Kogan Page, London, pp 61–72

Quirke, B (2008) *Making the Connections, Using Internal Communication to Turn Strategy into Action* (2nd Edition), Gower Publishing, Farnham

Ruck, K and Trainor, S (2011) *Communicating for Engagement Research Report for the Chartered Institute of Public Relations Phase one: the internal communicator perspective*

Smith, L [accessed 16 April 2012] *Internal Communications: Communicating Change to Employees*; CIPR Skill Guides [Online] www.cipr.co.uk/content/policy-resources/practitioner-advice/skills-guides

Strauss and Hoffmann (2000) cited in Tench, Ralph & Yeomans, Liz (2006) *Exploring Public Relations* (1st edition), Prentice Hall, Harlow

Tench, R (2006) Managing Community Involvement Programmes, in *Exploring Public Relations*, eds Tench and Yeomans, Pearson Education, Harlow

Torbay Council (2011) [accessed 11 November 2012] Winner *Employee Engagement Campaign*, Chartered Institute of Public Relations (CIPR) Excellence Award 2011 [Online] www.cipr.co.uk/content/news-opinion/press-releases/103195/cipr-excellence-awards-2011-winners-announced

Yeomans, L (2006) Internal Communication, in *Exploring Public Relations*, eds Tench and Yeomans, Pearson Education, Harlow

Yeomans, L (2009) in *Exploring Public Relations*, eds Tench and Yeomans, Pearson Education, Harlow

CIPR Skills Guides [accessed 2 March 2012] (member access only) [Online] www.cipr.co.uk/content/policy-resources/practitioner-advice/skills-guides
  Internal Communications – Introduction by Di Burton FCIPR
  Internal Communications – Top Tips by Tricia Boyd MCIPR
  Writing internal newsletters by Paul Nero MCIPR
  Communicating to a Diverse and Dispersed Workforce by Kaego Uba ACIPR
  Communicating Change to Employees by Lee Smith FCIPR
  Running an Effective Internal Communications Department by Yvonne O'Hara MCIPR & Lee Smith FCIPR
  Internal Branding – Building from the inside out by Mark Terry
  Internal Communications Strategy by Howard Krais
  Internal Communications during a downturn by Sally Sykes FCIPR

# Chapter 7

Acharya, L (1985) 'Public relations environments', *Journalism Quarterly*, **62** (3), pp 577–84

Broom, G M and Dozier, D M (1986) Advancement for public relations role models, *Public Relations Review*, **12** (1), pp 37–56

Chartered Institute of Public Relations (CIPR) (nd a) [accessed on 10 November 2011] *About PR* [Online] www.cipr.co.uk/content/about-us/about-pr

CIPR (nd b)[accessed on 10 November 2011] *Local public services* [Online] www.cipr.co.uk/content/membership-networking/member-groups/local-public-services

Cziok, P (2011) *After the riots: rebuilding place and community*, CIPR, London

Dozier, D M (1984) Evolution of the manager role in public relations practice, *Journal of Public Relations Research*, 7 (1) pp 3–26

Dozier, D M and Broom, G M (1995) 'Evolution of the manager role in public relations practice', *Journal of Public Relations Research*, 7 (1) pp 3–26

Gregory, A (2010) *Planning and Managing Public Relations Campaigns* (3rd edition), Kogan Page, London

Hill, B (2011) Telephone interview on 5 September 2011

HMTreasury (2010) [accessed on 10 November 2011] Spending Review [Online] www.hm-treasury.gov.uk/spend_index.htm

Local Government Association (LGA), LGcommunications (LGcomms) (2010) [accessed on 10 November 2011] Reputation Guide [Online] www.lgcomms.org.uk/asset/69/WCC_LGcomms_ReputationGuide.pdf

LGcomms (2008) Chief Executives Challenge Report, LGcomms, London

LGID [accessed on 10 November 2011] Partnerships [Online] www.idea.gov.uk/idk/core/page.do?pageId=1174195

LGID (2010) Reshaping the Partnership Landscape [accessed on 10 November 2011] [Online] www.idea.gov.uk/idk/aio/23885112

Schmid, M (2011) Telephone interview with Wendy Moran, 15 September 2011

Talbot, D (2012) Interview with Wendy Moran, Tunbridge Wells

Tizard, J (2010) [accessed 10 November 2011] Public service partnerships – evolution and revolution [Online] www.govopps.co.uk/public-service-partnerships-%e2%80%93-evolution-and-revolution/

Toth, E L, Serini, S A, Wright, D K and Emig, A G (1998) Trends in public relations roles: 1990–1995, *Public Relations Review*, **24** (2) pp 145–63

Wakeman, S (2010) [accessed 10 November 2011] Thoughts from LGCommunication [Online] www.simonwakeman.com/2010/05/27/thoughts-from-lgcommunications-conference

# Chapter 8

Andreasen, A R (1995) *Marketing Social Change: Changing Behaviour to Promote Health, Social Development, and the Environment*, Jossey-Bass, San Francisco

Cabinet Office, Behavioural Insights Team (2012) *Applying behavioural insights to reduce, fraud, error and debt*, Cabinet Office Behavioural Insights Team, London

Cabinet Office, Behavioural Insights Team (2011) *Annual update 2010–2011*, Cabinet Office Behavioural Insights Team, London

CIPR (2011a) [accessed 23 July 2012] Winner Public Sector Excellence Award 2011, South Wales Fire and Rescue Service [Online] www.cipr.co.uk/content/events-awards/excellence-awards/past-winners

CIPR (2011b) *Research, Planning and Measurement Toolkit*, CIPR, London

CIPR LPS (2010) *Excellence Awards Presentation*, Grand Hotel, Brighton, 22 October

CIPR LPS (2011) *Excellence Awards Presentation*, CIPR HQ, London, 14 October

Gregory, A (2010) *Planning and Managing Public Relations Campaigns*, 3rd edn, Kogan Page, London

Harrison, S (2000) *Public Relations: An introduction* (2nd edn), Routledge, London

LGA, LGcommunications [accessed 10 November 2011] *New Reputation Guide* [Online] www.lgcomms.org.uk/asset/69/WCC_LGcomms_ReputationGuide.pdf

LGA [accessed on 7 January 2012] *Reputation Campaign* [Online] http://reputation.lga.gov.uk/lga/core/page.do?pageId=1

Powell, M (2010) '*CIPR LPS Campaign of the Year Judges' Comments*', Presentation at London Thistle Barbican, 14 September

Smith, R (2005) *Strategic Planning for Public Relations* (2nd edition), Lawrence Erlbaum Associates, Mahwah, NJ

Thaler, R H and Sustein, C R (2008) *Nudge*, Yale University Press, London

Wakeman, S (2012) Public sector communications, in *The handbook of public relations* (4th edition), ed Theaker, A, pp 331–54, Routledge, London

Watson, T and Noble, P (2007) *Evaluating Public Relations: A Best Practice Guide to Public Relations Planning, Research and Evaluation* (2nd edn), Kogan Page, London

Yeomans, L (2009) Public sector communication and social marketing, in *Exploring Public Relations* (2nd edition), eds Tench, R and Yeomans, L, Prentice Hall, Harlow

# Chapter 9

Aitken, A (2012) TV bidding comes during regional comms crunch time, *PR Week online*, 28 August 2012

Barcelona Principles (2010) http://amecorg.com/2012/06/barcelona-declaration-of-measurement-principles/

Birmingham (2010) Online newsroom spreading the word in Birmingham, *Birmingham City Council Press Release*, 2 February 2010

BBC online (2011) Scottish councils slash newspaper advertising, *BBC Scotland news online*, 17 May 2011

BBC (2012) *Editorial Code of Conduct*, www.bbc.co.uk/editorialguidelines/

Chivers, T (2012) Daily Telegraph blog *'Thus I refute them: Argyll and Bute Council don't just censor little girls, they also hate English'*, 15 June 2012 http://blogs.telegraph.co.uk/news/tomchiversscience/100165609/thus-i-refute-them-argyll-and-bute-council-dont-just-censor-little-girls-they-also-hate-the-english-language/

Coleman, A (2012) Interview with *PR Week*, 12 October 2012

COI (2009) Standardisation of PR Evaluation Metrics

*Daily Telegraph* (2012) Mystery Blogger praising council was its leader, 11 September 2012

Dale, R (2012) Public Notices: the case for radical reform, *Local Government Information Unit*, September 2012

DCMS (2011) *Department of Culture Media and Sport*, press release no. 076/11, 9 August 2011

Diamond, H (1995) *Can you get my name in the papers?* Haruth Publishing

Diamond, H (1996) *Can you get my name in the papers?* Neil Wilson Publishing, Glasgow

Esler, G (2012) The art of great storytelling, The big interview, *PR Week*, 19 October 2012

Fletcher-Brown, M (2009) Blog 'Making an Impact', www.reputation.stuff.com

Francis, R QC (2013a) quoted in Press Release 'Publication of the final report of the Mid Staffordshire NHS Foundation Trust Inquiry', 6 February 2013, www.midstaffspublicinquiry.com

Francis, R QC (2013b) *Report of the Mid Staffordshire NHS Foundation Trust Public Inquiry*, Executive Summary paragraph 70 Stationery Office, London HC 947 February 2013

Highfield, A (2012) 'My ambition is for all our titles to be more relevant in this digital age' says Johnston Press CEO Ashley Highfield, *The Drum*, 11 May 2012

Hillsborough (2012) *The report of the Hillsborough Independent Panel*, Chapter 12, London: The Stationery Office

Independent (2012) Quality newspaper market welcomes surge in online traffic, *The Independent*, 12 September 2012

Jenkins, B (2012) Better Journalism in the Digital Age, Carnegie *UK Trust*

Kynel, R (2012) 'YouTube chief: mobile will soon eclipse TV', *Daily Telegraph*, 11 October 2012

Leveson, L J (2012) The *Leveson Report: Culture, Practices and Ethics of the Press*, The Stationery Office, London, Executive Summary Media Week (2012) 23 July 2012

MacMillan, G (2013) 'Mail Online is like "journalism crack", says editor', Media Week, 11 March

Nesta (2013) *UK Demand for Hyperlocal Media*, Research report, April [Online] www.nesta.org.uk

Neverseconds (2012) Blog of Martha Payne neverseconds.blogsport.com

Ofcom (2011a) Media Tracker Survey 2011

Ofcom (2011b) [accessed February 2011] The *Ofcom Broadcasting Code* [Online] http://stakeholders.ofcom.org.uk/broadcasting/broadcast-codes/broadcast-code/

Ofcom (2012a) 'Communications Market Report – Scotland' 18 July 2012

Ofcom (2012b) [accessed 1 May 2013] *Local Media Omnibus Survey for Ofcom* May 2012 Tables 62–64 [Online] http://stakeholders.ofcom.org.uk/binaries/research/research-publications/LMTables.pdf

Payne (2012) *Never seconds: the incredible story of Martha Payne* by Martha and David Payne, Cargo Publishing, Glasgow

PCC (2011) 'PCC Censures local newspaper for intrusion into child's privacy', *Press Complaints Commission*

PCC (2012) [accessed 1 May 2013] *The Editors' Code of Practice*, January 2012 [Online] www.pcc.org.uk/cop/practice.html

Shewell, J (2011) How I see it, *PR Week*, 22 June 2011

Short, A [accessed 15 June 2012] *How not to write a press release* [Online] http://blog.adrianshort.co.uk/2012/06/15/how-not-to-write-a-press-release-argyll-and-bute-council-style/

Social Journalism Study (2012) *Report by Cision & Canterbury Christ Church University UK*. Based on online survey of 769 UK journalists, June & July 2012

Webb, R 'Week in' column, *Team Spirit magazine*, Monmouthshire County Council, February 2012

# Chapter 10

Barcelona Principles (2010) [Online] http://amecorg.com/2012/03/knowledge-share-essentials/ [accessed on 11 June 2012]

Azyan, L [accessed on 2 June 2012] *Government-to-Citizen Communications: Utilising multiple digital channels effectively*, Local Government Engagement [Online] http://img.en25.com/Web/GovDeliveryInc/%7Bb8bb56ad-9343-4852-831d-1dbe4085fbbc%7D_Using_Multiple_Digital_Channels_Effectively.pdf

CIPR [accessed on 11 June 2012] *Social Media Measurement Guidance*, CIPR [Online] www.cipr.co.uk/sites/default/files/Final_Social_Media_Measurement_Guidance%20_March_2011.pdf

Fox [accessed on 11 June 2012] *Directgov 2010 and beyond: Revolution not Evolution*, Raceonline 2012 [Online] https://update.cabinetoffice.gov.uk/sites/default/files/resources/Martha%20Lane%20Fox's%20letter%20to%20Francis%20Maude%2014th%20Oct%202010.pdf

Gibson [accessed on 11 June 2012] *Local by social. How local authorities can use social media to achieve more for less* NESTA. [Online] www.idea.gov.uk/idk/aio/17801438

Govdelivery [accessed on 11 June 2012] *Norfolk County Council achieves channel shift cost savings using efficient digital communication*, Govdelivery [Online] www.govdelivery.co.uk/docs/pdfs/Norfolk_SuccessStory.pdf

Grunig [accessed on 11 June 2012] *Words of James and Larissa Grunig*, Pristop [Online] www.bledcom.com/academic/article?aid=51

Grunig, J E and Hunt, T (1984) *Managing Public Relations*, Holt, Rinehart and Winston, New York

Kay, N (2012) 'News and Social Media Course from the Emergency Planning College', Worthing and Adur Councils, Worthing

Local Government Information Unit [accessed on 2 June 2012] *Going where the eyeballs are*, Local Government Information Unit [Online] www.govdelivery.co.uk/docs/pdfs/lgiu-report.pdf?elq=7bf68761c338453aa942349bba58b25b&elqCampaignId=

Ofcom [accessed on 11 June 2012] *The Communications Market 2011*, Ofcom [Online] http://stakeholders.ofcom.org.uk/binaries/research/cmr/cmr11/UK_CMR_2011_FINAL.pdf

Prescott, J [accessed on 15 May 2012] Life is tweet, says John Prescott, as Twitter reaches 10m milestone in UK, *Guardian* [Online] www.guardian.co.uk/politics/2012/may/15/life-is-tweet-john-prescott

Reynolds, H (2012) *Social Media Interview with Wendy Moran*, Monmouthshire, 29 May 2012

Reynolds, H [accessed on 11 June 2011] Ace Digital Comms [Online] http://acedigitalcomms.wordpress.com

Slee, D [accessed on 11 June 2012] *Social photo: 11 groovy ways Flickr can be used by local government*, The Dan Slee blog [Online] http://danslee.wordpress.com/2010/06/16/social-photo-how-flickr-can-be-used-by-local-government/

Socitm (2012) [accessed 8 May 2013] *Better connected 2012: a snapshot of all local authority websites* [Online] www.socitm.net/betterconnected

Wakeman, S [accessed on 11 June 2012] *Why local government shouldn't be on Facebook*, Simon Wakeman public sector communications and marketing [Online] www.simonwakeman.com/2009/02/25/why-local-government-shouldnt-be-on-facebook

Yaxley, H (2011) Digital public relations – revolution or evolution, in *The Public Relations Handbook* (4th edition), ed Theaker, A, pp 411–32, Routledge, Oxon

# Chapter 11

BBC [accessed on 13 July 2012] *Editorial Guidelines*, BBC [Online] www.bbc.co.uk/guidelines/editorialguidelines/page/guidelines-privacy-death-suffering-distress/

Civil Contingencies Act, Part One (c36) (2004) The Stationery Office Limited, London

Coombs, T W (1995) Choosing the Right Words: The Development of Guidelines for the Selection of the 'Appropriate' Crisis-Response Strategies, *Management Communication Quarterly*, 8, pp 447–76

Cornwall Council [accessed on 15 May 2012] (2011) *CIPR Excellence Award Winner Crisis Communication: Flooding in Cornwall* [Online] www.cipr.co.uk/content/events-awards/excellence-awards/past-winners

Defra (2011) [accessed 10 June 2012] *Exercise Watermark*, Defra [Online] https://www.gov.uk/government/uploads/system/uploads/attachment_data/file/69476/pb13673-exercise-watermark-finalreport.pdf

Emergency Planning College (2012a) Preparing emergency communications plans, Easingwold: Emergency Planning College, 2-page handout, distributed on 15 May 2012 in 'News and Social Media Course from the Emergency Planning College', Worthing and Adur Councils, Worthing, 15–16 May 2012

Emergency Planning College (2012b) The framework of multi agency emergency management, Easingwold: Emergency Planning College, 3-page handout, distributed on 15 May 2012 in 'News and Social Media Course from the Emergency Planning College', Worthing and Adur Councils, Worthing, 15–16 May 2012

Exercise Watermark Review Team (2011) 'Exercise Watermark Final Report', HMSO: London

*Guardian* (2012) [accessed on 13 July 2012] Reading the Riots [Online] www.guardian.co.uk/uk/interactive/2011/dec/14/reading-the-riots-investigating-england-s-summer-of-disorder-full-report

Hainsworth, B E (1990) The Distribution of Advantages and Disadvantages, *Public Relations Review*, **16**(1), pp 33–39

Hine, D (2010) *The 2009 Influenza Pandemic*, HMSO, London

HMGovernment (2004) *Preparing for Emergencies*, HMSO, London

Jones, B L and Chase, H (1979) Managing Public Policy Issues, *Public Relations Review*, 5(2) pp 3–23

Kay, N (2012) 'News and Social Media Course from the Emergency Planning College', Worthing and Adur Councils, Worthing, 15–16 May 2012

Langford, M (2009) Crisis Public Relations Management, in *Exploring Public Relations* (2nd edition), eds Tench, R and Yeomans, L, pp 385–408, Pearson, Harlow

Local Government Association (LGA) [accessed on 21 May 2012] *How to conduct crisis communication*, LGA [Online] http://reputation.lga.gov.uk/lga/aio/11478266

LGID (2009a) [accessed on 19 May 2012] *Communicating about contamination* [Online]
www.idea.gov.uk/idk/core/page.do?pageId=9623876

LGID (2009b) [accessed on 19 May 2012] *Swine flu: crisis management* [Online]
www.idea.gov.uk/idk/core/page.do?pageId=12283256

Meng, M B (1992) Early Identification Aids Issues Management, *Public Relations Journal*,
47(3), pp 22–24

Ofcom (2011) [accessed on 13 July 2012] *Communications Market Report UK* [Online]
http://stakeholders.ofcom.org.uk/binaries/research/cmr/cmr11/UK_CMR_2011_FINAL.pdf

Pitt, M (2008) *The Pitt Review: Lessons Learned from the 2007* Floods, TSO, London

Regester, M and Larkin, J (2008) *Risk Issues and Crisis Management in Public Relations*
(4th edition), Kogan Page, London

Skelcey, L (2012) Crisis communication interview, Worthing, 15 May 2012

Stamper, C [accessed 13 July 2012] *Top tips: improving local government communication*
[Online] www.guardian.co.uk/local-government-network/2011/nov/19/top-
tips-improving-local-government-communications

Thompson, D (2012) 'News and Social Media Course from the Emergency Planning College',
Worthing and Adur Councils, Worthing, 15–16 May 2012

Yaxley, H (2011) Risk, issues and crisis management, in *The Public Relations Handbook*
(4th edition), ed Theaker, A, pp 154–75, Routledge, Oxon

# Chapter 12

Abratt, R (1989) A new approach to the corporate issue management process, *Journal of
Marketing Management*, 5(1) pp 63–76

Hampshire County Council [accessed 19 March 2013] *Hantsweb Our Brand* [Online]
www3.hants.gov.uk/logos/cx-logos-brand.htm

Hatch, M (1997) Relations between organizational culture, identity and image, *European
Journal of Marketing*, 31(5/6) pp 356–65

Hemisphere (2012) Interview with Wendy Moran, Manchester, 22 June

Ind, N (2004) *Living the Brand* (2nd edition), Kogan Page, London

Local Government Association (LGA) (2005) [accessed on 7 January 2012] Reputation
Campaign [Online] http://reputation.lga.gov.uk/lga/core/page.do?pageId=1

LGA, Local Government communications (LGcomms) (2010) [accessed on 10 November
2011] Reputation Guide [Online] www.lgcomms.org.uk/asset/69/WCC_LGcomms_
ReputationGuide.pdf

LGID (2009) [accessed on 1 July 2012] *Branding and Place Shaping* [Online]
www.idea.gov.uk/idk/core/page.do?pageId=7816272

Meech, P (1996) Corporate identity and corporate image, in *Critical Perspectives in Public
Relations*, eds L'Etang, J and Pieczka, M, pp 65–81, International Thomson Business Press,
London

Morgan, G (1987) *Images of Organization*, Sage Publications, California

MORI (2006) [accessed on 1 July 2012] The Business Case for the Reputation Project.
Research conducted for the LGA [Online] http://reputation.lga.gov.uk/lga/aio/354546

Quirke, B (2000) *Making the Connections: Using Internal Communication to turn Strategy
into Action*, Gower Publishing Ltd, Aldershot

Reynolds, H (2012) *Social Media Interview with Wendy Moran*, Monmouthshire, 29 May

Semley, R and Powell, M (2010) The Bolton brand: place branding as an alternative approach
to local authority corporate identity, in *Public Relations Cases, International perspectives*,
eds Moss, P, Powell, M and DeSanto, B, pp 160–73, Routledge, Oxon

Southwark Council [accessed on 1 July 2012] *Corporate design manual, Partnership
branding*, Local Government Improvement and Development [Online]
www.idea.gov.uk/idk/aio/7881321

Talbot, D (2012) Interview with Wendy Moran, Tunbridge Wells, 28 June

Van Riel, C B M (1995) *Principles of Corporate Communication*, Prentice Hall, London

Wathen, M (1986) Logomotion: Corporate identity makes its move into the realm of strategic planning, *Public Relations Journal*, 4(5) pp 24–29

# Chapter 13

Anholt, S (2010) *Places: Identity Images and Reputation*, Palgrave Macmillan, London

Armagh City and District website (2012) [accessed 18 October 2012] Lord Mayor Message [Online] www.armagh.gov.uk/your-council/mayor-of-armagh-city-district

Baker, B (2011) Foreword in *City Branding: Theory and Cases*, Dinnie, K (Ed) Palgrave Macmillan, pp xii–xiv

Bedford, P (1973) Holiday resort publicity, in *Public Relations for Local Government*, ed Geoffrey Lewis, IPR/Business Books, pp 111–14

Carnegie, UK (2011) [accessed 1 May 2013] *Pride in Place Tackling Incivilities* [Online] http://carnegieuktrust.org.uk/changing-minds/people--place/pride-in-place--tackling-incivilities

Chelmsford (2011) [accessed 1 May 2013] *Application for Grant of City Status* [Online] http://213.121.205.231/fpdfs/citybid/index.html

Connor, S (2012) quoted in Stevens, A [accessed 17 May 2012] *City Brand Leaders – Manchester blog* [Online] www.creativebrief.com/blog

Department of Communities and Local Government [accessed 1 May 2013] *Place Survey Results 2008* [Online] data.gov.uk/dataset/england-place-survey

Dinnie, K (2011) Introduction to the Practice of City Branding, in *City Branding: Theory and Cases*, ed Dinnie K, Palgrave Macmillan, London, pp 93–98

Dinnie, K (2012) 'Ensuring world beats a path to our doors', *Edinburgh Evening News*, 7 June 2012

Gelder, S van (2011) City Brand Partnerships, in *City Branding: Theory and Cases*, ed Dinnie K (Ed) Palgrave Macmillan, London, pp 36–44

Houghton, J and Stevens, A (2011) City Branding and Stakeholder Engagement, in *City Branding: Theory and Cases*, ed Dinnie, K, Palgrave Macmillan, London, pp 45–53

Kapferer, J (2011) Paris as a Brand, in *City Branding: Theory and Cases*, ed Dinnie, K Palgrave Macmillan, London, pp 184–89

Kavaratzis, M (2012) From 'necessary evil' to necessity: stakeholders' involvement in place branding, *Journal of Management and Development*, 5(1), pp 7–19

Kotler, P, Halder, D and Rein, I (1993) *Marketing Places*, The Free Press, New York

Marketing Manchester (2012) *'Team Manchester' sweep three prestigious retail industry awards*, Press Release, www.marketingmanchester.com

Monmouthpedia (2012) http://en.wikipedia.org/wiki/Wikipedia:GLAM/Monmouthpedia

Ooi, C (2011) Paradoxes of City Branding and Societal Changes, in *City Branding: Theory and Cases*, ed Dinnie K, Palgrave Macmillan, London, pp 56–61

Perth and Kinross Council [accessed 1 May 2013] *Fair City of Perth: Application for City Status* [Online] www.pkc.gov.uk/NR/rdonlyres/6DC7236C-E725-489F-B247-DF3176466E37/0/CityBidMay11Final.pdf

Royal Horticultural Society (2011) [accessed 1 May 2013] *Britain in Bloom: transforming local communities* [Online] www.rhs.org.uk/Gardening/Community-gardening/pdf/Britain-in-Bloom-Impact-Report

Semley, R and Powell, M (2010) The Bolton Brand – Place branding as an alternative approach to local authority identity, in eds Moss, D et al *Public Relations Cases*, Routledge, London, pp 160–71

Sunday Herald (2012) 'Incredinburgh! The new slogan for Scotland's capital' 14 October 2012

Stevens, A (2012a) www.creativebrief.com/blog

Stevens, A (2012b) [accessed 20 November 2012] *City Brand Leaders – Edinburgh blog* [Online] www.creativebrief.com/blog/2012/11/20/city-brand-leaders-%E2%80%93-edinburgh/

Stevens, A (2012c) [accessed 17 May 2012] *City Brand Leaders – Manchester blog*

Wardrop, K (2011) Edinburgh: Scotland's Inspiring Capital, in *City Branding: Theory and Cases*, ed Dinnie, K, Palgrave Macmillan, London, pp 138–49

Waltham Forest London Borough Council (2005) *The Beckham Trail* [Online] www.walthamforest.gov.uk/pages/campaigns/beckham-trail.aspx

Wigley, P (1973) Selling an Industrial City, in *Public Relations for Local Government* by Lewis G IPR/Business Books, pp 107–110

# Chapter 14

Bore, A (2013) The end of local government, *C'llr* magazine, February 2013, www.lgiu.org.uk

Brindle, D (2012) 'Graph of Doom: A bleak future for social care services', *The Guardian* 15 May 2012

Butler, P (2012) 'Local Government cuts: the "Jaws of Doom" are ready to bite', The *Guardian*, 18 December 2012

Cartmell, M (2012) Mapping council comms budgets, *PR Week*, 9 November 2012

Cave, A (2012) *CorpComms*, Issue 72, November/December 2012

Chartered Institute of Public Finance and Accountancy (CIPFA) 2010 Findings of the Disciplinary Committee, 3 November 2010

Earl, S and Waddington, S (2012) *Brand Anarchy*, Bloomsbury, London

Footner, L (2012) quoted in 'What's wrong with local government communications?' [Online] The Guardian Local Government Network Blog – 14 March 2012 http://www.guardian.co.uk/local-government-network/local-government-network-blog

Heseltine, Lord (2012) *No stone unturned*, Department for Business, Innovation and Skills, October 2012, www.bis.gov.uk

Hope, S (2012) quoted in 'What's wrong with local government communications?' [Online] The Guardian Local Government Network Blog – 14 March 2012 http://www.guardian.co.uk/local-government-network/local-government-network-blog

L'Etang, J (2008) *Public Relations Concepts, Practice and Critique*, Sage Publications, London, p 196

LGA (2012) *Services shared: costs spared?* Report commissioned by LGA from strategic advisers Drummond MacFarlane Ltd, www.local.gov.uk

LGA (2013) Polling on resident satisfaction with councils Full report, Local Government Association, January 2013

LGCommunications (2009) The Commission on Competencies for Senior Communication Roles, LGCommunications [Online] www.lgcomms.org.uk

Moss, D and DeSanto, B (2012) *Public Relations: a managerial perspective*, Sage Publications, London

Mr Reasonable (2012) [accessed 1 October 2012] 'The graph of doom – Fact or Fantasy?' An alternative perspective by a Barnet Resident Blog – [Online] http://reasonablenewbarnet.blogspot.co.uk

PwC (2012) *The (local) state we're in*, PricewaterhouseCoopers LLP [Online] www.psrc.pwc.com

Roe, P (2013) Opportunity Knocks, *C'llr magazine*, February 2013

Thraves, L (2013) *A Dose of Localism: The role of councils in public health*, Local Government Information Unit/City of Westminster City Council, www.lgiu.org.uk

# INDEX

NB: page numbers in *italic* indicate figures or tables

Lightning Source UK Ltd.
Milton Keynes UK
UKHW020112190722
406021UK00002B/20